VILL

NO REMORSE

by

Al McIntosh

with Dean Rinaldi

Published by Blue Mendos Publications
In association with Amazon KDP

Published in paperback 2022
Category: Memoirs & Life Story
Copyright Al McIntosh © 2022
ISBN : 9798415476039

Cover design by Jill Rinaldi © 2022

Dedication

For my beautiful wife, Dionne, and your continued love and support. Had I not met you then I would almost certainly have ended up dead or banged up for life.

Acknowledgements

Jill Rinaldi, for designing the book cover and Dean Rinaldi, my ghostwriter and friend.

Author's Note

The life of a hardened villain was a marvellous, never-ending adventure and I have no remorse. However, prison is a brutal existence and no way to waste your life. No matter how tough, hard or resilient you believe you are, violence can and will come from the most unexpected direction on any day at any time. A man you believe to be your friend can turn to extreme violence in a heartbeat for the pettiest of reasons.

In the words of my Uncle Tommy:

'In this world you get nothing for nothing. If you're weak then life walks right over you, but if you're strong, you do the walking.'

My name is Al McIntosh, and this is my story.

Chapter 1

1981: Wandsworth Prison, South West London.

"Benny, what was all that commotion outside your cell last night?" Al said as he leant against Benny's cell door.

"Commotion? What do you mean?" Benny said as he stood up from his bed.

"I got out of my bed for a pee last night and I could hear one of the screws outside your cell muttering something," Al said.

The keyhole on the cell door had no glass in it and the metal ring on the outside of the door was missing. Al had been curious and took a peek, only to find one of the prison officers standing with his legs apart and his trousers and underwear down by his ankles. He was masturbating and muttering something.

"Oh, that," Benny said softly.

Al took a step closer.

"It's that screw, Cartwright. We have this arrangement," Benny said subtly.

"Arrangement?"

"Yeah, he likes to toss himself off while he orders me to do all kinds of kinky shit. He gets off on it and I get an ounce of tobacco," Benny said, shrugging his shoulders.

"No judgement here," Al said.

"You've got to do what you've got to do to get by," Benny said.

"Yeah, maybe," Al thought. *"But I ain't going to go pulling my old todger about so some dirty screw can get his rocks off. But I suppose it takes all sorts."*

"Keep it to yourself, though eh, Al?"

"Not a word mate," Al said as he ran his index finger over his closed lips.

"Here, did you hear what happened to Carty, the fucking kiddie fiddler, yesterday?" Benny asked as he slouched back against the wall and lit a roll up cigarette.

"I saw it," Al said. "That new con Edwards beat the living shit out of him with a metal mop pail. There was blood and broken teeth all over the landing."

"Fucking good job," Benny said as he drew hard on his cigarette and blew the smoke towards the ceiling. "Nonces, rapists and grasses deserve everything that's coming to them. It was only a matter of time before someone marked Carty's card good and proper."

The two men left the cell and looked out over the landing.

HM Prison Wandsworth has a population of over fifteen hundred inmates and is situated on the south side of the River Thames. It is one of the largest prisons in the UK. The prison had originally been built in 1851 and was named the Surrey House of Correction. It had been constructed in a panopticon architectural design so that officers could oversee the cells from a central tower. One of the most infamous villains to pass through HMP Wandsworth was the Great Train Robber, Ronnie Biggs. Just fifteen months into his thirty-year sentence Ronnie Biggs scaled the prison wall with a rope ladder and made his getaway in a waiting delivery van.

"That Welsh slag is down there giving it the big one again," Benny hissed.

The two men watched as the six-foot, four-inch former rugby player strutted around the wing like he was the wing's scrumhalf.

"He's a bully boy who enjoys intimidating people with his height and size," Benny muttered.

"He's a closet coward and better not try any of that shit with me," Al said through gritted teeth.

"I fucking hate bullies!" Al thought.

The two men watched as Dawson sauntered over to where convicted fraudster, Billy Conroy, was chatting with fellow cons. He stopped and reached out for the rolled-up cigarette behind Conroy's ear. The three other men went quiet. Dawson looked down at the roll-up and put it behind his ear. He shot a manic grin to the four cons and then slapped Billy on the back of the head as he strutted away victoriously.

"This is going to get nasty," Al said.

Benny nodded.

Al watched as Billy stepped away from the group. He had a slim build and was short at just five foot and one inch in height. Billy disappeared off the landing for several minutes. Dawson continued to prowl amongst the other cons, stopping every so often to exchange a glare or pass comment with the smaller, weaker, inmates.

"He's back," Tommy whispered, as he nodded towards Billy Conroy.

Billy was carrying a toilet brush that had been sharpened to make a spear and had purposely walked around the back of the tables and approached Dawson from behind.

"Dawson, you fucking gobshite!" Billy yelled in his distinct Irish accent.

As Dawson turned, Billy plunged the sharpened toilet brush into his left shoulder, then twice in the stomach.

"Arghh!" Dawson let out a long, loud, piercing cry before reaching for the bloody wounds. He staggered backwards, still howling in extreme pain. He swayed from left to right, then tripped over a chair and landed in a heap on the floor. The inmates looked on as Dawson writhed around on the concrete floor, crying out to the screws for help. Billy dropped the prison made weapon and quickly positioned himself amongst the inmates looking on.

Al watched as the screws picked Dawson up off the floor, took him out of the wing and down to the prison hospital. His shrieks could still be heard through the corridors.

"Violence can come at you at any time in a place like this. The man was a fool and a bully. Justice was served up. There's no room for bullies in a place like this," Al said.

The screws invaded the wing en-masse, ordering inmates back to their cells.

"No one is going to grass Billy up. The inmates know it and so do the screws," Al thought.

"See you later Al," Benny said as he entered his cell.

"Yeah, it's not like we're going anywhere," Al replied as his cell door slammed behind him.

Al climbed onto his bunk and lay back with his hands behind his head. He looked around at his six-by-ten-foot one–man cell with the unscreened toilet at the end of his bunk and stared aimlessly up at the ceiling.

"How the fuck did I end up locked away in here?" Al thought. *"I never saw this coming. Not even for a single moment did I imagine I'd get caught for doing a bit of villainy. None of us convicted inmates ever do, which is probably why places like this are packed to the rafters the entire length and breadth of the UK."*

Al settled back and found his mind wandering back to his home on Scotia Street in Glasgow. It was the early 1960s and he had been out during the day with his younger brother, Brian, and friends Charlie and Rob. Al and a gang of local lads known as the Scoshees had visited their arch enemies, the Catholic gang known as the Gayfeelies, on Gayfield Street. Neither Al nor the other kids were bothered by religion. It mattered not if you were Protestant or Catholic, only the area you came from mattered. The previous day the Gayfeelies had jumped over a neighbour's fence and set fire to his 'dookits'. The aviary was home to scores of prized pigeons and was the neighbour's pride and joy. The lads were encouraged by the men in Scotia Street to take revenge. If you burn one of ours then we burn one of yours was the motto. Al and the lads had crept down Gayfield Street, and through the back alleyways until Rob peered over a fence and spotted a 'dookit'.

"I don't want to do this," Brian muttered.

"Well go back home then!" Al growled through gritted teeth.

"Come on Brian, we have to. They did one of ours, so we have to. You heard what the grownups said," Rob said, patting Brian on the shoulder.

"I'll tell Mammy," Brian said abruptly.

"If you say just one word to Mammy, I will beat the living crap out of you!" Al said, clenching and unclenching his fists.

There was a moment's silence.

"I'll do it," Rob said as he reached into his pocket and produced a box of matches.

"Alright," Al said, "Just be careful."

Rob scampered over the Victorian iron railings and warily made his way up the cracked, fractured and ruptured concrete to the 'dookit'. Al, Brian, and Charlie peeked over the fence as their friend tiptoed towards the 'dookit'.

"Hey, you!"

The boys looked over to see an elderly man in an open shirt with bare feet come out of the back door. He took a long drag on his cigarette and flicked it across the concrete.

"What do you think you're doing?"

"Run!" Al yelled.

The man grabbed a yard broom that had been leaning against the wall and raced towards the intruder. Rob turned with a look of sheer horror as the armed, red-faced man came bounding towards him.

"You wee shit!"

Rob shot off to the left then quickly veered right as the man swung the stick which narrowly missed him. He was back across the cracked and broken concrete slab and scaling the fence in seconds. As he landed on the ground in the alleyway there was a loud thud as the broom struck the top of the fence. The four boys pounded down the alleyway. Al could feel the adrenaline racing through his body as they left the alley and bolted out onto Gayfield Street. Brian lost his footing and tripped. Rob and Charlie were scampering down the middle of the road, but Al turned back for his brother. He reached down and grabbed him by the hand and hauled him back onto his feet. The front door of the house opened and the man stood there with a broken broom handle shouting as the boys ran up the road and back to their home area and the den they had built on the edge of Scotia Street.

The den had been made from old wooden pallets, floorboards scavenged from empty houses, and a full window, complete with glass, they had managed to remove.

"That was a close one," Charlie said, as he leant forward to catch his breath.

"Are you alright, Brian?" Al asked.

"Yeah, I'm fine," Brian said with a wry smile.

"What are we going to do now?" Rob said. "They'll be ready for us if we go back today."

"We'll wait," Al said.

"Maybe get them back in some other way," Brian said. "If we go back to the same 'dookit' they could be waiting."

"I'll come up with something," Al said.

While the Scoshees chatted amongst themselves, several lads from the Gayfeelies had got together and were out looking for blood and revenge. One of the lads had spotted the homemade den and crept through the long green grass and weeds until he could hear Al and the lads talking. The Gayfeelies collected bricks and rocks while others bolted back to their homes in Gayfield Street. They returned minutes later with homemade bows and arrows made from bamboo with flat headed nails rammed into the end. One of the Gayfeelies had wrapped a rag around his arrow.

Suddenly, while in mid-conversation, a brick came crashing through the plate glass window, narrowly missing Al's head. The glass shattered into hundreds of pieces and scattered across the den. The Scoshees tried desperately to get out. The Gayfeelies, on their leader's command, launched brick after rock after brick at the den. The den began to fall apart around them as they scuttled out and into the open. Al looked up to see an arrow hurtling towards him. It missed, as did the three rocks that followed.

"Run!" Rob yelled as he darted away.

Al grabbed his brother by the arm and began to run. He looked over his shoulder and saw that one of the Gayfeelie lads had lit the rag attached to his arrow and fired it into their homemade den. The mound of broken wood and pallets burst into flames.

"Those damn Gayfeelies!" Al thought. *"I'll get even. I will have my pay back!"*

Once out on Scotia Street, the lads knew they were safe and stopped running.

It was getting dark, and from the road Al could see the lights on in his front room.

"We'll see you tomorrow," Al said, "and we'll show them Gayfeelies what for!"

"Damn right," Rob said, pounding his right fist into his open left hand.

"Scoshees forever!" Charlie called out as he turned and ran across the road to his home.

"Come on Brian, let's go home, and remember, not a word to mammy," Al said as he put his arm around his brother's shoulder.

"Yeah, I know," Brian said with a chuckle. "You do know they could have killed us, Al?"

"We just have to hit them back harder and smarter," Al said as he opened the front door.

In the front room their mammy had *'Heartbreak Hotel'* by Elvis Presley playing on the family's record player. Al opened the door to find both his aunties, Doreen and Mary, dancing in their high heels by the fireplace. Both aunts had blonde hair styled into the fashionable beehives. Al loved his aunts because they were always happy, positive and full of life. Aunt Mary's husband was sat on the threadbare settee smoking a roll-up cigarette and tapping his foot to the 'King of Rock 'n' Roll'.

Al had overheard the family saying that their Polish uncle Nicholas was a Nazi collaborator during the Second World War and with the fall of Nazi Germany he'd high tailed it across to Scotland to avoid being hanged as a war criminal. Nicholas had claimed to have been young and scared for his life. He was adamant that nothing he ever did cost the life of a single Polish citizen. Al didn't care either way. Nicholas was family and he liked him.

"Hello my little sweetie," Auntie Doreen said, throwing her arms around Al.

"Hello Auntie Doreen," Al said, stepping back and looking her up and down. "You look really nice."

Auntie Doreen beamed.

Al quickly turned to his Aunt Mary and with a big smile said, "And so do you Aunt Mary."

Mammy had her eyes closed and was dancing to her favourite tunes. Al could remember times when she would play her Elvis and Al Jolson vinyl records over and over for the entire day.

Al could feel his stomach grumbling. It had been several hours since he last ate anything. While mammy changed the record to 'Carolina in the Morning' by Al Jolson he slipped out into the hallway where he saw his seven brothers and sisters at the top of the stairs looking down at him. He went into the kitchen and opened the food cupboard. With the exception of one single onion on the middle shelf it was empty. Another day would come and go when neither Al nor his siblings would eat. Al closed the cupboard door slowly and then rubbed his stomach to calm the hunger pangs.

"I can't wait to go England," Al thought. "One of these days I'll just pack my bags and go to England. It's the best country in the world and you can eat like a king every day of the week!"

Al would often talk about going to live in England at the family home. His mammy would shout at him to shut up while his father, Albert, would simply roll his eyes.

Al was brought back to reality as his cell door was unlocked and swung open. He immediately recognised the screw as the one that had been masturbating outside Tommy's cell the night before.

"McIntosh, your solicitor is here to see you," the screw said as he opened the cell door fully.

"Can't be for me. I haven't had a letter and you always get a letter before a visit from your solicitor," Al said as he sat upright and swung his legs around and onto the floor.

"You have got a letter. It was mislaid after that incident on the wing yesterday."

Al remembered that the previous day a young lad been badly beaten over a tobacco debt.

"Come on McIntosh, move!"

"You wouldn't be so fucking brave without that uniform to back you up," Al thought as he stood up.

Al followed the officer along the corridor and off the wing to the interview rooms. As he entered, he saw Detective Sergeant Skinner and his guvnor Detective Inspector Young sitting alongside his solicitor, Mr Edwyn Hawthorne.

"What the fuck is this?" Al thought as he stared blankly at his nemesis DI Young.

Al had several run ins with both DS Skinner and DI Young while he'd been living at the squat in Finsbury Park. On one occasion, the pair, while he was in custody for a crime he did not commit, had pulled in two additional uniformed officers. They closed the interview room door and at first tried to intimidate Al into signing a confession for a series of robberies that he hadn't committed. They played the usual good cop, bad cop routine without success. It was then that DI Young threw the first punch. Al had tried to fight back and had landed several good right handers before being overpowered with a succession of punches and body kicks. Al had rolled himself into a tight ball on the floor while the police officers administered their own form of criminal justice. Al refused to comply and was eventually released with several fractures to his ribs, left arm and ankle.

"What's all this then?" Al said cautiously.

"Please, take a seat," his solicitor, Edwyn Hawthorne said, motioning Al towards the wooden chair next to him.

Al sat down and stared at the police officers opposite him.

"Did you not get my letter Al?"

Al shook his head while maintaining constant eye contact with the officers opposite him.

"So what is it you two want then? Here to gloat, are you?"

DI Young grinned. He sat back in his chair and put his hands on the table.

"Mr Alan McIntosh I am arresting you for murder. You do not have to say anything, but it may harm your defence if you do not mention, when questioned, something that you later rely on in court," DI Young said with a broad, smug, grin.

The murder and the victim they were referring to had made national headlines. It had been featured on television, in the newspapers and had been talked about on the wing.

Al listened to what the officers had to say and took his solicitor's, advice to remain silent. He understood that most people, when arrested, begin to panic and incriminate themselves. The police are keen to solve a case by any and all means at their disposal. Al had seen this many times and with DS Skinner and DI Young, if it's not going their way then a damn good kicking would help the investigation along. The police can and will lie to suspects in a bid to have them waive their right to remain silent. There were stories out on the prison wing from first time offenders that the police had convinced them that they didn't need a solicitor. Al knew to restrain himself from pleading his innocence because you may well find yourself admitting to an offence without knowing it. The police were notorious for taking a small piece of information and then twisting the words into a motive when the case is presented in court. Experience had taught Al that you listen to your solicitor and do exactly what they tell you.

The interview concluded with Edwyn Hawthorne saying he would write again and arrange another meeting without the police being present.

"Checkmate McIntosh. You're going down for a long time," Detective Inspector Young said with a self-congratulatory grin.

"Nice one Guvnor," Detective Sergeant Skinner said with a short, sharp punch to the air.

Al was led back out of the interview room where he was met by six anxious, trouble ready, screws.

"You're being moved down to D Wing, McIntosh. You're a Cat A prisoner now so come quietly because we don't want any trouble lad," the principal officer said.

Chapter 2

1961 Grove Street School, Glasgow.

"Come in Mrs McIntosh."

Miss Campbell invited Al's mammy in to take a seat opposite her desk.

She had a supple hourglass figure, amplified by her tight fitting brown jumper and matching skirt. With her immaculate star flame golden beehive hairstyle, she attracted attention from fellow teachers and the council's workmen outside who would wolf-whistle when she arrived at school in the morning.

Al's mammy took a seat. She pulled the chair forward so she was closer to the desk that separated the women. Al fiddled with his fingers and looked down at the tiled flooring.

"I'm pleased you've come in, Mrs McIntosh, because your son's behaviour at school is simply unacceptable and he's given me cause to discipline him with the belt. He needs to settle down, do as he's told, and stop distracting the other pupils while I'm trying to educate the children and prepare them for the future," Miss Campbell said, sitting back in her chair.

The belt was officially known as the tawse. It consisted of a strip of leather split into a number of tails and was used in Scotland as corporal punishment in schools.

"My son is six years old," Mammy said firmly.

Al shuddered at the memory of the agonising pain the belt inflicted as it whipped across his wrist.

"Yes, and while he's in my class he'll do as he's told, or he'll be disciplined again. I simply will not tolerate poor behaviour from any of my pupils. This is a place of learning not a social club!"

"Right, so my six-year-old son spoke out of turn and you took the belt to him. Is that correct? Mammy said with a hint of aggression in her voice.

Al shook his head slowly.

"That is correct, Mrs McIntosh, and I would do it again," Miss Campbell said bluntly as she folded her arms triumphantly.

"I do not have any problem with you disciplining Al, if he played up then he deserves what he gets, but what I do take exception to is that you took the belt to his wrist and not the palm of his hand," Mammy said, as she leant a little closer to the table with her eyes firmly fixed on Al's school teacher.

"The palm or the wrist, it's all appropriate punishment as far as I'm concerned," Miss Campbell said adamantly.

Mammy leapt up from her chair and grabbed Miss Campbell by her golden hair. Al nearly fell off his seat as Mammy's wooden chair flew back across the classroom.

Shocked, Miss Campbell winced with pain as Mammy tightened her grip

"Appropriate punishment, is it?" Mammy said as she tightened her grip even more.

"Arghh," Miss Campbell howled.

Al looked up at his teacher. She was in excruciating pain.

SMACK!

21

Mammy slammed Miss Campbell's head down on the desk with a sickening thud.

"Arghh!"

"The tawse on the palm is one thing!"

SMACK!

Mammy yanked her head back before slamming it down on the desk a second time.

"Please, please!" Miss Campbell pleaded.

"But the wrist, that's not right! And you know it," Mammy said angrily.

With gritted teeth Mammy jerked her head up again before slamming it back into the desk with such force that the desk lurched forward.

SMACK!

SMACK!

"Please, please, I'm sorry. Please don't hurt me anymore," Miss Campbell implored as tears streamed down her face.

"Have I made myself clear?" Mammy said, with her hand clenched tightly around her golden blonde hair.

"Yes, yes, please let me go," Miss Campbell howled through the pain.

"If Al plays up then by all means punish him with the belt on the palm of his hand, but not the wrist. Do I make myself clear?"

"Yes, yes, whatever you say," Miss Campbell said with her head now held firmly down on the desk.

"Okay, then," Mammy said as she slowly released her grip.

Miss Campbell rose slowly and sat back in her chair, wiping the tears from her eyes.

Al glanced up and then back down at the floor again.

Mammy reached into her handbag and produced a metal horseshoe. She held it up in plain view. Miss Campbell looked petrified, like a rabbit caught in the headlights at night.

"This is the end of it," warned Mammy. "If you report this or break our understanding then I will be back, and you won't like it. That I can promise," Mammy said calmly.

"I won't say anything, I promise," Miss Campbell pleaded.

"Right, we're done then," Mammy said as she put the metal horseshoe back into her handbag. "Come on Al, we're going home."

Al stood up and briefly looked over at his teacher. She was no longer that stout figure of authority standing in front of the classroom but a weak quivering wreck at the hands of his mammy.

As they walked back home, Al found himself thinking back to a Christmas just two years ago. He had been excited that Father Christmas would be visiting with presents. Al had set his heart on the toy hunting rifle he'd seen in a book. It had been early; daylight was streaming through his window. He had been so excited about Christmas he hadn't been able to sleep, so he got up and made his way downstairs. He walked into the living room only to find the nine large stockings still lined up and empty on the mantelpiece. There were no presents. Al thought Father Christmas must have been running late. Then suddenly his attention was drawn to a noise from the kitchen. Gingerly he approached the kitchen door, turned the handle and peeked around. He could smell something strong, almost overpowering, and then he saw his mammy on her hands and knees with her head inside the gas oven.

"Mammy, mammy!" Al yelled, as he ran towards the crouching figure.

Mammy was crying uncontrollably and taking deep gulps of the gas. Al tugged at her cardigan.

"Mammy, mammy!"

Slowly Mammy's head emerged from the open oven with tears streaming down her red cheeks. Her eyes were bloodshot and looked sore. Al had never seen his Mammy look so desperately sad.

Mammy sat with her legs crossed, just staring down at the kitchen floor. Al clambered back onto his feet, turned off the oven and then raced over to open the back door. He opened the side window, kitchen door, and then the front door to let the fresh air in and the toxic gas out.

"What are you doing Mammy?"

"This is not the life I wanted for us," Mammy whimpered. "This is not what I expected when I married your Da. My family are good, educated, people, Presbyterians. My Daddy was a highly skilled engineer and we lived in a house that had been bought and paid for with blood, sweat and graft. Your grandparents own land with horses and cows."

Al looked silently down at his mother. He struggled to understand what she was saying.

"Your Da is lazy. A useless, father and a terrible husband, unlike his parents who are dead poor Irish, but they work hard and long hours in the iron foundry. They are a respectable working class family and what do we have? Nothing."

Al remained quiet while the cold, fresh, air filled the room. Mammy looked up and managed to force a slight smile.

"Silly me, I fell over," Mammy said, then muttered, "Now I've gone and wasted gas that cost good money."

"Mammy, I don't understand. Where is Father Christmas and our presents? I've been a good boy, Mammy, and Father Christmas always brings good little boys and girls presents. I have been a good boy, Mammy, honest," Al said sullenly as he looked down at his mammy.

Mammy wiped her eyes and scrambled awkwardly to her feet. She looked up at the ceiling and took a deep breath.

"I'm sorry, Al, but there are no Christmas presents for you or your brothers and sisters. Not this year," Mammy said, as she wiped away the last of her tears.

Even at just four years old Al knew better than to question Mammy further and accepted that he and his brothers and sisters must have not been as good as Father Christmas expected. There would be no Christmas this year.

Al and Mammy turned into their street. It was lined on both sides with scores of tenement homes which had small, fractured concrete slabs for a garden and identical Victorian metal fencing with missing railings. It was getting dark, and someone had turned the front room light on. Al could see the outline of his Da through the window.

Mammy took the key from her bag and opened the front door. As it swung open, Al caught sight of his Da standing by the front room doorway.

"Hello Da," Al said.

"I've told you before, boy. I'm not your da!"

Al could feel his heart skip a beat as his father shot him an angry, vicious glare. Even though his father, a large powerful man, had never taken his hand to him or any of his brothers and sisters, the threat of imminent violence was always in the air.

"Your Da is in Australia!"

Al, not wanting to aggravate the situation, nodded meekly before going into the kitchen where his younger brothers Charles, Brian, and Alexander, the triplets Elizabeth, John and David and the twins William and Doreen sat around the kitchen table. Charles was known as Charlie, Alexander had been named Sandra, William had become Wullie, and Doreen was simply Do-Do.

"What's for dinner?" Albert said as Mammy passed him in the hallway.

"Broth!"

"Broth? Broth again!" Albert growled through gritted teeth.

"Well, there would be more for all of us if you didn't drink away the money," Mammy said as she slid her hand inside her handbag.

Mammy would often make up a pot of broth and cook it over the open fire when the electricity had been cut off. It had to last the family of eleven for three days.

"Who do you think you're talking to?"

"You, you useless shite!"

Albert raised his hand and leapt forward. In an instant Mammy had the metal horseshoe firmly gripped in her hand and was ready to fight and defend herself. Despite Albert's fearsome reputation as the local hard man, mammy was utterly fearless and would never back down from confrontation from anyone.

The children all sat in silence as the threat of brutal violence enveloped their young, innocent, bodies.

Albert lowered his hand and reached for the bottle of Four Crowns wine he had put on the windowsill earlier and took three large gulps before skulking back into the living room and slouching back into the armchair.

Mammy smiled warmly at the children before dishing out a full bowl of a light, watery, liquid. Each slice of the stale white bread was cut into four and handed out to the children. Al dipped his bread into the broth and chewed it several times before swallowing. It was the first meal the children had eaten in two days.

Al's father, Albert, had served his country and seen active front line duty, battling the Nazis head on during the Second World War. Great Britain and its allies were losing the Battle of France on the Western Front against Nazi Germany. He and many young men fought desperately for their lives around the French port of Dunkirk. During the D-Day landing he suffered head injuries from shrapnel. Albert had never fully recovered from the effects of Dunkirk and would often wake up in delirious sweats in the dead of night, yelling out that the Germans were coming for him. It was a horrific, spine tingling, scream that sent shivers through Al's entire body. The State offered no help for Albert and thousands of young men like him who suffered the barbarous effects of war.

After their meal Al went upstairs to the bedroom he shared with his five brothers. In the room was a single bed that they all shared. It was held up by empty beer crates and was covered with a variety of coats to keep them warm at night.

"Do you think everyone lives like us?" Brian asked as he pushed himself up against the wall.

"Yes, of course. Everyone in Scotland lives like us. Well, except for the rich people on the west side of Glasgow. That's why, when I grow up, I'm moving down to England. They have big houses where children have their own bedrooms, and they eat meat every day. You know, chicken and beef, and even lamb with potatoes and greens. No one eats broth in England. Yes, I'm going to England just as soon as I grow up," Al said as he put his hand in his pockets and slouched back against the wall.

"What? Real meat?"

"Yep, roast beef with gravy and roast potatoes. I heard that in the summer people eat ice-cream every day."

"Maybe when I grow up, I might come down to England with you," Brian said.

"Maybe," Al said as he turned towards the bedroom window.

It was dark outside, but he could make out his neighbours arguing in the street opposite them. The husband was waving his arms around and shouting something. Al only heard 'cow' which he knew to be the worst thing that you could call a woman in Glasgow. The woman retaliated by throwing several clumsy punches which were easily defended. Al winced as the husband pushed her away and then launched a right hook that sent her sprawling. Her knees buckled as she fell awkwardly to the ground where she lay motionless. The husband then kicked his unconscious wife in the stomach before stepping over her body and marched off down the street.

"They're at again over the road," Al said, shaking his head.

"That's the second time this week," Brian said. "Why doesn't she just leave?"

Al paused for a moment before answering.

"Why doesn't he just stop hitting her?" Al asked.

The brothers talked about things that were happening in the neighbourhood when Al heard vehicles stop outside. The two brothers shot up from the bed and looked outside. A van and two cars were parked by their house.

Al and his brother raced out of the bedroom and down the stairs and joined their younger brothers and sisters who had been sitting on the settee. Albert had opened a second bottle of 'Four Crown' wine that he had hidden beneath the chair's cushion.

There were several loud knocks on the front door.

Al put his finger on his lips, indicating that his brothers and sisters should stay still and quiet. Albert, who was now drunk and delirious, just took another long swig from the wine bottle. Mammy opened the front door and was pushed back as six men in white overalls barged past her and entered the living room. The largest of the men stepped forward. He was holding an off-white garment with long sleeves.

"Alright, Albert. You know who we are and why we're here, so you best come quietly. We don't want a repeat of last time, do we?"

Albert looked up through slanted, drunken, eyes and began smiling.

"Fuck off!"

"There's no need for that Albert. Just do us all a favour and come nicely."

"I'll fight the fucking lot of yer," Albert slurred, clenching both fists.

Al knew the men were from the asylum from across the city. He had witnessed them come to the house several times in his life and his father never, ever went quietly.

Mammy entered the living room and walked around to where the children were sitting.

"Albert, we can do this the easy way or the hard way. It's your choice," the lead orderly said as he held out the straitjacket that had been designed to confine the arms of a violent prisoner or mental patient.

Albert leapt to his feet as the first of the orderlies approached him. With a swift kick between the legs the man screamed in pain as he dropped onto his knees, cupping his genitals. A second orderly ran forward. Albert side stepped him and threw a powerful right uppercut that sent the orderly down into the armchair. The lead orderly nodded to a colleague who was holding a syringe.

"When I give the word, get the bastard!"

The anxious orderly nodded and held up the syringe full of sedative.

"Well come on then," Albert taunted, holding his arms outstretched and beckoning them with his finger.

The lead orderly and his two colleagues moved together. Albert threw a left punch which caught one of the men, but they had overpowered him. He fell back on the floor still trying to throw punches. His legs wriggled and he lashed out as the men grabbed at his arms and legs. The syringe was plunged into his arm but still Albert yelled out and tried desperately to fight off the orderlies. Al and the children looked on as each kick and attempt to move became increasingly weaker. The orderlies pulled the straitjacket over his head and secured his arms across the front of his body. The men turned him over in one quick movement, with the lead orderly securing the sleeves at the back.

"Okay, get him up his feet," the lead orderly said as he stepped away.

"I'm sorry that it's come to this again Mrs McIntosh. You know where he'll be and if all goes well, he'll be back home in twenty-eight days."

Mammy nodded and looked on as Albert was bundled out of the family home and into the back of the van parked up the street.

Chapter 3

"I don't want to go to school," Brian said.

Why, are you ill?" Al said as he pulled his sweater over his head.

"No, I'm just embarrassed. None of my shoes fit me," Brian said as he held up a single scuffed black shoe with a severely worn heel.

"Look, I have a shoe that's a bit small for me but might fit you. What I used to do was wear whatever shoe fitted me and then I'd pretend to limp. If anybody said anything, I just said I had a bad leg. You could do the same, it worked for me," Al said as he reached down behind the bed and produced a single brown shoe.

"I don't know," Brian said.

"There's a flea market on this Saturday, maybe Mammy will get you another pair of shoes," Al said excitedly.

"Really, this Saturday?"

"Yeah, I think so," Al said.

Al could see Brian was hesitant. He held both up shoes and began to shake his head.

"Maybe I'll just go 'dogging' until I get some shoes on Saturday," Brian said.

Dogging was a term the neighbourhood kids used when they skipped school.

"Tell you what, put the shoes on and we'll both go 'dogging' and miss school today. Maybe take a walk around the city. What do you think?" Al said.

Brian perked up.

"Yeah, okay."

Al and Brian left home pretending to go to school but turned at the end of the street and headed towards the city. They had checked the broth pot but there was nothing left from the night before. They had learnt to control their hunger and had grown accustomed to starting the day without breakfast. As the brothers walked along the pavement they stared at the men and women going about their everyday business. They were oblivious to Brian's fake limp, his mismatched shoes or the boys and their decision to bunk off school.

"Do you like school, Al?" Brian said, putting his hands in his pockets.

"I hate it," Al said bluntly.

"Me too."

"I hate the way we all get jam packed into a classroom with someone telling you a load of boring stuff that has nothing to do with me or my life here in Glasgow."

"I know what you mean."

"It's like a prison. I can't stand the place," Al said.

"Do you think they have schools in England?"

"Yeah, course they do Brian, but I bet they're nothing like ours in Scotland. I bet they have really comfy chairs to sit on and teach you interesting stuff," Al said.

"Do you think they belt children in England?" Brian asked.

"Maybe if you're extremely naughty and not for just looking out of the window because the teacher and the lesson is so stupid and boring," Al said.

The boys stopped and watched as a large truck pulled out of the confectionary and sweet distribution centre. It was known by the locals as the Trebor factory. As the truck straightened up and drove away a single large box fell off the open back.

The two boys looked at each other and then at the box in the road. Al sprinted off down the pavement and crossed into the busy road. A car screeched to halt as he bent down to pick up the box. He left and right and then crossed back onto the pavement to join Brian.

"Quick, Brian, follow me," Al whispered.

The boys began to increase their pace down the pavement and then darted into an alleyway that led through to a play park with a climbing frame and swings.

"What do you think's in the box, Al?" Brian said, scanning the playground for adults.

"Only one way to find out," Al said as he tore the top of the box open, revealing the popular Mars chocolate covered caramel bars with the distinctive black wrapper and 'Mars' written in bold red print and 'A Mars a day helps you work, rest and play' in smaller white print.

"They're Mars Bars," Al said as he looked over at his brother.

"Hmm, Mars. I've never had a Mars bar," Brian said.

"Me either," Al said.

Al held a single bar up and read the print on both sides.

"What are we going to do?" Brian whispered.

"Keep them," Al said.

"What about the people in the factory or the police?" Brian said as he sat down on the swing.

Al put the box on the ground by his feet and sat back on the swing next to his brother.

"There you go," Al said as he handed Brian a Mars bar.

"I don't know," Brian said, fumbling with the chocolate covered caramel bar.

Al reached into the box and took out another bar. He looked around the play park and then tore the top of the wrapper off, revealing the delicious chocolate sweet. He looked at Brian, nodded and took a large bite out of the bar.

"What's it like?" Brian said as he watched his brother chewing, chomping and then finally swallowing.

"Fantastic!" Al said with a smile that reached from ear to ear.

Brian tore the top off his Mars bar and took a savage bite deep into the sweet. He gobbled hungrily at the bar and then took a second large bite before swallowing the first one.

"Slow down, there's no rush," Al said with a chuckle.

"I've never tasted anything like it," Brian said, popping the last piece of the bar into his mouth, scrunching up the wrapper and dropping it on the ground.

Al looked down into the box.

"There must be over a hundred bars in there," Al thought.

"Can I have another one, Al?"

"You can have two," Al said as he reached into the box and threw two bars over to his brother. "Now you've got one for each hand."

Brian didn't hesitate to tear open the wrapper and bite deep into his second bar.

"Thank You, Al," Brian said as he slurped and sucked the melting chocolate back into his mouth.

"What am I going to do with all these? It's too many to eat and I can't risk taking them home, not with how Mammy is about stealing." Al thought as he opened his second Mars Bar.

After the brothers finished eating their third Mars bar, Al closed the box.

"I'm full up, Al. I don't think I've been full before," Brian said, as he smiled and rubbed his stomach.

"Me too, and I like feeling this way," Al thought.

"Come on Brian, we're going to sell these," Al said, rising to his feet.

Al led Brian back towards his home area where he sold the chocolate bars to the neighbourhood kids and adults at half the shop price. For the first time in his life, he didn't feel hungry, had a pocket full of money and felt like he had choices.

As Al stood patting the pocket full of money, he had an epiphany. He was eight years old and made the decision that he would never allow himself or his family to go hungry again. He would, like his Victorian hero, Charles Peace, become a thief.

Al and Brian returned home with bread, milk, ham and sausages bought from 'Alex's Dairy,' the local shop. Proudly, Al handed the shopping bag to mammy along with three shillings. When mammy questioned him, he said he had been collecting wooden floorboards at the empty houses then chopping them up into sticks before selling them door to door as firewood. The McIntosh family ate well that evening.

Chapter 4

"I don't like it," Brian said.

"Brian, we're not going to find a box of sweets every day, are we, and you like to eat, don't you?"

Brian nodded.

It was Sunday and the Trebor factory was closed. Al had visited earlier in the week and walked around the outskirts of the entire site. He had found that by climbing up on the alleyway wall they could drop down inside the factory grounds without being seen.

"Come on, then."

The two boys clambered over the wall and then scuttled up the drainpipe until they reached the roof. Brian was clearly scared while Al was buzzing. He could feel the excitement stirring in the pit of his stomach as he peeled back the clear plastic sheet which led into the distribution centre.

"Right, you stay here, and I'll go in," Al said.

"Are you sure?"

Al shot his brother a harsh glare before dropping down inside the factory. Brian watched as his brother scampered around inside. He looked on as Al cautiously opened the back of a delivery truck, reached in, and took out a box before climbing up the storage racking with the box held firmly under his arm. Brian peeled back the plastic roofing sheet and reached down to take the box from his brother. He put the box on the roof and looked back, only to see that Al had already climbed back down and was taking a second box from an adjacent truck. He put it on the floor and then closed the back of each truck. With the second box of sweets under his arm he scaled the racking and joined Brian back on the roof.

"Why did you take two?" Brian asked.

"Because two is better than one," Al said, as he closed the clear plastic roof sheet.

"What if they notice?"

"Give it a break Brian, because you're beginning to get on my nerves!" Al said as he edged back across the roof.

"Do you want to go down first, Al, and then I'll drop the box down?" Brian said.

Al shook his head.

"No, the box might break and I'm not risking that," Al said as he turned and began to lower himself down with the box wedged tightly under his arm.

Brian looked on as his older brother slowly lowered himself and the box of sweets safely to the ground. Al placed the box by the wall before clambering back up the drainpipe where he grabbed the second box. With the lads both on the ground, they climbed over the wall and into the alleyway. Within minutes they were safely away with their haul of two full boxes of popular branded chocolate bars and sweets. Al and Brian were back amongst neighbours and friends. With almost all the sweetie bars sold in an hour they sat over at the play park and ate several Mars bars.

Al noticed a tall, stocky, lad enter the park. He knew him to be Sean Bullock, a local bully boy and self-proclaimed hardest lad in the class at school. Al slowed the swing down as Sean got closer.

"You got one of those for me?" Sean said as he pointed to the Mars bar sticking out of the top of Al's pocket.

"It'll cost yer," Al said, bringing the swing to a complete stop.

"You didn't pay for them though," Sean said.

Al could see that Sean was getting agitated as he began to clench and unclench his fists.

Al shrugged his shoulders.

"Do you know who I am? I could smash the pair of you up and not even break into a sweat, so you better just give me a Mars bar and some of that money in your pocket," Sean said as he raised his clenched fists.

Al rose to his feet and slowly looked Sean Bullock up and down.

"If you want sweets then go and get them yourself but you ain't getting none of mine."

Sean hesitated. Al could see that it wasn't the reaction he expected.

"I'll fight you if you want, but you're still not getting anything from me," Al said as he clenched both fists tightly and turned so that he was side on to Sean.

"So you fancy your chances, Al McIntosh?"

"Ready when you are," Al said confidently.

"This nutter might kill me and nick my sweets and the money," Al thought," *but I ain't backing off."*

Sean just stood and stared with his hardest and most menacing glare. Al met his threat and stood firm. No one was taking what was his no matter how much bigger a bully boy he was.

"You're on my list now McIntosh, and when the time is right you will get your fucking head kicked in," Sean said, still standing firm with his fists clenched.

"I'll be ready."

Al knew that the moment for Sean to make his move had passed. He might have a school ground fearsome reputation, but no one had ever stood up to him and Al figured that by standing his ground and meeting his threats head on, Sean had been rattled.

Al and his brother returned to the Trebor factory many times and took scores of boxed sweets. Increasingly he missed school as he also collected the floorboards from the demolished homes and sold them for a penny to neighbours as firewood. It hadn't been long before Trebor management cottoned on to the thefts and had a watchman patrol the distribution centre on Sundays. Even so, Al was earning between two and three shillings a day. Mammy had told him that he was like the real man of the house when he handed over money for food.

The twenty-eight days passed, and Albert was back at the house. Al and Brian had arrived home early to find their parents arguing outside in the street. Before Mammy could reach into her bag for the metal horseshoe, Albert pushed her away. Al looked on as she tripped backwards onto the road and into the path of a bus. The driver hit the brakes and burning tyre smoke belched out from the wheel arches just before Mammy was hit and knocked to the ground. Albert walked out into the road where his wife was lying. He stepped over her motionless body, picked up her handbag, reached in and took all the money she had in her purse. Albert dropped the bag onto the tarmac road. Al and his brother were now at the scene of the accident. Mammy let out a whimper as she came round.

"I'm going to the pub so don't bother waiting up!" Albert yelled as he marched off down the street.

The bus driver, Al and Brian helped Mammy back up onto her feet. Fortunately she hadn't sustained any serious injuries.

***

Later that night, after all the children had gone to bed, Mammy, still heavily bruised, searched the house for hidden bottles of Four Crown Wine with Al. Al found one hidden under the sofa. He raced into the kitchen carrying the prize find.

"He'll not be drinking this," Mammy said as she poured the contents down the kitchen sink.

Al looked on in silence.

"I should pack our bags and leave," Mammy said as she rubbed her swollen face. "But where, when you have nine kids?"

Al nodded.

"He wasn't always like this, you know. It was the war and those Germans. I know why he drinks but he can't be taking what little money we have to survive and waste it on booze down the pub. That's not right," Mammy said, shaking her head slowly. "We will have to take it back."

Al looked up.

"We must take the money back, Al. We need it back and so we'll have to take it," Mammy said as she reached down to the bottom drawer and produced a small claw hammer.

"I'm eight years old, what can I possibly do against a grown man?" Al thought.

Al was wide eyed as he watched Mammy hold the claw hammer up in front of her and then she offered it to him. He felt as though he didn't have any control of his hand. He found himself reaching out and gripping the handle. Mammy then took the metal horseshoe from her handbag.

"We're taking that money back," Mammy whispered.

Al and Mammy sat in the dark. They were both holding their weapons and waiting for Albert to come home from the pub. Al found himself thinking about the relationship between his parents. There had been violence for as long as he could remember. His Da would come home drunk and then Mammy, who was utterly fearless, would challenge him over something and it would erupt in an orgy of blood and broken bones. With a reputation as the local hard-man, Al had a grudging respect for him but hated it when he used his street fighting skills on his mammy.

Al tightened the grip on the claw hammers handle.

He remembered when, after one particularly violent attack that spilt out into the streets for all the neighbours to see, a social worker called round to visit. Al had expected his mother to reach into her bag and see the woman with the posh voice off. He was stunned when she smiled and invited her into the house. It was the role of the social worker to confront the problems of poverty and report their findings to social services. Mammy slipped Al a two-bob coin and then put her finger on her lips.

"Don't you say anything, okay?" whispered Mammy.

Al had nodded and followed Mammy into the front room where he sat opposite the posh woman in the pretty dress. Mammy had put on her best telephone voice as she spoke. Al had only ever heard her use that voice once before.

"Hello, my name is Claire. What is yours?" the social worker said to Al with a smile.

"Hello, I'm Al."

"Is that short for Alan?" Claire said.

Al nodded.

"Well, it's very nice to meet you Al." Claire said as she opened her notebook and began to scribble down notes.

"I'm a social worker, Al. Do you know what one of those is?"

Al shook his head.

"Okay, well my job is to help families resolve problems," Claire said. "Are you hungry, Al?"

"No," Al replied, shaking his head.

"I'm starving," Al thought, tightening the grip on the two-bob coin in his pocket *"I hope she doesn't hear my stomach rumbling."*

"What do you usually have to eat for dinner?"

"Mammy makes a lovely broth sometimes, and we have eggs and bacon," Al said enthusiastically. "That's my favourite."

"I wish I did have that," Al thought.

"That's nice, Al. Eggs and bacon is my favourite too. I see you have a bruise under your eye. How did that happen?"

Al rubbed the fading bruise.

"I was hit by a cricket ball at school," Al said, rubbing his eye. "It didn't hurt that much."

"That was no cricket ball. I got into a scrap with a lad two years older me than me," Al thought. *"When I got home Mammy yelled that the other boy better have two black eyes!"*

"Do you get hurt by cricket balls and things like that a lot?"

"No, that was the first time. It only hurt for a little while," Al said.

"How did your mother and father react to you being hurt?" Claire said, looking up from her note pad.

"Mammy washed my face and put something on it that stung for a bit," Al said, smiling at Mammy.

"What about your father, Al?"

"Da doesn't care about anything like that," Al said firmly.

"Do your parents ever leave you or your brothers and sisters alone in the house?"

"No, Mammy is nearly always at home or if she has to go out to the shops or something, then either Auntie Doreen or Auntie Mary will look after us," Al said.

"She must know I'm lying," Al thought.

"Al, when was the last time you had a bath?"

"I don't know," Al thought.

"Mammy makes us bath every Wednesday and Sunday before we go to school," Al said.

"That's good, Al," Claire said as she scribbled down her notes. "Has your father ever smacked you?"

Al shook his head.

"Has your mother ever smacked you?"

"More times than I can count!" Al thought. *"Mammy made me wear a dress and stand outside on the street so that everyone could see me. Then she belted me around the head and yelled out 'you'll never be a poof!'"*

"I get told off if I'm naughty, but Mammy has never smacked me," Al said.

"What about your brothers and sisters, has either of your parents ever smacked them?"

"We've all taken beatings, but William and Doreen get it worse. I've seen Mammy pull great chunks out of Doreen's hair, strip her naked and beat her until she couldn't get up off the floor and all because she took a lick of Mammy's ice cream," Al thought. *"She had bald spots on her head, so Mammy didn't send her to school. I've seen William be made to wear a dress and forced to sing 'everyone hates me' before getting beaten across the back with a dog chain."*

"No," Al said.

"Are you sure?"

"I've seen Beth slapped, punched and beaten again and again for no good reason," Al thought.

"Yes, I'm sure," Al said.

"Are you ever scared of making your parents angry?"

"Are you kidding me? Every bloody day! We all walk around the house never knowing when the next beating's going to come," Al thought.

"I don't like it when Da comes home drunk from the pub," Al said.

"Does he come home drunk often, Al?"

"All the time," Al said with a short nod.

"Does he argue with your mother?"

Al looked down at the floor and nodded.

"Does he ever hit your mother, Al?" Claire asked, as she looked up and put the tip of her pen on her lower lip.

Al looked back up and nodded again.

"We all love our mammy. It's our Da that causes all the problems," Al said.

"Okay, Al," Claire said as she wrote her notes. "Who is your favourite person in the family?"

Al thought about the question for a few moments.

"I think my mammy first and then my brother Brian. He's eighteen months younger than me," Al said.

"Do you have a hard time from anyone in your family?"

"Only Da," Al said.

"Do you ever think about hurting yourself?"

Al shook his head.

"Did your mother or father tell you what to say to me?"

Al shook his head and loosened the grip on the two-bob coin in his pocket.

"Are you sure?"

"Yes, I'm sure," Al said.

The social worker left shortly after. Mammy had waved her off with her best telephone voice but once the front door was firmly closed, she demanded the two-bob coin back. A few days later Albert was taken back to the asylum. He fought the orderlies right up until the sedative kicked in and he was bundled into the van.

**

Both Al and his Mammy sat in complete silence. Despite it being dark he could still make out her shape and the metal horseshoe. Al thought about the triplets, Beth, John and David. Al and the siblings had been excited by the prospect of more brothers or sisters but when Mammy returned from the hospital carrying the new-born triplets, she walked into the living room only to find that Da had ripped up all the floorboards, stripped out the lead and copper piping and taken it down to the scrap metal merchant so he could go to the pub. Albert hadn't even turned the water off. The floor was flooded. The carpet squelched as they stepped into the room. Mammy was distraught and took the triplets upstairs before going back down to turn the water off.

Al was brought back to the present when he heard the jingle of keys and then the lock turn.

"Da is home," Al thought.

Al could hear his heart thumping against his chest. Albert coughed and then staggered clumsily up the stairs.

"Drunk again!" Al thought as he tightened his grip on the small claw hammer.

The stairs thumped and thudded as Albert reached the top. He stopped and took a deep breath before staggering over to the bathroom. Al could clearly see his outline. Mammy had risen to her feet and was holding the metal horseshoe above her head. As Albert turned the bathroom light on, Mammy lurched forward and brought it down on Albert's head. Al scrambled to his feet and charged forward. He swung the hammer and hit Albert in the back. Mammy belted Albert a second and then a third time as he dropped to his knees. There were no cries of pain, just the thud of metal as it pounded Albert's flesh. Al had struck his Da several times before he noticed the pool of blood on the tiled floor. Mammy had a manic grin on her face as the giant of a man closed his eyes. She put the horseshoe on the windowsill and knelt to check his pockets for money. The first pocket was empty, so together they turned him onto his front so Mammy could get to the other pocket.

Mammy let out a shriek when she discovered that it too was empty. She clenched her fists and pounded Albert's motionless body several times until she slumped back against the wall. Al looked on as the tears began to stream down her face.

Al looked down at the claw hammer and then at his Da's still body. His right hand was outstretched showing the four tattooed crowns on his knuckles signifying his love of the wine.

"Go to bed, Al. You have school in the morning," Mammy said as she wiped away the tears and hauled herself back on to her feet.

Chapter 5

"Where are we going, Al?" Brian said, as he scampered to keep up.

"Up West," Al said, as he turned and slapped his brother on the back.

Al had heard a few of the local kids talking about the things they had found in the West of Glasgow, an area associated with people who have money. He had ventured up on his own at first to see exactly what could be found in and around the bins of rich people. At the very first bin he found a television set. It appeared to be almost new and in far better condition than the one they had at home. Al had struggled to carry the television set all the way home. He remembered there being an old television in the alleyway close to home and decided that he would take the two back home, so he had one for spares. Within minutes of changing a valve at the back of the television, it lit up. Al turned it off and then sold it to a neighbour in the next street for five bob. Immediately he ran down to Alex's Dairy and bought eggs, bacon, milk and bread and took it home.

Al had brought his friends Rob and Charlie to join in as they had been helpful in gathering up wood to sell and he didn't want to leave anything of value behind up West.

"What kind of stuff do they throw out?" Rob said as he skipped along the pavement.

"I don't know," Al said.

"Maybe they throw away their gold watches, rings and necklaces," Charlie said.

"Yeah, of course they do," Al said with a chuckle. "Probably throw out their old, crinkled pound notes too."

"Really?" Rob said.

"Who knows?" Al said, shrugging his shoulders.

The four boys walked through the tenement home filled streets until they found the tree lined avenues and large detached homes up west.

"I'm going to live in a house like this one day," Charlie said as he pointed to a large detached Victorian home with two wrought iron gates and a semi-circle driveway.

"I'll move in with you then," Rob said with a giggle.

"No, you have to get your own house because I'll have my wife living with me and who knows, maybe some children," Charlie said.

"Wife and children?" Rob said.

"Yeah, probably. I mean that's what you do when you grow up isn't it?" Charlie said.

"So, what are you going to do for a job? You'll need to earn a lot to live in a house like that with a wife and children," Rob said as he picked up the pace to walk alongside Charlie.

"I don't know?" Charlie said.

"Well, what are you good at in school?" Al asked as he looked over his shoulder at his friends.

Both Charlie and Rob were silent for a moment.

"Nothing," Charlie said finally. "I hate school. I suppose we'll have to go work with you Al."

"Yeah, we'll come and work with you Al. You always know how to make money from something," Rob said.

The four boys stopped by the first bin. On the ground beside it was a crystal chandelier. Al picked it up and inspected the light fitting. Two of the glass crystals were cracked.

"This should sell. Rob, you carry this, alright?" Al said as he handed the light fitting over.

"Yeah, sure.

At the second bin they found several suits which all appeared to be in good condition. Brian picked them up and slung them over his shoulder.

"These are really heavy," Brian said as Al placed the last suit jacket on his shoulder.

"Just think of the money," Al said.

Brian smiled.

The boys collected a number of bits and pieces, including a pair of full-length curtains and a boxed tea set that included a pot and four cups and saucers. Once Al was sure no one could carry any more they set off for home. Al was totalling up how much he wanted to get from the haul and how they would share the money out when he spotted his Da. They stopped briefly when he asked what they had and where they were going. After Al said that he was selling them locally, his Da told him to cut out the middleman and go directly to the rag and bone man in Balnain Street. Al, for the first time in his young life, marvelled at the business advice his Da had passed on. The rag and bone man bought everything and paid them the market rate. Al took the opportunity to ask what else he would buy so he could keep an eye out on his travels.

Once they were back on the street, Al split the money four ways and handed the coins to the boys. Brian wanted sweets and to go to the play park while Charlie and Rob wanted to go to the cinema. Al patted the money in his pocket. He knew that he wanted more, so he left and made his way alone back up west.

"I wonder what's in there?" Al thought as he peered over the fence at the padlocked dustbin. *"It must be worth something to have a padlock on it."*

Al clambered over the fence and jumped down into the garden. The padlocked dustbin was by the back of the house. Cautiously Al made his way across the garden, stopping momentarily behind a tree. He peeked out to check that no one could see him before racing up to the bin. Al tugged at the bin's lid. The padlock was slim and flimsy but held firm. To his right was a small rockery with plants and foliage. He leant down and picked up a broken house brick. Al took aim and with one almighty swing he brought the brick down on the base of the padlock. It broke open.

"Brilliant!" Al thought, as the thrill of finding something else created a buzz in the pit of his stomach.

Al lifted the dustbin's lid expecting to find something of great value but... it was empty.

"What! Who would padlock an empty bin?" Al thought.

Suddenly Al felt a drizzle on his head. He looked up to see if it was raining. A boy, Al thought was about ten years old with smartly cut hair into a side parting style, had opened his bedroom window and was holding a pot.

"What are you doing in our garden, scum?"

Al rubbed his wet hair and then sniffed his hand.

"It's piss! The kid's just thrown piss on me!" thought Al.

"Get down here, you!" Al yelled, "I'll beat you to a pulp!"

The young boy laughed and then turned the pot over completely so the full contents rained down all over Al.

"He's thrown more piss on me!" Al thought as the rage fired through his body.

"Get off our property before I call the police!" the boy called with a nasty laugh.

The stench of piss was overwhelming to Al. He was covered from the top of his head right down to his shoes. Al waved his fist angrily at the boy.

"You're going to really get it now!" Al warned.

"That's it, I'm calling the police," the boy said as he closed the window and disappeared inside the house.

Al wanted to beat the life out of the kid for what he'd done but he had to leave and leave quickly before the police turned up. Al knew they wouldn't take too kindly to a kid from his area up in the West of Glasgow.

He ran across the grass, vaulted over the fence and then broke out into a run down the avenue. The stink of piss was revolting. It was on his hands, in his hair, on his face and clothes and the deep breaths he took while running made him feel like his body was being infected. By the time he arrived back in Scotia Street it was getting dark. He stopped by the entrance to his house and shook his head in disgust as he still reeked from the smell of piss.

Once inside, he bounded up the stairs to the bathroom where he stripped off and waited for the bath to fill with hot water. He scrubbed his hair and body with soap, muttering under his breath all the violent things he would do to the boy that had poured the piss pot over him.

***

The following morning Al was up early, out of the house and back up West where he waited at the end of the avenue for the boy that threw the piss over him. He watched closely as the lad came out of the house with his mother, a well-dressed, blonde woman wearing a long brown coat and boots. Al kept his distance and followed them until they reached the gates to a school several roads away. The boy's mother kissed him on the cheek, turned and began chatting with another mother. Al watched the boy join a bunch of lads playing with a ball. He was laughing.

"He'd better not be laughing at me!" Al thought.

Al spent the day going through bins and took what he got down to the rag and bone man before returning to the boy's school. From across the road, he watched a sea of pupils leave the school gates. When he spotted his target he moved out slowly to follow him. The boy was alone and walking back towards the avenue where he lived. Al was on the opposite side of the road and quickened his pace. The boy was oblivious to Al and just skipped happily along the pavement. As he turned the corner, Al raced across the road. He grabbed the boy by the scruff of his neck and swung him around. The lad was startled and before a word was spoken Al threw a right hander that him to the ground. Al dropped down onto one knee and threw a second punch before turning the lad onto his back and sitting on his chest.

"Remember me, piss pot?"

Al punched the boy in the face with such ferocity that his head hit the pavement with a thud before bouncing back up.

"Please, I'm sorry" the boy pleaded.

Al punched him again with his left hand.

"Sorry? Sorry you're not talking your way out of this!" Al said as he grabbed the boy by his shirt collar and smashed his fist into the boy's face.

"Now you listen to me, piss pot. I know who you are and where you live and I'm going to beat the shit out of you every time I see you unless you have a ten bob note for me!"

"Yes, okay," the boy cried. "Anything, just please don't hurt me."

Al let go of the boy's collar and got back on his feet.

"How much money have you got on you now?" Al said menacingly.

"About five bob," the boy said, sobbing.

"Well that's mine, alright?" Al said, his eyes firmly fixed on the boy's.

The boy didn't answer but reached into his trouser pocket and produced a handful of coins. Al snatched them away, counted them quickly and then put them into his own pocket.

"Remember, I know where you go to school and where you live so trust me, piss pot, you will not see me coming. So you better have that ten bob or it will get nasty, very nasty!"

The boy nodded his head and wiped the tears from his face.

Al spun around on his heels and strutted away, patting his pocket full of money.

"Serves the little piss pot right," Al thought. *"No one does that to me and gets away with it."*

Chapter 6

"What's going on downstairs?" Brian said as he pulled his brown jumper over his head.

"They've come for Da again?" Al said as he opened the bedroom door and peered out into the hallway.

The boys could hear their Da shouting and yelling obscenities downstairs in the living room. There was a sudden thud.

"Who?"

"The people from the asylum," Al said as he stepped back into the bedroom and picked up his black jacket.

"Where are you going?"

"Out," Al said as he tugged on the zipper.

"Out where?"

"Just out."

"Can I come?"

Al turned and looked down at his brother.

"Alright, but you have to do as I say, okay?" Al said as he turned back to the bedroom door.

Brian beamed and scampered off the bed to join his brother.

The two boys walked cautiously down the stairs. They could hear the violent struggle as their da fought ferociously to keep the hospital orderlies from taking him back to the asylum.

Mammy passed calmly by the orderlies as they struggled to tie the back of the straitjacket and went into the kitchen. With the front door open Al shot across the hallway and out into the street with Brian close behind.

"So where are we going? The Trebor factory or out to collect some wood to sell?" Brian said, putting his hands into his trouser pockets.

"No, we're going up West," Al said.

The two boys stopped as an argument broke out between two neighbours on the opposite side of the road. The husband was shouting at the top of his voice at his pregnant wife.

"You've been at it; I know you have!"

"I haven't, please come inside and calm down."

"Calm down? Calm down? Don't you tell me what to do, cow!"

"Cow? Cow? Don't you call me no cow!"

"You're a no good cow!"

"My da said you were no good and he was right!"

"Well fuck off back to them then!"

"Why should I? It's my name on the rent book!"

"Yeah, but it's my hard graft that pays the rent you lazy fat cow!"

"I'm pregnant, not fat, you animal!"

"All the same!"

"Go on then, fuck off down the pub with your so-called mates!"

"Don't you tell me what to do!"

Al and Brian watched as the husband reached down and picked up an empty milk bottle from the doorstep. He turned sharply and smacked his heavily pregnant wife around the head. The boys heard the dull thud clearly from across the road and watched helplessly as her legs buckled before she slumped down onto the pathway.

"Fucking serves you right you lazy fat cow!"

The husband dropped the milk bottle and walked past his wife's motionless body. He turned abruptly at the gate and stormed off down the street.

"That was nasty," said Brian. "Someone should call for an ambulance or something."

"They will," Al said, as he nodded towards a couple looking out of their front room window from behind the curtains.

"Come on, we need to get a move on."

The boys travelled at pace across Glasgow until they reached the affluent West.

"Right, now follow me," Al whispered, as he darted down a side alleyway between two large, detached homes.

"What? Are we raking the middens?" Brian whispered.

The local boys coined the term 'lucky middens' as a rich person's dustbin and 'raking the middens' was stealing from them.

"No, now keep quiet and follow me," Al said as he opened the wooden gate that led into the back garden.

Brian followed his brother across the grass until they reached the back door.

"What are we doing?" Brian whispered.

Al tugged on the door handle and then opened the back door slowly.

"We're going in," Al said.

"The door's unlocked. What if they're at home?"

"They're not Brian. There's three days of milk on the doorstep. They must be away and have forgotten to cancel the milkman," Al hissed.

Al closed the back door gently and then tip toed through the kitchen. Brian stopped and opened one of the cupboards.

"Al, look. I've never seen so much food in one place."

Al turned back to see a cupboard full to the brim with tins of beans, peas, Spam, cakes and biscuits. Brian reached in and took out a Battenburg cake, a light sponge cake with different sections held together with jam. He unwrapped the packaging to reveal the white marzipan covered cake with chequered pink and yellow sponge.

"Do you want some Al?"

Al nodded.

Brian opened a nearby drawer and took out a bright silvery dinner knife. He sliced the cake into four large pieces and then handed his brother a large chunk of the sponge cake.

Brian bit into his slice first. He closed his eyes as the wonderful taste teased his taste buds.

"This must be the best cake in the world," Brian said, taking a second bite.

Al took a bite from his own slice.

"This is what it's like to be rich or living in England," Al whispered. "You can eat cake like this every day."

Brian had swallowed both his slices before Al had finished his first.

"You must have been hungry," Al chuckled.

"Always," Brian said, licking the jam and marzipan from his fingers.

Al left his slice on the kitchen work top and edged out towards the hallway.

"This hallway is bigger than our bedroom," Brian whispered.

The two boys peeked around the first door into what looked like a library with a large hand carved desk and matching chair.

"This room is bigger than the whole downstairs of our house," Brian said as he scanned the room. "They must have more books than the Glasgow University Library."

Al walked up to the bookshelf and read some of the titles. They included:

A History of English Law Vol 3: The Reform of The Police

A History of English Law Vol 4: Grappling for Control

"He must be a lawyer or something," Al thought.

Al picked the book up and flicked through the pages before putting it back on the bookshelf. He then walked around to the back of the large ornate desk. He tugged on the handle of a drawer a couple of times but found that it was locked. He was just about to tell Brian to go and get him the knife from the kitchen, when he spotted the drawer's key next to a set of Parker Pens. The pens had a black base with a stainless-steel cap with a gold arrow etched into it. Al took the key and opened the drawer.

Inside, he saw a wooden box with a label reading 'Esplendidos Cohiba'. He took the box out and opened it to find just four cigars left in the box and a pair of silver cigar cutters. Al closed the box and just as he was about to put it back in the drawer, he spotted a black leather wallet. He quickly reached in and opened it. Inside he saw a business card with 'St Mark's Masonic Lodge No 102' written on it. At the back of the wallet were notes. Al plucked them out and, with a huge smile on his face, held them up for Brian to see.

"We've hit the jackpot," Al said as he counted the one pound notes out on the desk.

"We're rich," Brian said as he threw his arms up into the air, "We're rich!"

"Ten, eleven, twelve, thirteen, fourteen, fifteen. We've got fifteen pounds," Al said as he held up the tidy bundle of pound notes.

"Can I touch them?" Brian asked as he approached the desk.

"Yeah, of course," Al said, handing the bundle of notes over to his brother.

Brian's eyes lit up as his hands closed around the money.

Al watched his brother finger the money before reaching out his hand. Without any hesitation Brian handed his brother back the money. Al folded it and placed it firmly into his pocket. The boys ventured from room to room. Upstairs they stumbled across a child's bedroom.

"I would love a bedroom like this," Brian said as he gazed at the bed with matching coloured pillows and cushions. On the floor was a box, full to the brim with metal toy cars. Brian's gaze landed on a children's Beano annual. The front cover featured Biffo the Bear holding up some circular weights while being tickled with a feather.

"Look at this," Brian said as he picked up the Beano annual and flicked through the coloured pages. "It's got Dennis the Menace, Minnie the Minx and the Bash Street Kids.

Al took the annual and flicked through the pages quickly.

"We don't have time for this," Al said.

"Can I take it?"

"No, it has no value," Al said as he glanced out through the upstairs window. "We have to go."

Al had a few bits and pieces, but the day's prize was finding fifteen one pound notes hidden inside the lawyer's desk drawer.

"Close the door behind you," Al said, as Brian left the house.

The boys opened the garden gate and peered down the alleyway.

"It's all clear, come on." Al said as he ushered his brother through the gateway into the alleyway before closing the gate firmly behind him.

The boys travelled back to their home area, stopping off at a sweet shop where they indulged themselves with the branded chocolate bars and sweets they had seen on television adverts or heard friends talk about. In the corner of the shop was a rack of magazines. Al spotted a Beano comic. He picked it up, smiled, and added it to the assortment of sweets on the counter. In the park near home, they ate sweets while Brian read his comic book. Before returning home Al went into Alex's Dairy and bought groceries for the family. In the following days Al replaced the food that was eaten by the family. It had been the first time that he could remember when the family all ate a full meal every day.

Over the coming months Al and Brian broke into seventeen homes up West. He had developed contacts for jewellery, radios and other small electrical items. He liked to focus on cash and small, high value items that would sell quickly and easily.

"Maybe this house will have more money that that lawyer's house," Brian said.

The two boys had ventured up West again on the thieve. Al had taken time out to scope a home that he thought would deliver a decent haul of goodies. For Brian the money they made was the prize, but Al had increasingly become addicted to the tremendous high of being on the thieve and walking away with a pocket full of money to help support his family and live the kind of life that he'd seen people from the luxurious homes that he robbed have.

"Come on, follow me," Al said as he scaled over the five-foot brick wall that surrounded his target home. The boys crouched down behind a tree in the garden. Al peeked out.

The house was having a large double storey extension built. Al thought that the extension was larger than four of the houses in his home road combined, so he assumed that the owners must be rich. Scaffolding had been erected around the house with all the brickwork now at almost roof height. The window frames had not yet been fitted, so a flimsy sheet of plastic had been placed over the hole to keep the weather out. Al took a second peek at the house and then scuttled across the garden with Brian close behind. They stopped at the base of the scaffolding and looked up.

"This should be easy compared to the Trebor Factory," Al said as he reached up to the temporary structure's scaffold tube. He heaved himself up and rolled onto the scaffold board before reaching down to help Brian up.

"I'm alright," Brian said as he dragged himself up onto the board and sat beside Al.

"We'll go in through the upstairs window," Al whispered, pointing up at the plastic covered hole.

The boys reached up and pulled themselves up to the second floor of the huge extension.

"Are you alright?" Al said as he looked down at a small cut on his brother's hand.

"Yeah, I caught myself on a nail," Brian said, holding his bleeding hand up.

"Be careful, Brian," Al whispered before turning and pulling the corner of the plastic sheet away from where the new window would be fitted.

With the corner prised open, Al hauled himself up and into the room. As his feet landed with a thud, he turned to find a large man dressed in work clothes behind him. He had a bushy black beard and moustache.

Al turned quickly to make his escape, but the builder grabbed him firmly by the arm.

"Run, run!" Al shouted as he wriggled, tugged and pulled to get away.

Brian spotted what had happened and quickly scaled down the scaffolding tubes after Al called out for him to escape. Once back on the ground, Brian raced across the garden and leapt up and over the garden's brick wall. With his hands in his pockets and looking down he waked back out into the avenue quickly and didn't look up until he was out of the West of Glasgow.

Al fought to escape but the builder's grip was too strong. A second builder appeared carrying a brick trowel and a black plastic bucket full of fresh cement.

"Norman, call the police!" the builder yelled.

Norman dropped the bucket and trowel and raced downstairs into the house.

"Let me go, let me go!" Al yelled as he slammed his free arm down onto the builder's grip.

"You're not going anywhere you wee thief!" the builder hissed as he tightened his grip.

"That hurts, let me go!"

A few seconds later Al could hear the pounding of feet on the wooden staircase. The door was pushed open, and Norman entered, trying to catch his breath.

"They're on their way," Norman said as he looked down at the nine-year-old boy.

The adrenaline rush that Al had experienced during his struggle to escape capture began to wear off. He had stopped struggling as he realised the enormity of what he was facing. As he slumped back onto the steps of a timber ladder he became overcome by a mixed range of emotions. He was in shock at being caught; frustrated by not being able to get away, confused because he didn't know or understand what would come next. He only knew that the police were the enemy and not to be trusted, and he was scared of how his mammy would react when she discovered that her son was a thief. Al was, however, happy that his brother, Brian, had got clean away. In Mammy's eyes Brian could do no wrong and he didn't want to think about how she would be when she discovered that Brian had been out housebreaking with him.

"Please let me go mister. I was just playing on the scaffolding. I promise not to do it again," Al said as he looked up at his captor.

The builder slowly shook his head.

"The police are on their way."

Al quickly concluded that there would be no reasoning with the builder and hung his head until two uniformed police officers arrived. The door swung open and the officers walked into the newly constructed room.

"Is this him?" one of the officers asked, pointing to Al.

"Yeah, that's him," the builder said.

"You've certainly been busy for a wee fella," the second police officer said. "Come on, up you get."

The builder finally released his grip on Al's right arm. Al looked up at the two officers and slowly got up. The first officer took hold of Al's left arm and led him through the newly built red brick extension, down the stairs and out onto the avenue where he spotted a black Austin Cambridge police car. Al could see the curtains twitching from the house across the road while a man in a long black raincoat walking his overweight golden Labrador stopped by the lamppost and shook his head as the police officers opened the police car's rear door and sat him inside.

"I've never been in a police car before," Al muttered.

"People that steal end up in police cars, court and eventually prison. After all the burglaries that have been committed in this area, I'm sure this will not be your last time in a police car," the second officer said as he reached down and turned the ignition key.

The police car roared to life. The officer slipped the gear shifter into first gear and pulled away slowly. Al looked over to his right. The man walking his dog stood motionless, staring blankly at Al inside the police car.

"How am I going to explain all this to Mammy?" Al thought. *"She will beat the living crap out of me."*

The police car turned right into St Georges Road and pulled into the police station's car park area. Al was led into the station and down into an interview room.

"I never thought this could happen to me," Al thought. *"Will they send me to prison?"*

The officers left Al alone in the room. He sat silent and listened to the conversations, scuffles and arguments in the hallway outside. Finally, an officer entered the room. He took out his notebook and asked for Al's full name and address. Al gave it willingly. To his surprise the officer closed the notebook, stood up and opened the interview room door.

"Gone on then, get yourself home and tell your parents what you've been up to. We'll see you shortly," the officer said as he motioned Al to leave the room.

Al returned home and scampered straight upstairs to the boy's bedroom where he found Brian reading his Beano comic.

"What happened Al?" Brian said as he put the comic on the bed.

"They got me, but I didn't say anything about you," Al said as he sat on the corner of the bed.

"I just ran as soon as you said to," Brian said.

"Good, because Mammy will go mad if she finds out you were with me," Al said.

"Are you going to tell her?" Brian asked, twiddling his fingers nervously.

"The police said they will be coming back but I'm not saying anything to Mammy," Al said.

"Why?"

"Just in case they forget," Al said.

The police didn't forget. Four days later they arrived at the McIntosh's family home. The police told Mammy that they believed him and one other to be responsible for seventeen housebreakings in the West of Glasgow and that charges would be brought against him. They strongly suspected that Brian had been Al's accomplice but didn't have any evidence to bring charges. Mammy remained quietly stunned throughout their visit. She could not believe that her son, Al, would rob people's homes. Minutes after the police left Al was savagely beaten red raw with a dog chain for robbing homes and involving his brother, Brian.

The court case came round quickly. Al was held downstairs in a room with several lads waiting to appear before the judge. The officer looked down at the nine-year-old and warned him to behave himself. Al sat amongst the other lads waiting. Each one remained silent, lost in their own thoughts.

Finally the court officer led Al up before the judge. The whole experience had been a little overwhelming but the excitement and rewards from the crimes outweighed the consequences. The judge looked down at the young boy as the charges were read out. The judge raised a single eyebrow as he passed down three a year probation order.

The court official explained that probation was the release of an offender from detention subject to a period of good behaviour under supervision.

The McIntosh family moved, albeit in the same area, shortly after the court case, so Al never attended a single session.

Chapter 7

Al and Brian were talking in the backyard when, Jimmy, an old drunk, staggered past the metal railings.

"Alright lads," Jimmy said as he tripped over the kerb and fell against the railings.

"Yeah, alright," Al said, nodding his head.

"You haven't got a few pennies you can spare for a drink, have you?"

Al patted his empty pockets, shrugged his shoulders and called back "Can't help you, Jimmy."

"Alright, thank you lads," Jimmy said.

"Is that you Jimmy?"

Al and Brian turned to see Mammy standing behind them.

"It is Hen," Jimmy called back.

"Are you looking for a few pennies?"

"I am Hen."

"I'll see what I have if you'll give us a tune," Mammy said, turning and winking at Al.

Jimmy pulled himself upright and pushed his shoulders back.

"I can do that. What would like to hear?"

"The sound of your footsteps fucking off," Al thought.

"What about *"I can hear a Lassie?"* Jimmy said. "I know every word."

Mammy shook her head.

"I've got it Hen, I've got it," Jimmy said, wiping his mouth.

"Alright then Jimmy, you sing, and I'll see what I can find you," Mammy said as she turned and went back into the house.

Jimmy placed a hand on each hip, took a deep breath and began to sing:

'I belong to Glasgow

Dear old Glasgow town

Well what's the matter with Glasgow

For it's goin' 'roon and roon'

I'm only a common old working chap

As anyone can see

But when I get a couple of drinks on a Saturday

Glasgow belongs to me'

"What a racket," Al thought.

Jimmy broke into the second verse. He was wailing so loud the dog from down the street began howling along.

Mammy returned to the backyard holding a coal fire shovel with a thru-penny bit in the middle.

"There you go Jimmy," Mammy called out as she tossed the coin into the air. It landed on the pavement a few feet away from where Jimmy was standing.

"God bless you Hen," Jimmy said as he bent down to pick up the coin.

"Arghh!" Jimmy yelled, as he picked the coin up and immediately dropped it and cradled his hand.

Mammy burst out laughing.

"You bitch! You fucking horrible bitch," Jimmy shrieked as he frantically waved his hand around.

Al and Brian laughed with Mammy. They had both seen this before. Mammy had gone inside the house and placed the thru-penny bit into the open fire and then, when it was seriously hot, she took it out of the open fire with the coal shovel.

Jimmy called Mammy every name under the sun while he waved his hand around and blew ferociously on his burnt fingers. Al, Brian and Mammy continued to laugh long after Jimmy picked up the cooled down thru-penny bit and wandered off, muttering to himself.

Al and Brian left home and joined a game of football at the end of the road. They arrived back later in the afternoon.

"Is that Wullie?" Al said as he approached the house.

Wullie was dressed in a dress and had been painted blue. He was dancing awkwardly and singing 'I'm the Wizard of Oz'. Several of the street lads were laughing and pointing at his brother.

"It's Mammy, she's been at it again!" Al thought.

"Come on Wullie, let's get you inside," Al said, while Brian shot up the pathway and inside the house.

"You're an evil bully, Mammy!" Al thought.

"Alright that's enough," Al said to the small crowd of lads jeering and pointing at Wullie.

"It's okay Al, I am the Wizard of Oz," Wullie said.

"Of course you are," Al said as he put his arm around his brother's shoulders.

Once they were inside the house Mammy stormed into the front room.

"You wee bastard, you've been embarrassing me in front of the neighbours!" Mammy bellowed, swinging the dog chain around her head.

SMACK!

The dog chain caught Wullie on the arm.

"Please Mammy, please don't hurt me again," Wullie whimpered.

"That's enough Mammy, come on!" Al said as he stood in front of his brother. "You must have painted him blue because he wouldn't have done it himself."

"Do you want a beating too?" Mammy shouted as she swung the heavy dog chain towards Al.

Al ducked and slipped into the hallway and raced upstairs to the bedroom he shared with his brothers.

"Poor old Wullie's getting it again," Al said.

"If it wasn't him, it'd be Beth," Brian said.

"We all get beaten, but never as bad as Wullie or Beth," Al said.

"She hates us all," Brian said.

"She belongs in a nut house along with Da," Al said.

There was a stomping on the stairs as Wullie scampered up them, promptly followed by Mammy. Al could hear Mammy scrubbing the blue paint off his brother. He imagined the look of sheer delight as she scored his young skin. There was another thumping of footsteps across the landing before a barrage of blood curdling screams could be heard from the back bedroom with Mammy screaming obscenities at the top of her voice. The violence finally came to an end with Mammy slamming the bedroom door and stomping on the landing and stairs.

***

The following morning, when Wullie hadn't returned to their bedroom, Al went to find his brother. He was lying on the threadbare carpet in the girls' room, holding his legs.

"Are you okay, Wullie?" Al said as he crouched down.

"Look at my knee," Wullie whimpered.

Al glanced over at Wullie's heavily swollen knee.

"You evil witch," Al thought as he looked down at the swelling.

"What did she do to you?" Al said.

Wullie wiped a tear from his face.

"She took a needle and hammered it into my knee," Wullie said with a snivel.

"No!" Al said as he looked closer at Wullie's knee.

"Can you stand up?" Al asked.

Wullie shook his head.

"It hurts too much," he replied.

Al got up and raced off downstairs to the kitchen where he saw Mammy standing by the sink with a handful of pills she had got from the doctor and a teacup full of tap water.

"Wullie needs to go to the hospital," Al said calmly.

"I'll be having no poofs in my house," Mammy said.

"His knee is swollen right up, and he can't walk. We need to call an ambulance," Al said.

"I said no!"

"Mammy, he's really hurt and needs help," Al pleaded.

Mammy swallowed the last of her medication and put the teacup in the sink.

"Alright, well you take him," Mammy said bluntly.

"But it's well over a mile away," Al said.

"You take him and don't you be telling those damn doctors anything that happened here. He fell over, alright? Do you understand me?"

Al nodded, raced back up the stairs and helped Wullie to his feet. With Wullie's arm around his shoulder he gently helped him down the stairs, out through the front door and onto the street. Al turned back to see Mammy, expressionless, standing by the window.

Al carried Wullie in his arms the full mile to the hospital. They had to stop several times as Al was physically exhausted. His arms, legs, and back ached, but he finally got to the hospital entrance. A passing nurse caught sight of Al struggling and ran over to help.

"What happened?" the nurse said as she placed Wullie's arm around her neck.

"It's my brother, he's hurt himself," Al said taking a deep breath.

The nurse, having looked at Wullie's knee, took Al and Wullie straight through the emergency waiting room and into a cubicle. Between Al and the nurse, they managed to haul Wullie up onto the hospital bed. She rushed out and returned seconds later with a doctor. Al stepped back to let the doctor examine Wullie's knee.

"This is serious, what happened?" the doctor said as he turned to Al.

"My brother and I were playing football and he fell over on something," Al said.

"I should be telling you that this kind of thing happens weekly in our house. I should tell you that Wullie gets beaten black and blue with the dog chain for no reason and his twin, Doreen, has her hair ripped out from the roots by Mammy. We are all systematically beaten with the dog chain and then we're told to lie about it," Al thought.

"Where's your mother?" the doctor said.

"She's not well, sir, so I just brought him here straight away," Al said in a sullen tone.

The nurse let out a minor tut and shook her head.

"We need to get this boy to x-ray, nurse," the doctor said.

"What, you believe that my brother's leg would look like that from a fall playing football?" Al thought.

The nurse put her right foot on the bed's wheel brake to release it and then pulled it out and away from the wall. Al stepped forward to help.

"No, no, young man. The best thing you can do now is go and sit yourself down in the emergency waiting area. We'll take good care of your brother," the doctor said.

"What is your name?" the nurse asked with a smile.

"Al."

"Well don't worry Al. I'll come and find you when we know what we're dealing with," the nurse said as she pulled on the bed.

"You'll be alright now, Wullie," Al said.

An orderly rushed up the corridor between the cubicles and took the other side of the bed. Al watched as his brother was wheeled away.

He returned to the emergency waiting area and took a seat. Al slouched back into the uncomfortable metal and threadbare fabric chair and looked up at the sunlight and dust particles floating about in front of the window. He felt his throat tense up when he imagined Mammy hammering a needle into Wullie's knee. Al looked around at the scores of people waiting to be seen. An older woman held her wrinkled hand. Her eyes were red, and Al could see they were filled with tears. The younger woman next to her was staring into space, emotionless. Al watched as she turned to the older woman, said nothing, and then looked at her watch.

"I'm not sitting about in here," Al thought. *"I'm going to check the place out."*

Al approached the receptionist and smiled.

"If that nice nurse comes looking for me, please tell her that I won't be long. I'm just going to go outside for some fresh air," Al said.

"Err, oh yes, alright," the receptionist said as she looked up briefly and peered over her glasses.

Al went outside and followed the perimeter of the building. He peeked down the alleyways and through the windows. He passed an old ambulance that was sitting on three flat tyres. The windscreen was cracked, and somebody had removed the passenger side door. Al smiled to himself, climbed up through the passenger side and sat in the driver's seat. He placed his hands on the steering wheel and his right foot on the pedal.

"Neer-ner, neer-ner," Al yelled, pulling the steering wheel from left to right and crunching the gearstick back and forth.

"This must be what it's like being an ambulance driver racing to the scene of a big pub fight in Scotia Street, and then, when you arrive, you see Da drunk, screaming at the top of his voice, surrounded by all the neighbours. Then he starts punching Mammy over and over," Al thought.

Al let go of the steering wheel and sat back in the seat.

"If I were an ambulance driver I'd come and save all my brothers and sisters," Al thought. *"I would never believe any of the stories that Mammy makes up."*

Al clambered back out of the ambulance and continued to explore the hospital grounds. He came across an area that had three large black bins.

"I wonder what's in there?" he thought.

Al looked around to make sure he was alone before climbing up onto the top of the bin. He checked around him again then opened the lid. Al peered down at several greeny-yellowy coloured bags. He reached down and hauled one up onto the top of the bin.

"This could be some kind of treasure," Al thought as he tore the bags open.

A blood-stained hand fell out.

"What the fuck?" Al cried out as he scuttled back, almost falling off the bin.

Al stared at the hand, and after a few seconds he composed himself. He slowly reached out and touched a finger.

"It doesn't feel like anything," Al thought. *"Somebody must have had their hand chopped off by a surgeon."*

Al picked up the hand, held it up and gazed at the crooked fingers.

"Imagine having no hands," Al wondered. *"You can't eat properly, wash, or go to the toilet. I'd hate that."*

Al put the hand down on the bin, opened the bag wider and peeked in.

"Bloody hell! There's legs and arms and a load of fingers!"

Finally, Al put the hand back inside the bag and dropped the bag down into the bin. He closed the lid, scrambled off the bin awkwardly and jumped onto the ground. He continued to investigate the hospital grounds and then returned to the emergency waiting room. The seat he had been sitting on was taken so he sat by the window. He smiled when he noticed that the old lady cradling her injured hand was no longer there. Moments later the nurse appeared at the door; she scanned the room and walked over to Al.

"Is my brother alright?" Al asked.

"Come with me Al," the nurse said, motioning him to join her.

She led Al through the corridor and then down onto a ward where he found Wullie lying in bed. The doctor was standing over him looking at the x-ray.

"Your brother is a very lucky young man. It was fortunate you brought him in when you did," the doctor said, holding up the x-ray.

Al stepped forward and gazed at the x-ray sheet.

"Do you see that?" the doctor said.

Al nodded.

"That is a pin and it's buried in your brother's knee," the doctor said. "We'll need to operate."

"Will Wullie be alright?" Al asked.

"He will now, but if it had been any longer, your brother could have lost his leg," the doctor said, pointing down at the bandaged knee. "There are early symptoms of gangrene setting in."

"Gangrene?" Al said with a gasp.

"When body tissue dies due to lack of blood flow, gangrene can set in. Your brother could have lost his leg or worse still, died. Well done young man for bringing him in when you did," the doctor said, putting the x-ray back inside the envelope.

"When can I take Wullie home?" Al asked.

"We will be operating on your brother shortly. The best thing you can do is ask your mother to come in tomorrow and we'll be able to give you more information," the doctor said.

"Okay, I'll do that," Al replied.

"How could you have done this, Mammy?" Al thought, trying hard to contain his anger.

"Fell on a needle while playing football," the nurse said.

"Yes," Al said.

"Please, just force me to tell you the truth," Al thought.

"Okay, on your way," the doctor said.

Al thanked the nurse and the doctor for caring for his brother. He left by the emergency ward door and had an overwhelming need to go back and check out the hospital grounds some more. He scanned the grounds for anything that he might have missed and then stopped by the black bin that housed the amputated limbs.

"I could have a laugh with these," Al thought as he scaled the bin, tore open the lid, and grabbed hold of a bag full of amputated body parts.

***

Al carried the bag back to Scotia Street where he met up with some of his friends. He took them to one side and opened the bag. One lad reached in and pulled out an arm.

"Whoever lost that is 'armless' now," Al said with a raucous, laugh.

"Cool," one lad said.

"Where did you get them, Al?" another asked.

Al told them of his adventures at the hospital and how he stumbled upon the black bin full of body parts.

"We could make a person," one lad said.

"Yeah, like Frankenstein," said another.

"Or we could just have some fun," Al said with a mischievous grin.

Later that night, Al and a few of the boys watched a neighbour stagger drunkenly along the street. He tripped, recovered and then tripped again.

"Are you alright?" Al said as he ran over the road to steady the drunk.

"Yeah, yeah," the man grunted.

Al had been holding a severed hand behind his back and when the drunk leant on his shoulder to steady himself and get back onto his feet, Al slipped it into the drunk's coat pocket.

"Alright, alright on your way then," Al said as he waved the drunk off.

Al was struggling to contain his laughter as the image of the drunk waking up in the morning, reaching out for his something in his pocket and finding the hand played over and over in his mind.

Over the next few days, the boys tied some string to a leg and then tied the other end to the knocker on a neighbour's front door. The boys knocked on the door, ran and hid behind a delivery van on the opposite side of the road. The door was yanked open by a woman in a checked apron who stood looking up and down the road. She finally looked down and saw the human leg dangling from her door knocker. She fainted and fell onto her back in the hallway. The boys, in fits of laughter, got up and ran down the road.

Al had always been a dog lover and had often gone to the butcher's and asked for bones to feed the street dogs. The butcher gave him a bag which he used to encourage dogs from all around the Cowcaddens to follow him back to Scotia Street where he fed them the bones. It was not unusual for a dog to recognise Al and come up to him, wagging their tail, hoping to get a treat. A black mongrel dog with a curly tail spotted Al and bolted across the road. Al patted him while the dog sniffed the bag of limbs.

"Gone on Al, give the dog a bone," one of the boys said.

"Yeah, go on Al. It'll be a laugh," another said.

Al reached in and pulled out an arm. The mongrel dog turned and snatched the last of the limbs and scooted off across the road. The boys, who were still laughing at seeing the dog with the arm in its mouth watched as a woman carrying a paper bag of groceries, spotted the dog, screamed, dropped the bag and ran wildly up the street, hands flailing. The boys quickly ran across the road and collected the tins of beans, Spam and the loaf of bread. They left the broken box of eggs on the pavement.

***

Wullie was allowed to return home and Mammy had been full of apologies and promises to never hurt or harm them again.

"I've heard all this before Mammy," Al thought. *"Give it three or four days and you'll be back to yourself."*

Al didn't return to the hospital and take any more bags of amputated limbs. However, when the other kids in the area found out where they were, they had gone down and taken bags for pranks themselves. The police were called in, believing that people were being murdered and hacked up in the area. The newspapers carried out their own minor investigation and put the whole incident down to university students carrying out practical jokes.

Chapter 8

Glasgow Council had approved plans to build the M8 Motorway right through the heart of the City. Slum areas that included Townhead, Charing Cross, Anderston, Kinning Park and Al's home district, Cowcaddens, were rife with poverty and overcrowding. They had all been destined for demolition.

Al had taken a walk to where the construction had begun. He looked at the men and machinery and then at the empty houses. He spotted an electrical shop with a television in the window and a large sign saying 'Sale'. Al crossed the road and stared at the television set.

"I'd love a television set like that in our house," Al thought as he studied every button and curve on the set. *"It wouldn't last long though. Da would have it sold and spend the money getting drunk."*

Al looked over at the empty house next door to the shop. He turned quickly and walked up the concrete pathway and found that the door had already been opened. Al pushed it open further and stepped inside. The house was full of dust and bare floorboards. He walked from room to room.

"It's good to check it out because you never know what you can find," Al thought.

When Al spotted the stairs leading down to the cellar area, he walked down cautiously, leaving the door open to let in some light. Once inside, he found himself looking at the wall that separated the empty house and the electrical shop.

"I wonder what's on the other side of that wall?" Al thought. *"There might be a television just like the one in the window."*

Al rubbed his hand against the brick wall.

"I need to find out what's on the other side of you," Al muttered under his breath.

Al left the deserted house and returned to Scotia Street where he found Brian and the other local boys huddled together.

"What's going on?" Al said.

The lads turned to face him.

"It's those Gayfeelies," Brian hissed. "They beat Trevor's brother up."

"Right, we can't be having that. We need to hit them hard and fast," Al said.

"What are we going to do?" Billy Bunter said.

Billy Bunter was the only overweight boy on the street. At just ten years old he was already bigger than some of the teenagers. Al and the Scoshees would go on Gayfeely raids after being attacked. They would grab a lad, beat him and then hold him down so that Billy Bunter could drop his entire body weight down on them. On one occasion the Scoshees grabbed a lad and took him to Billy Bunter's home. They called up to his bedroom window. When Billy Bunter saw the frightened boy, he produced a pot full of piss and shit from his grandma's room and poured it onto the Gayfeely.

"Come on, follow me," Al said as he led the boys down Scotia Street.

The boys hid behind a car at the entrance to Gayfield Street. They watched as two boys kicked a football back and forth.

"Let's get them," Al whispered.

"It wasn't them that beat up Trevor's brother," Billy Bunter said.

"That doesn't matter," Al whispered. "They're Gayfeelies, which means they're automatically affiliated to the street just like we are to Scotia Street.

"I'll make you pay for what you did to my mate, Larry White, that time," Al thought.

Weeks earlier Larry had been caught and battered by a mob of Gayfeelies. They dragged him by the hair to the rear of a deserted house, beat him, and then tied him to the back door. They taunted him by showing him their home-made arrows with nails in the end and bashed him around the head with their crude, homemade, bows. The weaponized arrows had narrowly missed his head, arms and legs. Had it not been for Al leading the Scoshees charge to save his friend, Larry could have been seriously hurt.

One of the lads kicked the ball and it shot up the street and hit the tyre of the car that the Scoshees were hiding behind. The Gayfeely boy came bounding up the street with a smile on his face which quickly disappeared as Al and the boys jumped up and ran around the car. The boy tried to stop and make a dash for it, but he was quickly brought down.

"Jump on him Billy," Brian called.

"He needs more than that," Al said.

The Scoshees dragged the boy by his hair and arms out of Gayfield Street and around to the back of some waste ground.

"Crucify him, the bastard," one of the kids shouted.

"Let me go, please," the Gayfeely yelled.

SMACK!

Billy Bunter smashed him in the face with his monster sized fist.

The Scoshees held out his arms, pulled the barbed wire down from the top of the fence and bound it tightly around the boy's wrists. Al could see the blood dripping from his tightly bound hands. The mob had taken on a life of its own. Without any instruction, the Gayfeely was now being systematically tortured by the gang.

"Burn him!" Billy Bunter shouted.

Al looked on as the Scoshees gathered up twigs, paper and broken furniture and placed it around the boy's feet.

"Burn the Gayfeely!" Billy Bunter screamed.

"Burn him, burn him, burn him!" all the Scoshees shouted together.

Al stepped forward and put his hand inside his trouser pocket. He produced a small box of matches.

"Burn him, burn him, burn him," the gang of eight-, nine- and ten-year-olds chanted.

Al took another step forward and leant down on one knee. The Gayfeely was bawling uncontrollably but Al couldn't hear his pleas for mercy. Just as he was about to strike the match he heard:

"Stop!"

Al and the Scoshees turned to see a grown man racing towards them. He knocked Billy Bunter over and charged over to where the boy had been bound to the fence with barbed wire.

Al was up on his feet and scarpered with Brian and the others. The man yelled when he saw the distressed boy and the blood streaming from his hands. The Scoshees dashed out of the gate and scuttled up the street and into the heart of Scotia Street.

"We could have killed him," Brian said as he bent over to catch his breath. "That must have been his Da."

"They'll come back hard now," Billy Bunter said as caught up with the boys.

"So, we'll burn them too," Al said coldly.

As the sun went down, Al and Brian took a walk back to where the M8 Motorway was being constructed. Al led Brian to the house next door to the electrical shop with the television on sale in the window, lit a candle and walked down into the cellar.

"What are we doing?" Brian said.

"See this wall?" Al said as he pulled out a large flat piece of tapered metal from his trousers.

Brian nodded.

"Well, there might be a television set on the other side and we're going to get it," Al said.

"Do you think we should?" Brian asked.

Al ignored him and began to dig out the cracked mortar that bonded the bricks together.

"What if the police come?" Brian asked.

"Brian, are you in or not?" Al said bluntly.

Brian hesitated for a moment and then nodded.

"Good. Now find something to help me get these bricks out," Al said as he finished digging out the first brick.

He put his eye up against the hole in the wall.

"What's in there?" Brian asked as he scouted around the cellar looking for something to help his brother.

"I can't see anything yet," Al said. "But there's definitely something in there. I can feel it."

Al, now fully motivated, dug harder, deeper and faster with his piece of metal. Brian grabbed the bricks and yanked them out. As each brick was forcefully removed, taking down the wall became easier and easier. Within half an hour the brothers had created a hole in the wall big enough to step through.

"We're through, come on," Al said as he picked up the candle and stepped into the cellar of the electrical shop.

Al held up the candle and lit the room. The boys gasped when they saw that the cellar was stacked from floor to ceiling with brand new, boxed television sets.

"We're rich," Al gasped.

"There's loads of them!" Brian said.

"Yeah, and we're taking them all," Al whispered, punching the air with excitement.

Al and Brian took the televisions one by one and hid them in an empty house three doors down.

"How many have we got?" Brian asked.

"Fourteen brand new television sets. We're in the big time now," Al said with a huge grin.

"Who are we going to sell them to?" Brian asked.

"Don't worry about that," Al said, as he patted a television. "I'll have all these sold."

It was the early hours of the morning before Al and Brian got home. The boys crept into the house and up to their bedroom.

***

The following day Al was up, washed, and out early. He was excited and wanted those television sets sold. Al loved the feel of money in his pocket. Only this time it would be more than coins.

"Uncle Tommy," Al said as his uncle opened the front door.

"Hello Al, what can I do for you?"

Uncle Tommy and Uncle Yank were not family members, but Al had been them calling uncle for as long as he could remember. Uncle Yank was an American who got married and stayed in the UK after the Second World War. Uncle Tommy was a ducker and diver. He would always have his hand in some scheme that would afford him to wear nice, well made, clothes and look smart. He enjoyed a drink on a Saturday night but wasn't a slave to alcohol like his Da.

"Can I have a quiet word?" Al said.

Uncle Tommy closed the front door and stepped outside.

"Sure, what's the problem?"

"I've found a television," Al said.

"What, an old television that someone has dumped?" Uncle Tommy chuckled.

"No, it's brand new and still in the box," Al whispered.

Uncle Tommy stopped laughing.

"You found a brand-new television set?"

Al nodded.

"Can I see it?" Uncle Tommy asked.

"Do you want to buy it?" Al said bluntly.

Uncle Tommy smiled and then brushed his hand over Al's head.

"Sure, I'll buy it."

Uncle Tommy paid fifteen pounds for the television set. Al had argued that it cost over one hundred pounds in the sale, but Uncle Tommy just laughed it off saying he would only waste the extra money on sweets. Al took the money and shared some with Brian before going to the shops and buying food for the cupboard. He handed three pounds over to Mammy, telling her that he had found a wallet on the streets. She didn't question the find and promptly put the money into her purse.

"Keep that hidden from Da," Al said.

Al sold several television sets to Uncle Tommy over the next few weeks. He was on his way to the shops when he caught sight of his Da.

"Al, Al," his Da called.

Al stopped and waited for his Da to catch up.

"I've just seen your Uncle Tommy," Da said.

"Oh no, what's Uncle Tommy been saying," thought Al.

Da started to smile once he caught his breath.

"Listen, son, you don't want to be selling those televisions to your Uncle Tommy. He's not even real family. Let me have them and I'll see you right. We're family so you can trust me to get the best deal," Da said.

"What do I do?" Al thought. *"Fuck it I'll let him have some."*

Al brought six television sets for his Da to sell on the understanding that he would get twenty pounds for each one. The following day Al asked his Da for his money.

"You ain't getting fuck all!" Da growled.

"But you promised," Al said.

"Well, let this be your first lesson in life. Never trust anyone, not even your own family!"

"You're nothing to me, you drunken old man. Just shit on my shoes. I'll never do anything, ever, with you again," Al thought as he turned sharply and walked away.

Al sold the remainder of the televisions sets to his Uncle Tommy with a price increase and an undertaking to take everything that Al brought to him. Al returned home with the money hidden in his underwear.

Later that night Al and Brian crouched down by the bedroom window in the dark. They occasionally peeked out over the windowsill when they heard voices.

"Do you remember when Mammy left us?" Brian said, rubbing his hands together.

Al nodded as the memory came flooding back.

On the corner of Scotia Street and Gayfield Street was the local pub, 'Gayfield Bar'. Because their Da spent almost every day in there, Mammy sarcastically renamed it 'Albert's Bar'. Mammy had told Al to take his brother out to play in the streets earlier. She had seemed somehow distant, as if she had a lot on her mind. Brian had asked about dinner and received a glare that all the children knew meant that violence was imminent. Al grabbed his shoulder and took him back outside.

Minutes later Mammy appeared at the front door in her coat, carrying a large bag. She was agitated. She called all the children together and without a word she led all nine of them up Scotia Street to 'Albert's Bar'. She stopped briefly, took a deep breath and pushed the door open with such force it slammed against an empty chair. Mammy had all nine children troop in one by one and then stand in a parade at the end of the bar. Al could see his Da propping up the bar, chatting with neighbours and friends. He stopped briefly to turn and look at his wife and children. A number of those close by had stopped talking; they knew Mammy and her violent capabilities. Da ignored them and took a long slurp from his glass. Mammy turned abruptly and walked out. The nine children watched as she left, slamming the pub door behind her.

"She was gone for eight weeks," Al said.

"I know, we were all so hungry," Brian said, rubbing his stomach.

"You mean hungrier than usual," Al said.

"I remember how he just locked us all in the house in the morning and didn't get back until the pub had closed," Brian said.

"A nine-year-old shouldn't be expected to look after eight brothers and sisters," Al said with a hint of resentment.

"I can remember how the front door would open and the smell of chips would just fill the house. Da would lay them out on the table and we would scoff them down like vultures," Brian said.

"You probably wouldn't remember this, but it was me that climbed down the drainpipe and went down to Woolworths so I could steal the broken biscuits that they would sell for tuppence, so you all had something to eat," Al said as he leant back against the wall and closed his eyes for a moment.

"I know," Brian whispered. "We all knew."

"It wasn't just me though," Al said with a broad smile. "I used to watch as Auntie Doreen and Auntie Mary climbed up the drainpipe with food for us. It was funny seeing her clamber up with her beehive hairstyle and high heel shoes.

"They're good aunts," Brian said.

"The best," Al said firmly.

Al loved his aunts for the care, love, and stability they brought to the house whenever they visited.

"Then Mammy came back, and it just went back to how it was," Brian said. "Do you know where she went?"

"No," Al said, shaking his head.

The boys sat in silence for a few moments.

"Da did save you from a beating once," Brian said breaking the silence.

Al thought back to when all his siblings were at home in his care. Mammy was out and Da was at the pub. The children had been sitting together in the front room when they all jolted upright when they heard three aggressive thuds on the front door. Finally, the front door's lock flew off and the door swung open. A large, drunken, bearded man staggered into the front room with his fists tightly clenched. The younger children darted behind the settee while the man stood with his legs apart scanning the room through blood shot eyes. Finally, his drunken gaze fell upon Al. With a mighty roar he stomped to where Al was sitting, reached down and grabbed him by the jumper, lifting him clean off his feet. Al let out a yell as the drunken intruder turned and began to march back towards the door. The children cried out with tears streaming down their faces as their older brother swung like a rag doll under the man's grip. As the drunk stepped outside the house, with Al still firmly in his grip yelling out for help, he saw Albert standing in the road. The drunk dropped Al instantly and took several steps forward. Al had hit the concrete slab with a thud but quickly gathered himself up and scampered back so that his back was against the house. Al watched as Da raised his arms and clenched fists in line with his head. The drunk shouted something and threw a clumsy punch which left him wide open. Da's right punch hit the drunk with such ferocity that Al could hear the crunch of bone. A quick fired left punch had the drunk staggering back. Da stepped forward with punch after relentless punch. The drunk's legs collapsed, and he dropped onto one knee. Al could see the blood pouring from the drunk's facial injuries. However, he got no mercy from Albert who stood over the intruder. He grabbed him by the scruff of his neck with his left hand and looked down with a menacing glare as he raised his right hand. The final blow had the drunk sprawling backwards and lying flat out on the road.

"Yeah, I remember that," Al said. "That's probably the only good thing he has ever done for this family."

"That drunken man could have killed you," Brian whispered.

"Probably," Al said.

"You've always looked out for us, Al," Brian whispered.

Al nodded.

"Yeah, I can remember having to change the triplet's nappies and then wash them out because Mammy would never do it," thought Al. *"I've probably done a lot more than you know or can remember."*

Al, having had the taste for money and being assured that his Uncle Tommy would take everything he stole, went to work screwing electrical shops from neighbouring districts. He and Brian would take the radios, stereo systems and television sets and hide them in the empty homes where the M8 motorway was being constructed. Al continued to fill the cupboards with food, he bought clothes for his siblings and gave his Mammy the money that he always claimed he had found. Uncle Tommy showed Al how to fix the electricity and gas meters, so they had a constant supply without any bills. Al returned home and 'screwed' their own meter immediately. When he told Mammy she stepped back in amazement and looked the young boy up and down before telling him:

"One day you'll be Prime Minister because you're so smart."

Chapter 9

Al and Brian had been walking around the neighbouring areas on the lookout for opportunities when a car stopped on the opposite side of the road. The driver tooted the horn and wound down his window.

Al looked over and saw that the driver was smiling and waving him over.

"Stay here," Al said.

"Why?" Brian said.

"Can you please just do as I ask?" Al said firmly.

Al looked left and then right before crossing the road.

"Hello," the man said with a crooked grin.

"Hello," Al said cautiously.

"What are you boys playing at today?" the man said.

"We're just out having a walk," Al replied.

"Do you live far from here then?" the man said, looking in his rear-view mirror.

"Not far," Al said evasively.

"Do you like animals?" the man asked.

Al shrugged his shoulders.

"What about little white baby rabbits?"

"Yeah, I suppose so," Al said, turning briefly to see that Brian was still there.

"Would you like to come to my house and see my baby rabbits?" the man said.

Al shook his head.

"Oh, come on they're ever so nice and I'll bring you straight back in the car."

"I said no!" Al said firmly then turned and walked across the road back to his brother.

Al watched as the driver wound up his window and drove away.

"Brian," Al said.

"Yes."

"Don't ever get into a car with someone you don't know, alright?" Al said as he put his hands in his pockets and started walking.

"Why?" Brian said.

"Because I said so, okay?"

"Okay," Brian said.

The brothers returned home to find that while Mammy was paying the milk bill with money Al had given her a few days before, she saw the milkman had a friendly boxer dog with him. When she asked about the dog, the milkman told her that it would be going to the vets to be put down because they could no longer afford to keep it. Knowing how much Al loved dogs and how he would lead them home with bags of bones from the butcher's she agreed to take it into the McIntosh family home.

Al was thrilled. He patted and stroked the dog while its little tail wagged frantically.

"Let's call him Rebel," Al said, stroking the dog's head.

"Whatever you like," Mammy said.

"I can help pay for your food with the money I'm making from 'screwing' the electricity meters for the neighbours and from the stuff Uncle Tommy buys from me, boy," Al thought.

Rebel followed Al all over the house when he was home, and during the day the dog would roam the streets in a pack. Al would smile as he watched Rebel impose his authority on the other dogs. Al sat back on the kerb and watched as the dogs leaped around playing in the streets. From the corner of his eye, he saw a large black, scruffy Labrador known as Jet that he'd seen in Gayfield Street while out on raids with the Scoshees. Rebel stopped playing and stood firm as the black Labrador approached. The two dogs circled each other, growled, bared their teeth and then Rebel leapt forward and sank his teeth into the Labrador's neck. Jet shook his neck violently and Rebel lost his grip. Jet bit his leg, then tore into his neck and finally sunk his teeth into Rebel's ear.

Rebel yelped as Jet tightened his grip. Al leapt up and ran across the road yelling at the pack of dogs. Jet bit down hard and Rebel howled as part of his ear was torn off. Jet spat the ear onto the road, saw Al steaming across the road with fists clenched and gritted teeth, turned, and bolted away back towards Gayfield Street.

"Are you alright boy?" Al said as he crouched down.

Rebel was lying on his side whimpering.

"You let him beat you, Rebel. You should never have given up," Al said, gently stroking Rebel's back.

"The king is dead," Al thought as he coaxed Rebel back onto his feet and led him home.

Rebel didn't run wild with the pack of street dogs anymore but took to lying outside and watching the other dogs and children playing in the street.

Al and Brian had stayed out all night chatting over an open fire in the woods. They talked about their earliest memories of school and how the children would hang from a metal rail which the sliding door ran along. Every boy was expected to do this as part of an initiation. Al, aged five, clambered up onto the desk and then onto the rail while the other kids pulled the door closed. He let go and dropped to the ground just before it ran over his fingers. Al was instantly accepted by all the boys. The next lad was a little hesitant, but succumbed to the chanting of 'coward, coward,' and climbed up to hang off the rail. The boys pulled the door shut but the little boy didn't let go in time and the door running gear nipped off the end of two of his fingers.

As they left the woods, they were stopped by a police car. Al said that they were playing in the woods and were on their way home. The officer insisted on taking them. The boys got into the police car and were driven back to Scotia Street. The officer got out of the car and opened the back door for the boys. He turned to see a woman bounding towards them with a large stick. It was Mammy.

"See this?" Mammy yelled as she smashed the stick down hard against the pavement. "This is what you'll be getting when we get inside. I've told you before, don't you ever bring the police to my door!"

"Mrs McIntosh," the police officer said calmly. "I was just giving your boys a lift home."

"Okay," Mammy said, lowering her aggressive tone. "Thank you, Officer."

"You're welcome," the officer said as he got back into the police car, started the engine and drove away.

"Inside, you two, now!" Mammy yelled.

The two brothers ran up the pathway and into the house.

"Into the living room!"

The brothers stood side by side by the open fireplace.

Mammy reached down to the armchair cushion and picked up the bright stainless steel dog chain.

"Get undressed, now!"

Al and Brian slowly undressed until they were standing naked.

"You will wear this dress and stand out on the streets until it's dark!" Mammy shrieked, pointing to a blue dress she made the boys wear after a naked beating with the dog chain.

With a venomous, malignant expression spread across her hate filled face, Mammy swung the steel dog chain and belted Al across the arm with such force that his whole body shuddered.

He didn't react to the vicious attack but remained still.

Mammy was used to seeing the boys buckle, cry out and plead for mercy. She pulled her arm back and swung the chain with all her might. It slammed hard into the side of Al's chest. Still Al showed no emotion. Mammy screamed and whipped the heavy dog chain across his naked body several more times.

"I will feel no pain, I will feel no pain, I will feel no pain," Al thought to himself over and over.

Mammy stopped and looked at the red marks on his body, pulled the chain back, and with a wild, manic, grin she dispensed more powerful, lethal lashes on Al's body.

Al could no longer feel the pain. He slowly looked up with a fixed glazed expression. He met Mammy's eyes, and for the first time in his life he witnessed her fear.

"You wanted to whip the devil into me, well now you have your wish, and he's never getting back into his box again," Al thought as he maintained his rancorous, hardened, scowl.

Mammy coughed to clear her dry throat, dropped the steel dog chain and took two steps back. Al could see sheer terror in her eyes. He slowly stood up, maintaining his menacing glare, reached down and picked up his clothes.

"Pick up your clothes, Brian," Al said calmly.

Brian wiped the tears from his eyes, bent down, collected his clothes and scurried away towards the living room door. Al turned and took two steps forward before turning back slowly.

"Never again! Do you understand me?" Al said as the anger and hatred stirred in his stomach.

Mammy stood motionless; both her hands held out to her side in a submissive pose, her mouth partly open. She was petrified.

Al looked down at the steel dog chain lying on the carpet and then looked back at Mammy, his eyes burning into hers. He calmly shook his head twice before turning his back and leaving the room.

Chapter 10

While waiting for his lads Al found himself thinking back to New Year's Eve. There had been an altercation earlier in the year with a local kid throwing a stone at the McIntosh family's window. Al took it upon himself to return the gesture by throwing a brick through the kid's front room window. Albert, the kids Da, was drinking whiskey at a New Year's party at the McIntosh's home. He was becoming increasingly provocative by calling Mammy Mrs 999, a name that had stuck with many of the residents, and eventually he spat a mouthful of whiskey into the open fire. Mammy took a red-hot fire poker and said, 'Let me have a quiet word' and then proceeded to smack him over the back of the head with the poker. The shriek of pain could be heard all over the house. Albert's hair caught fire, he screamed, burst through the door, and out into the open air, running and shrieking at the top of his voice while frantically trying to put the flames on his head out.

Albert's family, like the McIntosh's were a fearsome family and they had taken it upon themselves to wreak revenge. Al, now aged thirteen, had become the target. Albert had a younger brother, the same age as Al. Albert stopped Al in the street and told him that he had to fight his brother. At first Al was reluctant but Albert's persistence led to a swift right hander followed by several powerful kicks while the kid rolled around on the ground. Al had beaten him while Albert looked on.

Then Albert, later that week, lined up another kid of the same age. Al fought and beat the second, third, fourth and fifth kid that Albert brought before him. Al, during his final fight had become increasingly confident in his abilities and would knock the kid over, kick him a few times and then let him back on his feet out of a sense of fair play. Finally, the kid placed a punch that shook him, his legs buckled, and the kid punched and kicked him again until he lay on the ground. Fuelled by hate and ego the kid continued to pile in one kick after another until a girl who had witnessed the fight threw herself over Al and pleaded with them to stop because she could see that Al was concussed and something was desperately wrong. Al had been rushed off to the hospital where the doctor confirmed that the girl had probably saved his life.

Failing to finish the kid off when he was on the floor was a life changing lesson for Al with regards to violence. Never again would he show mercy to anyone, anywhere.

The lads all arrived as arranged.

"Right," Al said, "I've checked out the church and there's definitely a box of Ranger's football kits that will sell well."

"Nice one," Jack Glasgow said. "I might even keep one for myself."

"You don't want to do that," John McDaid said. "

"Why?" Jack asked.

"Ain't it obvious?" John said, shaking his head. "The police will know what's been taken and you walking around in a new football kit will attract attention."

"Yeah, and we want the money from selling them and anything else the house of God has to offer," said Al.

"I'm not sure about this," Brian said.

"Sure about what?" Al said.

"It's not right, screwing a church," Brian said. "We might lose a bit of our soul and go straight to hell."

"We'll worry about that when we get there," Al said with a broad smile.

"I don't like it..." Brian said cautiously.

"Well fuck off back home then and we'll share the spoils out three ways," Al said firmly.

Brian hesitated for a moment.

"Are you sure about the Ranger's football kits?"

Al nodded and winked to Jack.

"And will Uncle Tommy take them?" Brian said.

"Uncle Tommy will take everything we take from inside the church, and I've lined up the scrap man for the lead on the roof," Al said triumphantly.

"Sounds like you've got it all organised," Jack said.

"I have," Al chuckled.

"Alright, I'm in, but I'm not happy about it," Brian said.

"If the demons from hell come looking for you, Brian, just tell them they have to go through me first," Al said.

Al had brought Jack Glasgow and John McDaid into his team of burglars. Brian, despite his reservations, was always game in the end. Al saw Jack Glasgow and John McDaid as a pair of staunch lads who were always up for making a few pounds.

Al led the lads through the church grounds to the back door of the vestry. Within a few minutes the door had been broken open and they were in the church.

"Are you sure there's no one here?" Brian whispered.

"What do you think, Brian? When the front and back doors are locked?"

"Yeah, I'm just a bit worried about it being a church, Al."

"Think of the money," Al said bluntly.

The lads began to open and empty the cupboards.

"Jackpot Al, there's six bottles of wine in here," Jack said as he put them on the table.

"Quick over here," John said, looking into a large pantry style cupboard.

"What is it?" Brian said as he scampered over to join him.

The two lads looked at scores of pop bottles.

"There's Coke, Fanta and my favourite.... Irn-Bru," Brian said.

"I'll be having one of those Irn-Bru's later," Al called out as he forced the door open and entered the church.

"Now where is that poor box?" Al thought, as he threw gowns over the seats. *"There it is!"*

Al managed to break the locked poor box open only to find it was empty.

"Shit!" Al thought as he looked over the pulpit.

He stood up and threw the poor box across the church before walking over to the pulpit and climbing up into the box so he could see over the church to where the parishioners would be sitting.

"Well what about that then, God?" Al shouted, pounding his fist. *"You can't be that all-powerful because you can't even protect your own house!"*

Al picked up the hymn sheets from the shelf below and threw them into the air.

"Brian," Al called as he climbed from the pulpit.

"What?"

"Let's go and see if we can get that lead from the roof," Al said as he charged across the church and up through the stairway.

"Sure," Brian called out after him.

While Al and Brian removed the lead from around the windows and roof lights, Jack and John brought everything thing of value together and put it on the table.

"Here, what's this?" John said, pointing at a metal cylinder object.

"It's a fire extinguisher," Jack laughed.

"Is it worth anything?"

"Probably not, but you can do this," Jack said as he picked up the fire extinguisher, broke the seal, and proceeded to spray a thin layer of white foam over the walls, stained glass windows and seating areas.

The two boys laughed raucously.

Al called down to the lads to help bring the lead down.

"This is heavy," Jack said.

"The heavier the better," Al said. "We're paid by the weight."

"What have you done?" Brian said, looking around at the mindless act of vandalism.

"We thought we'd do the place up a bit. Give it a bit of a fresh coat of... foam," Jack said with a giggle.

"This isn't right," said Brian. "It's a dreadful violation and we could go straight to hell for this."

"What if I do this then, Brian?" Jack said as he undid his trouser button, unzipped himself and pulled both his trousers and pants down before squatting over the altar.

The boys looked on as Jack scrunched up his face.

"What is it with you, Jack? You always have to take a shit when we rob a place," Al said as he turned around and wandered into the back room to see what the boys had brought together.

Brian followed Al.

"Not a bad haul," Al thought as he scanned over the goodies on the table.

Minutes later Jack and John joined Al and Brian in the vestry. They gathered up what they could carry.

"The wine and the lead will bring the most money," Al said, pointing out what he wanted each of the boys to carry.

"I love thieving," thought Al, *"I'm pretty damn good at it too!"*

Al and his lads left the church carrying the football kit, lead, soda pop and wine, and made their way down to the old railway tracks at the back of the church. The lads had only carried their haul a few hundred yards when Jack started complaining about the weight of the lead he was carrying. Al ignored him and led the group further up the tracks. Then both Brian and John started to complain.

"Look, it's a just bit further. I know a place where we can bury it and then come back for it later," Al said, cracking open a bottle of Irn-Bru.

He lifted the bottle to his lips and took a long, satisfying gulp, belched loudly and wiped his lips with his sleeve. Al thought he saw something in the bushes to his right but quickly dismissed it.

"Right, everybody rested and ready?" Al said bending down to pick up the lead.

"What's that?" Al thought as he looked back over at the bushes.

"Stop, police!"

Al looked up to see eight police officers racing towards them over the embankment.

"Run!" shouted Al.

All the lads scattered with the police in hot pursuit. Al dropped the lead and bolted over towards a street to his left. He puffed and panted, pushing himself to outrun the police officer behind him. Al turned a corner sharply then turned briefly to see how close the police officer was. The red-faced cop was gritting his teeth, he was just a few feet away. Al turned back and ran headfirst straight into a lamp post.

SMACK!

Al was lying unconscious on the road by the side of a Morris Minor delivery van.

A tingling sensation raced through Al's body as he slowly came around. He found himself on the back seat of a police car.

"Where am I?" Al groaned as he rubbed his sore head.

"You're under arrest for robbing the church, you little bastard!" the police officer said, looking in his rear-view mirror.

"Shit, where are Brian and the others?" Al thought while he continued to rub his sore head. *"I hope they got away."*

Al was taken to the police station where he refused to say who was with him. Later that afternoon a police officer entered the room with a broad grin on his face.

"We know all about your escapades over the last two years, McIntosh," the officer said. "We know the places, dates and what you stole. You've been a busy little boy."

"What do they know?" Al thought anxiously.

"We have your whole little gang. Your brother Brian, Jack Glasgow and John McDaid," the officer said as he pulled out the chair and sat down.

"Who's been clyping?" Al thought. *"It wouldn't have been Brian, never. Jack is staunch and John, well, I just can't see him grassing us up."*

"You might as well come clean, McIntosh, because a little birdie has been singing his little heart out and it looks like you've been the ringleader of this motley crew," the police officer said, producing a pack of cigarettes.

Al shrugged his shoulders.

"Breaking into factories and stealing crates of whiskey and clothes by the tonne by all accounts, and then there was the railway depot for the perfume and jeans

"No way would Brian tell the police anything," Al thought. *"Some silly sod has fallen for the good cop / bad cop routine."*

The good cop/ bad cop routine is a classic police interrogation tactic that's been used since the dawn of policing by every police force in the world. An officer will enter the interrogation room, slam his hands down on the desk, make aggressive threats and accusations while using every psychological trick he can muster. It's then that the 'good cop' enters feigning sympathy and respect for the suspect while promising to keep him safe from the bad cop in a bid to gain his trust. Once that has been established, the suspect will open up and tell all in a bid to protect himself.

"Shitting on the altar! Did you agree to Jack Glasgow's dreadful behaviour?" the officer said with a wry grin.

"He knows everything," thought Al. *"Jack wouldn't have told on himself and Brian despite all his reservations wouldn't say a word so it must have been John, John-fucking-McDaid who clyped on us all."*

xxx

While waiting in the courthouse, Al found himself thinking about what had brought him before the court. His Da had suffered with mental health issues since the war which often led to spells at the asylum. Al remembered the stories he had overheard about how the German SS would simply shoot British soldiers that found themselves separated from their buddies and their dead bodies were left for the crows. He also learnt that the British Army carried out their own atrocities too. Da could never hold down a job, so they existed on what little benefits they could get their hands on. It was the thrill and excitement of thieving that encouraged Al to rob, and the overwhelming sense of achievement when he saw his poverty-stricken family eat the food that he alone, as a child, had brought in.

Al thought back to how the police had chased him through the streets but somehow he always got away. He loved his life of criminality and savoured all its proceeds.

Al, Brian, Jack Glasgow and John McDaid were brought before the Sheriff (magistrate) on one hundred and ten robbery charges. Al had been identified as the gang's ringleader, and before being sentenced to three years in an approved school, was given a lengthy lecture by the presiding Sheriff for desecrating the house of the Lord. He warned Al that if he continued with his anti-social behaviour his soul would be damned to hell. Brian was sentenced to two years. Jack Glasgow was given one year while John McDaid was set free.

"You clyped on your mates, John McDaid, and you will pay with blood," Al thought as he was led away.

Chapter 11

1969: Thornley Park Approved School, Paisley.

As he rode in the back seat of the court official's minibus, it suddenly dawned on Al that he was wearing his cheap coat from Martha Street.

"Oh, fucking hell! This Martha Street coat is a right give away. I'm going to look like some kind of pauper turning up dressed in this," Al thought as the overwhelming feeling of shame, humiliation and indignity washed over his entire body.

Martha Street was where the poor of Glasgow were clothed once a year.

Al lifted his head and stared out of the side window.

"I'll miss my Aunt Doreen and Aunt Mary. They've always been good to me. I wonder if they'll come and visit. I love my aunts." Al thought, as he stared aimlessly out at the passing traffic. *"Maybe I'm not even allowed to have visitors. Three years was harsh, bloody harsh. I want to go home."*

The vehicle stopped outside the aged Victorian building with its unapologetic devotion to ornament and flourish.

"Right, McIntosh, Anderson and Ferguson, out the vehicle!"

"Yes, sir," the boys replied as they scampered out of the vehicle and stood in a line, military style.

"You, McIntosh, stand up straight, legs together and get those shoulders back, you scruffy street urchin!" the master ordered.

"Yes, sir," Al replied as he slowly straightened himself up.

"Who the fuck do you think you're talking to, you long streak of piss?" Al thought. *"Out there on the streets I'd batter seven sorts of shit out of you for giving me attitude like that."*

The school master wore a shabby dark blue suit with an off-white coloured shirt and a blue striped tie. He was only a few inches taller than Al, but carried himself like he was six foot tall.

The two lads stood either side of Al. One of the boys could only have been about twelve years old. He wore black short trousers and a green woolly jumper. His hair had been cut into a side parting with the side of his head being shaved a good two inches up from his enormous ears.

"Mate," Al thought. *"You look like a fucking wing-nut with ears like that."*

On Al's right was a tall lad. He was skinny and towered over the school master. He hadn't looked up since he was ordered out of the vehicle.

"Right, now listen you street scum. My name is Mr Douglas. You call me Sir or Mr Douglas, do you understand?"

"Yes, sir," the three young offenders replied as one.

"You will call all masters here by their title and surname or sir. Am I making myself clear?" Mr Douglas said as he walked slowly past each of the new arrivals.

Al and Anderson replied 'yes sir' together.

Ferguson, the tall, lanky, kid, didn't reply and just stared blankly at the ground. Mr Douglas quickly turned on his heels and stood in front of the boy.

"Didn't you hear me, Ferguson?"

Ferguson tried to reply but the words were muffled. He looked up at the school master. His eyes were red, puffy and full of tears.

"I just want to go home, sir," Ferguson cried as he fell to his knees onto the cold, cracked concrete pathway. The tears streamed down his face as the young boy struggled to catch his breath.

Al looked down and slowly shook his head.

"What is the matter with you? You can't show weakness here or anywhere, or you'll become a victim," Al thought.

"Get on your feet, boy! What are you, some kind of poofter?" Mr Douglas yelled, reaching down and grabbing the teenager by his collar and forcefully pulling him back up.

"Poofters and cry-babies don't last long here, son, so you better get a grip on yourself." Mr Douglas bellowed, his face just inches from Ferguson's.

Ferguson tried to pull his shoulders back as the torrent of tears continued to stream down his face.

The three new arrivals were marched across the cracked concrete parade ground. Scores of boys dressed in short black trousers, army style jackets and boots yelled, jeered and shook their fists while others ran a finger across their throat. Al kept his head down and entered the building. He looked up to see the ornate maximalist interior design and the sign on the wall that read:

'Every lie is a little bit of your soul dead'

Mr Douglas marched them through the hallways quickly until they reached a large oak door with a plaque that read 'Headmaster'.

"Halt!" Mr Douglas shouted before knocking on the door.

Mr Douglas and the three new arrivals waited in silence for several seconds.

"Enter!"

Mr Douglas reached down and opened the door.

"In, in, quick march!"

Al and the two new lads stood in a line facing the headmaster's desk. He had his head down and was writing in a large book. To his right was another master sitting in an armchair. Finally, the headmaster put the pen down and closed the book. He looked at the boys over his thick black rimmed glasses.

"My name is 'Wee Garry' and I'm Headmaster. Mr Wilson is the Assistant Head, and this is my school. Take a moment and let that sink in... this is my school!"

There were a few seconds' silence.

"You boys have been sent here by the courts because you've either committed a criminal offence or they deem you to be out of parental control. Here at Thornley Park Approved School we take each boy as we find them. If you keep your head down, do as you are told, and follow the rules, you will have the opportunity to receive academic tuition. In addition, there is scope for some of you boys to become assigned to work groups where you'll learn building, brickwork, metalwork, carpentry and gardening," Wee Garry said as he sat back in his leather chair and looked at each of the boys one by one.

"However, be warned, I run a tight ship and corporal punishment will be administered without hesitation either by me or any of my school masters for anyone not following the rules," Wee Garry said as he reached into his desk drawer, brought a leather belt out and put it on the

117

desktop. "I insist on a minimum of eight lashes and for your name to be entered into the school's 'Good Book'. Persistent offenders will also forfeit any privileges. That includes pocket money and losing the right to use the school's recreational facilities, loss of meals for up to three days and finally, complete separation from the other boys."

"Where the fuck have I ended up?" Al thought.

"Make no mistake, this is my school," Wee Garry said sternly. "I've seen countless smart arse back street hooligans thinking they can get the better of us."

Wee Garry stared long and hard at each of the teenagers.

"None have succeeded. Work hard, do your time and you'll leave here with qualifications and a skill that will make you a living out there. But try to beat the system, and we'll come down on you like a tonne of bricks and the chances are you'll go from here to a Borstal and for some of you, on to prison. Your future lies in your hands," Wee Garry said as he leant across the desk and held the leather belt firmly in his right hand. "Mr Wilson, have you anything you want to add?"

"Yes Headmaster," Mr Wilson said as he turned to the three boys. "We operate a points system here. Good behaviour results in a 'good' mark and any breach of the rules or poor conduct results in a 'bad' mark. Each and every Friday, directly after dinner, everyone will be reviewed for their week's performance. Three good marks will result in a weekend's leave. At 10.00am sharp on Saturday you can leave here but must return by Sunday at 4.00PM. Two good marks and one bad will allow you a day out. Three bad marks and you're 'snibbed' and that means discipline plus you lose all privileges."

Mr Wilson got up from his chair and walked past each of the boys staring hard into their faces.

"Thank you, Headmaster, that's all," he said.

"Right, do any of you boys have a question?" said Wee Garry.

One by one the three boys answered 'No, sir'.

"Good, then follow Mr Douglas to the shower block.

"Attention! Right turn!" Mr Douglas shouted.

The three boys promptly turned right and quickly marched off through the hallway.

"Halt!" Mr Douglas yelled.

The boys stopped and stood to attention outside the shower block.

"Right, you lot, strip off," Mr Douglas commanded.

Al and the two boys reluctantly peeled off their clothes and folded them neatly.

Al was the first to move towards the shower.

"You, McIntosh, stop!" Mr Douglas yelled.

"Yes sir," Al said, standing to attention.

"Hold your arms out to your side, boy!"

"Pardon, sir?"

"You heard me, vermin. Hold your arms out to your side and do as you're told!"

Al held both his arms out to his sides.

"I'd like to punch the fuck out of your face," Al thought.

"Right, now pull your arse cheeks apart," Mr Douglas said.

"You fucking what?" Al thought.

"Now, vermin, now!"

Al closed his eyes, took a deep breath and did as he was ordered.

"You nasty, dirty, horrible bastard!" Al thought.

Mr Douglas strode around behind Al, bent down and peered at his nakedness.

"You're sick, bloody sick!" Al thought.

"Right, stand to attention, lad!" Mr Douglas shouted.

"Yes sir," Al said as he stood upright and put his arms by his sides.

"In the shower! Move, move, move!"

Al darted into the shower. The water was boiling hot and felt good on his body. He scrubbed himself clean while Mr Douglas had Ferguson and Anderson bend down for him.

"Right," Mr Douglas said as all three lads stood naked and to attention in front of him. "This is your uniform."

Mr Douglas handed Al a pair of black short trousers, a white shirt, tie and a black jacket.

"What's this short trouser lark?" Al thought. *"You, John McDaid, are a no good grass! If and when I ever see you again I'm going to smash seven sorts of shit out of you and then stamp on your fucking head for good measure. It's all your fault I'm in here!"*

Al was then handed a brand new pair of army style boots.

"Now you're probably thinking why am I being given short trousers?" Mr Douglas said, handing Ferguson his pair of army boots. "Well, the Headmaster, Wee Garry, has said that if young girls can walk around in short mini-skirts then short trousers are good enough for you lot."

Al pulled on the short trousers, buttoned his shirt, did up his tie and then sat down to put the tightly fitting army boots on.

"Short trousers, mini-skirts.... what kind of sick mind arrives at that?" Al thought.

"Right, you lot," Mr Douglas yelled. "Attention!"

Al, Ferguson and Anderson stood to attention in a line outside the shower block.

"Move, move, move!" Mr Douglas screamed.

The boys began to race down the corridor towards a set of stairs.

"Left, left, left you vermin. Up the stairs... run!"

Al darted to the left and bolted up the stairs and waited, still standing to attention, in the hallway outside a large dormitory. The three boys stood together.

"This is where you'll be sleeping," Mr Douglas said as he pointed into the room. "Your beds are the last three on the left... move!"

Al stood to attention at the end of the third bed in.

"You'll be sleeping in here for twelve months and then, if you have enough good points, you'll be moved into a cubicle with three other lads.

"I've got to sleep in here with thirty other kids? You must be joking!" Al thought.

"Right, now get yourself settled and be down at the canteen for 5.00pm sharp for food," Mr Douglas said as he turned sharply on his heels and marched away.

Al sat back on the bed and put his hands behind his head. Moments later three older lads entered the dormitory. They walked past Al and stopped by the bed next to his.

"You, Anderson, on your feet!" the largest of the boys ordered.

"What?" Anderson said as he sat up.

"On your fucking feet!"

Anderson leapt off the bed.

"Stand to attention!"

"Every Friday you give ten pence of your wages to Bam Bam here," the biggest lad said, pointing to his scruffy looking sidekick.

"Bam Bam?" Anderson said, looking confused.

Bam Bam slapped Anderson in the face.

"You fucking heard him, every Friday you give me ten pence from your wages, got it?"

Anderson rubbed his face and nodded.

The three lads looked at Ferguson and then at Al before walking off and laughing to themselves.

"What the fuck was that all about?" Ferguson said.

"Don't ask me," Al said. "I've just got here.

***

At 5.00pm Al joined the other one hundred and twenty boys in the canteen. At each table sat six boys. There was a master placed in all four corners. They stood on a small box so they could monitor everything that happened in the room. Al was ushered over to a table where he sat with his arms tightly folded like all the boys in the canteen. At 5.00 sharp there was complete silence. Al looked down at the table. In front of each boy was a knife, fork and a plate. In the middle of the table was a bowl of potatoes, greens and twelve sausages. It was then that a master used his whistle and the five boys around Al began diving in with their forks to get the sausages, potatoes and greens, and then spat on their food once it was on their plate.

"What the hell is going on here?" Al thought.

Al looked on as the boys spat on the food before ramming fork loads of it into their mouths. They swallowed and then rammed more food in. Al put his knife and fork back down on the table.

"I'm not eating anything some dirty bastard has spat on," Al thought.

Within just a few minutes everything on the table had been eaten and every boy sat bolt upright with their arms crossed. Al was still hungry; he hadn't eaten that day.

"What's your name?" the lad next to him whispered.

"What's yours? Al said.

"Adam, we're in the same dorm," Adam said.

"Al, Al McIntosh," Al said.

"Good to meet you Al. I have to say though, mate, you're going to go hungry if you're not 'dicking'.

"Dicking?" said Al.

"Yeah, you've got to spit on your food before someone else eats it," Adam said.

"Fuck that," Al said.

"Trust me mate, you need to be dicking to survive food times," Adam said. "What are you in for?"

"Three years for robbery," Al said.

"I'm doing two years for stealing cars," Adam said. "Where are you from?"

Al turned to face Adam.

"Cowcaddens," Al said bluntly.

"Me too," Adam said. "Do you know Diablo?"

"No," Al said.

"Oh, he's a mad man. He stabbed six lads before he was fourteen. We were best of mates," Adam said.

"Who gives a fuck about who you may or may not know? It doesn't make you sound tough to me," Al thought.

"Who is that?" Al said as he nodded towards a table with a large, overweight, lad sitting on his own.

"That's Gudgey," Adam said. "The masters make him sit on his own because of his disgusting habit.

"What's that?" Al said.

"He swallows his food and then brings it back up again, you know, regurgitates it. It made the lads sick, so he was made to sit on his own."

"That's revolting," Al said as he scrunched up his face at the repulsive thought of watching someone do that.

"He's a proper poof too," Adam said. "He'll suck you off for ten pence."

"Not for me!" Al said firmly.

"No offence, Al. I'm just putting you in the picture," Adam said.

Wee Garry, the headmaster, entered the room and immediately every boy shot up onto their feet. Wee Garry sauntered round to the table at the far end and then placed a book in the middle before taking a seat. Once Wee Garry sat down everyone else returned to their seats.

"That's the 'Good Book'" Adam whispered.

Al remembered Mr Wilson, the deputy headmaster, telling him earlier about the point system.

Wee Garry opened the book and flicked through the pages. He stopped, read the page and then looked up.

"Trevor Johnson, on your feet lad," Wee Garry said as he peered over the top of his black rimmed glasses.

There was a screech as a chair scraped across the tiled floor and a lad at the next table stood to attention.

"Johnson, you have three good marks. You can go home tomorrow for the weekend," Wee Garry said.

"Thank you, sir," Johnson said before sitting back down.

"Miller!" Wee Garry said as he put the book down on the desk.

The lad opposite Al pushed out his chair and stood to attention.

"Yes sir," Miller said.

"You, Miller, are a continual disappointment. You have three black marks this week. Come out to the front now," Wee Garry said as he reached into his brown leather briefcase and produced the leather belt.

Al could see the look of sheer dread on Johnson's face as he reluctantly walked towards where Wee Garry sat.

Wee Garry stood up and stretched the belt between his hands.

"Hold your hand out, lad," Wee Garry said as he took a short step back and raised his hand.

"Please, sir," Johnson pleaded.

"Get your hand out, boy, and take your punishment like a man," Wee Garry growled with a look of utter contempt.

Johnson held out his hand. Wee Garry whipped the leather belt. Al watched as Johnson flinched.

"Please sir, that really hurt," Johnson pleaded, tears streaming down his face. "No more, please, no more, sir."

"He's for it now," Adam whispered. "The lads in here don't like cowardice. Johnson is in for a right kicking. He should have just kept his mouth shut and taken it."

Johnson, despite his pleas, received six from the belt. From the look of sheer agony after the final whip, Al, having had it himself, knew that the leather belt must have caught the lad's wrist. Johnson, bawling uncontrollably, was led out of the canteen by Mr Douglas.

"He's off now to Matron," Adam said. "He'll get no sympathy there."

"Adam?"

"What?"

"Who are the three lads on the table on the far right?" Al said, nodding towards the lads.

"Oh, you'll come across them sooner or later. That's The Don, Don Mitchell. He's pretty much the toughest kid here. Rumour has it that he killed two kids in a gang fight. The two sidekicks are Bam Bam and Mallison. They prey on the weak. Nasty bastards," Adam said. "You'll need to watch yourself with them."

"Noted," Al said.

"They better not try any of that old bollocks with me," Al thought.

The evening continued with kids being told they could go home for the weekend, were 'snibbed' or received six lashes from the belt.

Wee Garry read the final name in his 'Good Book' and then closed it.

"Patterson," Wee Garry said.

A lad on the table to Al's left stood up.

"Now we have it," Adam said. "This is the walk of shame."

"Patterson, get yourself up here boy!"

Patterson pushed back his chair, lowered his head and walked towards Wee Garry.

"You've been caught at it again! Patterson, I despair, you know that self-abuse is against the rules and yet you persistently abuse yourself, Wee Garry said as he put the 'Good Book' back into his brown briefcase.

"Did you abuse yourself, Patterson?"

"Yes sir," Patterson said as he tried to lower his head even further.

"What did you do Patterson?"

"I abused myself, sir," Patterson muttered.

"What did you say? Speak up Patterson!"

"I said that I abused myself, sir," Patterson said.

The boys around the room began to mumble 'wanker...wanker...wanker'.

"You're fined fifty pence and don't let us catch you abusing yourself again," Wee Garry said.

"Yes, sir."

"Wanker...wanker...wanker...wanker," the boys were becoming louder and louder. Finally, Bam Bam shouted 'WANKER!' as Patterson walked back to his chair. All the boys joined in yelling 'wanker, wanker' at the top of their voices.

"Right, that's enough," Mr Wilson said as he stood up and waved both arms in a downward motion.

The boys ceased immediately.

"Like I said," Adam said. "That's the 'walk of shame'. Wanker, that's what we call the night watchman, sneaks around the dorms in his slippers after lights out, listening out for kids having a crafty wank. Once he finds a kid at it, he leaps up and shouts out at the top of his voice, 'Wanking!' That,

Al, is when you're written into the 'Good Book' with a black mark. Being caught wanking carries an immediate 'snibbed' and a fifty pence fine."

"Now, it's Friday and that means it's movie night. This evening we have 'A Hard Day's Night."

"Brilliant," Al thought. *"I love the Beatles."*

The boys were allowed to buy sweets before going into the room prepared for the movie night. Al caught sight of Bam Bam and Mallinson taking ten pence each from a number of the younger kids. With his Mars Bar held firmly in his hand Al walked into the room with Adam and enjoyed the momentary escapism the movie gave.

After the movie it was back to the dormitory. The lad walking in front of him and Adam was pulled to one side by a master and then slapped around the head.

"What's all that about?" Al whispered.

"That's old Jonesy. He makes up this hair cream at home and forces some of the kids to buy it for ten pence on a Friday. Sometimes he'll make them buy two or three jars of his 'Jit'.

"Jit?" said Al. "You mean he bashes one into a jar and flogs it as hair cream?"

Adam chuckled.

"No, it's a proper home-made hair cream. He just calls it 'Jit'," Adam said, pausing for a moment. "Well at least I don't think it's real 'Jit'.

Al understood that the slang for sperm was 'Jit'.

The two boys walked down the corridor towards the stairway that led to the dormitory. Standing by the stairway was a master with his arms crossed. He had wild, mousey coloured hair that looked as though it hadn't been washed in a week.

"You, new boy!" the master said as he unfolded his arms and pointed to Al.

"Here, now!"

Al stopped in front of the master and stood to attention.

"Yes, sir."

"Open your mouth, now!"

Al did as he was told.

"Wider, boy, wider!" the master shouted in his broad Yorkshire accent.

He grabbed Al by the ear and stuck his nose just inches away from Al's open mouth. He began snorting loudly. After the third loud sniff he let go of Al's ear.

"I'll be keeping an eye on you!" the master said, then promptly called another lad over and did the same thing.

"Adam, what's that all about? Is he off his rocker or what?" Al said as they walked up the stairs.

"That's Mr Sykes, and yeah, he definitely isn't all there. Every day he will just call kids over at random and then sniff their breath for signs of smoking," Adam said.

"You're kidding me. You mean that's his job here?" Al said.

"It gets worse, mate. If he can smell peppermint on your breath, then he takes it that you've been smoking and trying to cover it up. That's automatic 'snibbed' and a fine."

"Looks like it's just Mars bar for me then," Al said with a sarcastic laugh.

Al undressed and got into his bed. Once the lights went out, he could hear movements from around the dorm. One boy was pleading to be left alone as a larger boy climbed into his bed.

***

The following morning, Al made his way to the canteen after he washed up in the shower room and got dressed. Other than the Mars bar, he hadn't eaten in over twenty-four hours. He sat at the table of six with his arms crossed. Each of the boys had a breakfast bowl and a single spoon. In the middle of the table was a large bowl of porridge. One of the masters sounded the whistle and immediately the lads began 'dicking' on the food. Al placed the spoon by his empty plate and shook his head. Adam was amongst the first to spit on the food and then swooped up a large spoonful. Al felt that he could have been sick. He turned his head to where 'Gudgey' sat alone at his own table. The boy took a big spoonful of porridge and shovelled it into his mouth. He chewed for several moments then made an exaggerated attempt of swallowing it all. As hard as he tried, Al found it difficult to look away until Gudgey's chest began to rise and fall until his throat filled and the porridge was regurgitated and back in his mouth. Al felt as though he would have heaved if he'd had some food in his stomach.

There were no formal school classes on Saturday, so Al decided he would walk around the grounds and familiarise himself with the place where he would have to spend the next three years. He passed one boy performing a sex on act on another, and then witnessed Johnson being beaten by Bam Bam, Mallinson and three other lads.

When the clouds opened, Al decided to go back to the dormitory and stopped on the way to use the toilet. He opened the cubicle door, pulled his shorts down and sat on the toilet seat. Moments later he heard voices whispering. Then, there was a massive crashing noise as the door of the cubicle next to his was smashed open. Al could hear the yells of a boy he thought was Anderson as his attackers punched and kicked him.

"Please, please, don't make me do that" Anderson begged.

Al pulled up his trousers and flushed the toilet. He opened the door to find that two lads were holding Anderson while a third, with his trousers around his ankles, was performing a sexual act. Anderson pleaded again, but the lads showed no mercy. They continued to punch him in the stomach and chest while their friend committed rape.

Al ignored the commotion and washed his hands in the basin.

"I can't fight everyone's battles," Al thought.

Al returned to the dormitory and lay back on the bed with his hands behind his head.

"I'm starving, bloody starving, and this place is full to the rafters with twisted, nasty, pieces of work. I'm going to have to make some changes to survive this shit hole," Al thought. *"There's no time to feel sorry for myself or anyone else. I need to embrace these changes, stay focused and not waste any time or energy on things I can't control."*

At 5.00pm, when the masters blew the whistle in the canteen, Al was the first 'dicking' and swiftly followed with his fork digging into what was more than his fair share of the evening's meal. He gulped the food down and shovelled a second, then a third forkful into his mouth and swallowed. Al and Adam finished eating within seconds of each other.

"Not bad for a new kid," Adam chuckled.

"Needs must," Al said, as he put his knife and fork neatly on the empty plate.

Later in the dormitory, as the lights went out, Al could once again hear the pleas to be left alone. He turned over, closed his eyes and slept.

Chapter 12

"You'll love this," Adam chuckled as he did his tie in front of the mirror.

"Love what?"

"Sundays, mate. We have to march off down to the church in Paisley.

"Oh yeah," Al said with a chortle." It'll be the highlight of the year."

Out in the yard, Al, Adam and the other boys, in full school uniform and army boots, were formed into lines like soldiers.

"Attention!" Mr Douglas yelled.

The boys quickly brought themselves to attention with their shoulders back and facing the front.

"Right turn!" Mr Douglas said as he moved closer to the boys and then turned right so that he was positioned by their side.

"By the left, quick march!"

The boys strode off as one leading with their left foot. Mr Douglas marched down the road towards Paisley. Residents would look through their windows at the marching boys while others stood on the side of the road holding their Sunday newspapers.

Mr Douglas and the boys began to sing:

> *Onward Christian soldiers*
> *Marching off to war*
> *With the cross of Jesus*
> *Going on before*
>
> *Christ, the royal Master*
> *Leads against the Foe*

Forward into battle
See, his banners go!

Onward Christian soldiers
Marching off to war
With the cross of Jesus
Going on before.

Al mouthed the words while others sang out loud. Mr Douglas marched the boys down through the town centre and finally called them to attention outside the church at the West end of the High Street. Al looked up at the dominant feature of the town's skyline and the striking crown steeple. He felt nothing by being in the presence of the alleged home of God.

Members of the congregation were welcomed into the church while the boys from the approved school were ushered up to the gallery.

The minister walked out and greeted his congregation in his clerical robe. He said a few words before climbing up into his pulpit. Al and the boys sat in silence while the minister read passages from the bible.

"Do you go in for all this bollocks?" Adam whispered.

"The only time I've been to a church is to screw the place," Al said.

"I know that my feet are bloody killing me though," Al thought.

"They're hypocrites. The lot of them," Adam said. "Christianity is supposed to be the fulfilment of God's plan to restore a broken world through his son Jesus. This lot in here, with their narrow-minded views, believe that it all went wrong when Adam and Eve ate the apple from the tree of knowledge. I bet they all claim to have read the bible and yet not one of them knows who Lilith was."

"Nor do I," Al said, shrugging his shoulders.

"These boots are a bloody nightmare. They're just not giving at all," Al thought.

"Lilith is mentioned, albeit briefly, in the bible. She was God's first creation of woman and Adam's first wife. She was created as an equal to Adam, but Adam and God didn't like that she refused to be subservient. She didn't want to live in Adam's shadow, so she was quietly fucked off and replaced by Eve. I would have a bet with you right now that this lot of knee bending God botherers wouldn't have a clue who she was."

"So how do you know?" Al said as he put his hymn book on his knees.

"I've read the bible, Al, because I'm interested in the big questions like what is life all about and why are we here," Adam said.

"Any conclusions?"

"Not yet, but I do have some observations," Adam said.

"Like what?" Al said as he reached down and rubbed the back of his ankle.

"Have you ever noticed that every picture of Jesus has him as a white person?"

"Well, he must have been white," Al said.

"On the contrary Al, Jesus was born in Bethlehem in the Middle East. That would mean Jesus would have been black, possibly brown, but almost certainly not snow white like that," Adam said as he pointed to an image of Jesus on the church wall.

"Black?"

"Yes mate, and this lot would lynch you as a heretic for even suggesting it," Adam said.

"I've never thought about it," Al said. "Making money for my family and getting by has pretty much been my life's priority."

"I don't want to oversimplify things, but if we were all nicer, more honest, more selfless, more giving and more genuinely concerned about those less fortunate than ourselves, then the world be a far better place," Adam said.

There was a moment's silence as they listened to the minister deliver his pre-prepared sermon.

"We as human beings are fundamentally flawed. In theory, we all want to live consistently with things we believe are true, noble, right, pure and … well, nice, but in reality, we don't," Adam said.

"He's not far wrong there. Just a couple of days at Thornley Park Approved School would open people's eyes to what life can really be like," Al thought.

"Adam, I never asked. What are you in here for?" Al whispered.

"I robbed a church," Adam said with a smile. "Six times."

The minister turned his sermon towards the boys in the gallery.

"You see those sinners up there in the gallery? My friends, you do not want to be like them. You must not allow your children to grow up like them because those boys are destined to burn in the fires of hell," the minister said, as he pointed to Al and the boys around him.

"Let that sink in, burn for eternity in the fires of hell. These boys are lucky that the death penalty has been abolished," the minister said, pointing and shaking his head vehemently. "Because these sinners will all have been hung by their neck until they were dead. It would be then that Satan's demons would take them down into the fiery pits of hell where they would have remained for all eternity."

"Listen to him," Adam hissed. "He's probably messing with the kids in the choir. If hell exists, then it's him and others like him that will be the ones that'll go there. You can't be taken in by the uniforms that men hide behind. Ministers messing with kids, preaching faith in a God that sits on a cloud saying do as I say and not as I do, police officers that fit you up or bash seven sorts of shit out of you because they can. Doctors who prescribe drugs because they're paid to by pharmaceutical companies and politicians who send young working-class kids off to fight wars when they fall out with politicians from another country. You have to wonder how many of the politicians, judges and senior bureaucrat's kids were sent off to fight the Germans in the last war."

Al didn't reply.

"Like I said, Al," Adam said. "I take an interest in the big questions and the world around me."

"You! Yes, you," the minister said as he pointed to the lad to Al's right. "Stand up!"

The congregation turned in their seats to look at the twelve-year-old boy.

"Get up then boy!" Mr Douglas hissed. "On your feet now lad and do as you're told!"

Warily, the boy stood up and put his hands at his sides.

"Sinner! You are a sinner, boy. I want to hear your confession. Tell the good people here what you did," the minister shouted.

The boy covered his mouth and coughed.

"Speak up!" the minister said.

"I climbed over the wall at the back of the local off-licence and stole empty pop bottles and soda syphons and then took them to another off-licence for the returns money," the boy said.

"So you stole from your fellow man?"

"Yes," the boy said.

"What did you do with money you gained from stealing the owner's bottles?"

"I put some of it into the electricity meter at home so we could keep warm and bought sweets with the rest," the boy said.

"You bought sweets?" the minister said in a condescending tone.

"I did."

"Now, do you repent, sinner?" the minister said, with both his arms and outstretched fingers pointing towards the boy.

"I do, sir," the boy said, nodding his head frantically. "I don't want to go hell."

"Good, now sit down," the minister said. "If you want forgiveness from our Lord God then you must read your bible and pray to God to absolve your sins."

"I will sir," the boy said as he sat down.

"Anything to add to that, Adam?" Al whispered.

"Yeah. Christians believe they are called to perfection when in fact perfection is something that no person can attain in this life. But this lot," Adam said nodding towards those sitting around the minister. "Pretend they are perfect and therefore they are better than everyone else, when in fact they have just as many skeletons in their closets if not more than the rest of us. They act nice but really, they backstab and manipulate while living a life of deception. Pride wouldn't allow them to admit that they cannot attain perfection and that's when hypocrisy comes into play."

"So here endeth the lesson," Al said with a chuckle.

"Sorry about that. I have been known to get on my soapbox sometimes," Adam said.

"None of these kids deserved that disgraceful lecture," Al thought. *"Most of the kids in here are from broken homes. They're already traumatised by being in a place like Thornley Place with real criminals like me. Now the older kids that sexually abuse and bully the younger lads can burn in fucking hell."*

The boys were told to wait until every member of the church's congregation had left before they were allowed down from the gallery. Mr Douglas had them fall into line, military style, and then marched them back through Paisley town singing *'Onward Christian Soldiers'* and on to Thornley Park Approved School.

"My foot is killing me," Al said, as he removed the army boot from his foot. "It started with just a slight ache, then a burning tingle and now it bloody well hurts."

"That looks nasty," Adam said as he looked at the blister on Al's ankle. "You better get yourself over to Matron's."

"Where's that?" Al said, carefully pulling his sock back up.

"I'll go with you," Adam said.

Al limped down the hallway where he saw Bam Bam standing over a young lad that was cowering down on his knees in fear of being beaten. Mr Douglas came bounding up the stairs, turned into the hallway right by where Bam Bam stood. He looked at Bam Bam and then looked down at the lad on his knees being bullied before moving swiftly on.

Adam took Al through to Matron's office. Al knocked on the door.

"Wait outside until you're called in!"

"She sounds like a right battle axe," Al whispered.

"Trust me, Al, she is," Adam chuckled.

The door swung open and a large, overweight woman in a green full length medical gown stood in the doorway. Her hair had been cut into a 'bob' style that ended just above her collar.

"Yes?" Matron said as she chewed furiously on a sandwich.

"It's my foot Matron," Al said.

"Yes, yes we all have them," Matron said.

"I've got a blister from wearing the boots," Al said as he pointed down to his ankle.

"Yes, they do that," Matron said, as she put the last piece of her sandwich into her mouth and began chomping.

Al remained in the seat rubbing his ankle.

"Okay, okay come in," Matron said.

Al followed her into the office. Matron pointed towards a chair while she opened a cabinet drawer.

"Take your sock off," Matron said.

Al peeled the sock down slowly to avoid the pain. Matron held his ankle firmly and looked at the large, angry looking, blister. She produced a large pair of steel scissors from behind her back and swiftly cut the blister clean off.

Al let out a sudden yelp as the pain surged through his body

"That's it," Matron said. "On your way!"

Al scrambled awkwardly to his feet. He clenched and unclenched his fists as the pain from his ankle affected every nerve in his body. He hobbled back out into the hallway.

"She's a fucking butcher," Al whispered.

"Rumour has it that her husband buggered off with her best friend and she's had a hate for men and boys ever since," Adam whispered back.

"Really?" Al said.

"No, I just made that up," Adam chuckled.

Al managed to hobble back to the dormitory only to find Gudgey down on his hands and knees performing a sexual act on a boy by his bed. There were three more lads waiting in a queue, each holding a ten pence piece in their clammy hands.

"What the fuck?" Al said. "I ain't hanging about in here," as he turned and hobbled back into the hallway.

"Tell you what," Adam said. "Let's go down and see Mr Brown the boiler man.

"Anything but that," Al said. "You'd think the masters would do something about what goes on in here."

"That will never happen," Adam said as he jumped the final two steps down the stairs. "The kids in here aren't the only ones abusing each other. Believe me, some of the masters are it too. One kid fought back, and I mean he beat the shit out of the master we call Willy Green. Everyone started calling him 'Willy' because he would make boys show him their willies and, well, you can guess the rest. After this kid beat him up all the masters got together and kicked the fuck out of the thirteen-year-old. He was so badly beaten that he had to go to hospital. Then they falsified all the records to show that he had a history of violence against both us boys and the Masters. He never came back. Willy Green is still here as is his psychopath mate 'Wee Buck.' That bastard takes great pleasure in inflicting violence on the younger kids. They'll both be back next week."

***

Adam took Al down to meet Mr Brown. Several of the lads would stop by Mr Brown's place of work. He would tell the boys stories about the First World War and how they should never, ever trust any German. He described his part during the battle of the Somme in great detail and how he had been shot. The boys would take turns to tell jokes and then Mr Brown would have them all singing anti-German songs at the top of their voices. Al had taken an instant liking to Mr Brown and found himself laughing out loud when he told the boys that he called the school's boiler 'The Kaiser', and promptly stood up and gave it a good bashing. He told Al he should join the school's army cadets because World War Three was coming and it would be started by the Germans. Mr Brown stood up, grabbed his broom, and demonstrated how he should stab the cadet's scarecrows with his bayonet. He emphasised how it was important to turn the blade because those bloody Germans will just keep coming otherwise.

Al was still in pain but chatting and laughing with Mr Brown had taken his mind off both the blister and being away from home and his brothers and sisters.

"He's alright, Mr Brown," Al said.

"Yeah," Adam said. "Old Wee Garry tried to put a stop to us boys going down to see him, but Mr Brown was having none of it. He marched up to his office and slammed the door behind him and after that nothing was ever said."

"Really?" said Al

"No, I just made that shit up as well," Adam said, bursting into fits of laughter.

***

Al was standing in line to buy some sweets from the canteen.

"I didn't see any of this coming," Al thought. *"Three years, three bloody years! It's a lifetime. Mammy must be going mad and Da, well, he'll still be drinking his life away at the pub or fighting the orderlies before being hauled back off to the asylum. Brian's away for a year and he's still just a kid... damn it, I'm still just a kid. I'm fourteen years old and facing three years in an approved school. I wonder if people can visit me? Will they even bother? I can't imagine Mammy will find the time and Da won't even know I've gone unless someone tells him."*

Out of the corner of his eye he saw that Don Mitchell and his two side-kicks Bam Bam and Mallinson were heading his way. Al stood up straight and took his hands out of his pockets.

"Alright?" Al said, as the three lads crowded around him.

"Alright? I'll give you fucking alright," Don said as he quickly kneed Al's thigh, crushing the muscle against the bone. Al buckled down onto one knee with an extremely painful dead leg. He felt as though he were about to vomit.

"I'm the fucking number one in here, McIntosh, and you'll pay your fucking dues like everyone else. If you don't want to get sliced up, you'll give ten pence to Bam Bam every Friday.

Al took a slow, deep, breath as the blood began to flow back to his leg, then shot up like a tightly coiled spring. He head butted Don. Al felt his nose crack on his head. He launched a left hook followed by a heavy right uppercut. Don was stunned and caught off balance. Al took a quick aim and fired a powerful kick straight between his legs. He turned quickly to Bam Bam and caught him smack in the mouth. Al felt no pain. He dug deep and threw a heavy succession of punches and kicks, left hook, right jab, left hook, and an uppercut that jerked his head back. Seeing the opening, Al grabbed Bam Bam by the hair and brought his face down hard onto his knee. Blood spurted over the wooden flooring and cream coloured wall. Al looked down as Bam Bam wriggled, kicked and held his face. He gasped desperately for breath and spat out blood.

Mallinson held his hands up in the air in a submissive gesture.

"I don't want any trouble," Mallinson begged as he looked down at Don and Bam Bam both laid out on the concrete. Don was out cold with blood streaming from his nose while Bam Bam was still floundering and coughing and gasping for breath. Al stared deep into Mallinson's eyes before booting Bam Bam in the chest and stomach. Bam Bam yelped and twitched as the kicks lifted part of his body clean off the ground.

"You ain't no fucking number one, now," Al said as he turned to Don and kicked his motionless body several times.

"Fucking have that!" Al thought as he looked down at the bullies with utter contempt, his fists tightly clenched. *"There's plenty more if you want it!"*

"I don't want any trouble," Mallinson pleaded again, both hands still floundering above his head.

"Cross me, Mallinson, and I'll bite your fucking face off," Al said calmly.

"Okay, no problem," Mallinson said, shaking his head vehemently.

Al looked around him. Several lads from the dormitory had witnessed the altercation. He raised his right hand and placed a solitary finger on his nose indicating that were to say nothing. With Don and Bam Bam still on the ground he promptly made his way inside the building.

"McIntosh."

Al turned to see Matron walking up behind him.

"Yes Matron?" Al said calmly.

"How is your foot?" Matron said as she looked down at his army boots.

"I've had worse," Al lied.

"Good," Matron. "McIntosh?"

"Yes Matron?"

"Is your grandfather Charles Rose, Charlie?" Matron asked.

Al could see what looked like a sparkle in her eyes as she spoke the name.

"I'm not sure, Matron. But I can find out if and when I get home on a visit," Al said.

"You do that, McIntosh. Don't forget now. It's Charles Rose and he used to work here many years ago. He taught game keeping to the boys, okay?" Matron said with a broad smile.

"Was she having some sort of fling with this Charlie Rose?" Al thought. *"Maybe it was my grandfather. Who knows, but I will find out."*

Al could feel a slight pain in his knee. He went into the toilets and found a part of Bam Bam's tooth lodged in his skin. Al teased it out with his fingernail and then cleaned the minor wound before finding the master that ran the army cadets and put his name down to join. Adam raced up behind him.

"Al, Al," Adam called.

Al stopped and turned to face him.

"I've just heard what you did to Don, Bam Bam and Mallison, the spineless prick," Adam said as he patted him on the back.

"Alright, keep it down," Al said.

"Now you have a reputation, Al. You're the 'Daddy' and no one is going to fuck with you. I mean taking out on the Don is one thing, but to smash the shit out of him *and* Bam Bam? You ain't going to get any trouble from no one," Adam said.

The term 'Daddy' is prison slang for a tough kid.

***

It was seven months before Al earned enough 'good marks' to have a full weekend at home with his family. On his return, Mammy announced that his Aunt Doreen was ill and that she would be going out for the evening to help her out. Al had also found out that his da and mammy were now separated, and she had filed for divorce. Da was no longer living at the family home.

Al had been sitting in the front room warming his hands in front of the fire. It was late and all his brothers and sisters were in bed. He thought he heard something from the kitchen. He ignored it the first time, but when it happened again, he wandered out and put the kitchen light on. He stood motionless, listening out for the noise. Al heard a scuffling noise again. He looked over at the open window. The noise continued. He clambered up onto the kitchen worktop and peered out of the window.

"What the fuck is that?" Al thought. *"Some bastard is trying to break into our house!"*

Al jumped down quickly and ran over to the utility cupboard. He grabbed the door handle and tore it open, reached in and grabbed a mop, complete with the handle. He bounded back to the worktop, scrambled back on top, opened the kitchen window wide and then, with both hands, he began bashing the mop head as hard as he could on the head of the dark figure climbing up the drainpipe. They yelled out as Al pounded away furiously. Al could see that the burglar had lost their grip with one hand, so he battered harder and faster in a bid to shake him off completely.

"It'll serve the bastard right if he fell off and smashed his head," Al thought as he continued to batter the person.

"Stop, stop!" the person called out.

"Fuck off!" Al said, still smashing the mop head down.

"Al, Al! It's Da, it's your da!"

"You're not my da," Al said. "He's in Australia!"

Al pulled the mop back inside the kitchen and climbed down onto the kitchen floor. He stood back while his da, with blood running down his face scaled the drainpipe and scrambled awkwardly into the room.

"What are you doing Da?" Al said.

Da climbed down off the worktop and brushed himself down. He used his jersey sleeve to wipe the blood from his forehead.

"I need to see your mammy," Da said as he strutted out of the kitchen.

Al followed him into the living room.

"She's not here, Da. She's with Auntie Doreen," Al said.

"Yeah? Well, I'll just look for myself," Da said as he swiftly turned and left the room.

Al stood in front of the fire and warmed the back of his legs. Moments later he heard a thumping on the stairs, the kitchen door open and then a metallic clunk. Shortly after the front door opened and slammed hard.

"What was that all about?" Al thought as he walked back into the kitchen. The utility door was open. Al peered inside to see that his Da had broken into the gas meter and stolen the money.

The weekend passed and Al got back to Thornley Manor late Sunday afternoon. After he ate, he showered and went to bed early. The weekend away had been a disappointment. He had dreamed about leaving the approved school and returning home, but the reality was an overwhelming anti-climax.

"I need to start making some proper plans for when I get out of here," Al thought. *"Running up to a scarecrow and being ordered to stab it with a bayonet isn't going to help me out there in the big wide world."*

A nine-year-old boy whose parents had both been sentenced to a hefty prison sentence had been dropped off at Thornley Park Approved School for an overnight stay before being moved on to a children's home. Al could see the how lost and scared the young boy looked. Shortly after the lights went out, Al heard footsteps. He turned over to see a fifteen-year-old lad climbing into the boy's bed. Al shot out of his bed and grabbed the lad by his hair. He yanked him hard and then dragged him out and onto the floor. Al grasped the lad by his pyjama top.

SMACK!

Al drove his fist hard into the lad's face.

SMACK!

A second punch had the lad pleading to be let go. Al pulled him up so that his face was just inches from his own.

"Fuck off now before I fucking kill you!" Al hissed.

Al let the kid drop back to the floor with a thud and stood back while he scrambled onto his feet, still rubbing his face, and then disappeared back down to his own bed at the far end of the dormitory.

Al rubbed his hands together and then got back into bed. The nine-year-old boy climbed out of his bed and stood by Al's. He cautiously held out his hand. Al shook it.

"Thank you," the boy whispered.

Al nodded and smiled. He turned over and closed his eyes.

Al remembered the kid that had been made to carry out sexual acts in the toilets when he first arrived. Since then that same kid had turned into a right bastard and in addition to willingly taking part in sexual activity, could often be found in the showers flicking his wet towel at the naked new kids. The masters had witnessed the bully forcing himself on the younger boys and did nothing.

"I feel pretty damn proud of myself," Al thought. *"I'm pleased I helped that boy and kept him safe from some of the nonces in here.*

The following day after breakfast, the boy was taken to a children's home by social services. He smiled and waved to Al from the back seat as the car slowly drove away.

***

Al and the lads were playing football when the ball was kicked up onto the roof of the building. One of the boys asked a master if he could go up and retrieve it. The master shook his head vehemently as the boy had absconded the last time he climbed up on the roof. The master turned and told Al to climb the forty-foot drainpipe and get the balls down. Al nodded enthusiastically and scaled up the drainpipe then lifted himself up onto the flat roof of the building. He found fourteen footballs and kicked each one off the roof to the boys down below. After he threw the last one off, Al clambered around to the far side of the building and just sat on the tiles looking out at the road and the cars driving past.

"That's it. I've had enough. I'm done with this place and I'm out of here," Al thought as he shimmied down the drainpipe and dropped the last few feet down to the grass at the back of the building.

He crouched down and looked left and right before bolting across the field towards the road. His heart thumped as the adrenaline and excitement raced through his body.

"I'm going to England!" Al thought. *"Home of the Great Train Robbers and the jet set. To where five-pound notes hang from trees just waiting to plucked off, to the gold paved streets of London."*

Chapter 13

Al made his way to Mt Vernon, the Glasgow Motorway junction. He stood on the side of the motorway slip road thumbing for a lift. He had nothing but the clothes he stood in. Thoughts of the masters searching Thornley Manor looking for him plagued him. He imagined Wee Garry calling in the police to track him down with dogs. Al would look from left to right intermittently and kept his wits about him. He didn't want to raise any suspicion. As the time passed Al found himself thinking about leaving his family and Glasgow behind.

He had the strangest image of his da crying while watching the news in 1963. John Fitzgerald Kennedy, the 35th President of the United States had been assassinated while travelling through Dallas, Texas, in an open top Lincoln convertible. He watched the tears stream down his drunken da's face as the news commentator told how the First Lady, Jacqueline Kennedy, who rarely accompanied her husband on political outings but was sat beside him on this trip, along with the Texas Governor, John Connally and his wife for the ten-mile motorcade ride through the streets of downtown Dallas. The news reader told how the large and enthusiastic crowds gathered along the parade route. The reader's voice became sadder while announcing that as the President's vehicle passed the Texas School Book Depository building at 12.30pm, three shots were fired. John F Kennedy, age 46, was rushed to Parklands Hospital and was pronounced dead thirty minutes later.

"How could you have cried over somebody you don't even know, who had nothing to do with Glasgow or even the United Kingdom, when you've never shed a single tear for the unnecessary pain and hardships our family have had to endure, mostly by your hand?" Al thought. *"I just wanted you*

to shut the hell up and go to sleep so I could go through your pockets for change."

Several cars passed him. One looked as though he was going to stop but had actually slowed down so the driver could light his cigarette.

"I miss my mate, Larry," Al thought as the image of his friend entered his mind.

Al and Larry White had been the best of friends. Larry's parents were Londoners and had moved to Glasgow. Larry had been extremely tall for his age. When he was just eight years old, he looked more like a teenager because of his height. Al thought Larry and his English accent was the coolest thing on the planet. He always admired how Larry would stand his ground against the local kids who tried to bully him because he was a Londoner. Al had looked on as Larry fought one kid after another around the back courts. He was unbeaten. Another game local lad, who had been nicknamed 'Fatty', decided it was time to teach the English kid a lesson. He had been backed up by scores of street kids eager to see the English lad beaten. Larry, true to form, didn't back off, and proceeded to punch and kick 'Fatty' until he fell to the ground. It was then that Fatty's best friend ran forward and jumped on Larry's back. With his arms crossed tightly around Larry's neck he tried to bring him down and give Fatty a chance to get back on his feet. Al, instinctively, jumped into the fight and began to pound Fatty's friend with a quick succession of targeted punches. Larry managed to get free, and the two boys fought side by side. From that day on Al and Larry had become inseparable. Al saw him as smart and tough, both qualities he admired.

However, Larry's parents didn't like Al hanging around with their son and did little to hide their disdain for either Al or his father's violent, drunken, behaviour. He never forgot the look on Larry's mother's face when, as she passed by the family home, his da had come home paralytic and began to throw large stones and bottles through the windows. Al was ashamed and embarrassed by his da's behaviour as they had been condemned as pariahs by his best friend's parents and almost every other family in the street. From that day forward Larry would find himself punished by his father's leather belt if he was seen with Al. However, such was the bond the two boys had, that Larry would take the punishment and then go and find his friend.

Al had been cautious not to invite Larry when he was out thieving with Brian. He knew it was never Larry's thing. He did join them on a couple of jobs out of bravado and the sheer excitement of breaking the law, and would try to give Al advice on how the robberies should be planned and executed. Al would just smile wryly. He was the brains behind the robberies and most of Larry's advice made no sense. It hadn't been thought through. Al put it down to Larry, being the biggest, also thought he was the smartest. Larry had only played a very minor part in all the robberies and thefts that Al had organised or been involved in.

"You were probably the best friend I've ever had," Al thought.

After Al was handed down the three-year probation order, the police had gone to Larry's parent's home despite Al not giving either his brother Brian or Larry up. Grassing or 'clyping' as it was known in Glasgow, was an absolute no, no and Al remained staunch and took the rap for everything the police had. Larry's parents were outraged that the police had gone to their home. It didn't help that Mammy, who still didn't believe that Al was guilty of all the police charges, blamed Larry for being a bad influence on her son.

Al shook his head slowly as he remembered how the judge had told him that one of the conditions for the three year probation order was that he had to keep away from Larry White.

He was brought back by the sounds of air brakes. A large articulated truck was slowing down.

"Where are you going?" the driver, with a broad Liverpudlian accent, called out after he wound down the window.

"London," Al said with a broad smile.

"I can get you down as far as Charnock Richard Service Station between junction 26 and 27 on the M6 if that helps?" the driver said.

"That would be great, thank you," Al said as he raced around to the passenger's side of the truck, opened the door and climbed up inside.

As Al slammed the door shut, the driver shifted the gearstick into first, checked his wing mirror and began to pull back out onto the motorway.

"I'm Des," the driver said.

"I'm Al."

"So what takes you off to London?" Des said as he shifted the gear lever into third.

"I'm visiting family," said Al.

"I should have thought that through," Al up. *"I was bound to be asked why London."*

Al and Des spoke a little before he found himself staring out of the passenger side window. It had just started raining and the water on the glass window triggered a memory.

Al had scraped together a few pennies to go swimming in Kay Street with friends. As they swam around playing games and challenging each other to hold their breath underwater, several uniformed police officers came in and ordered everyone to exit the pool, get dressed and leave the area. The police gave no details, only that an incident was taking place. Al and the local lads had been intrigued. They did as they were told but instead of making their way back home, they hung around at the top of the road watching the police run between cars by the flats and order passers-by to turn back. Al heard a loud bang. It was a gunshot. Later that day he learnt that a deranged gunman named James Griffiths had gone on a shooting spree that had left one man dead and thirteen injured, including a seven-year-old boy. The gunman had tried to make his getaway in a stolen vehicle but was forced to take refuge in a top floor tenement. The unhinged psychopath began firing randomly at the people below, including scores of young children frolicking in a play park. Two armed detectives managed to sneak into the building undetected. The shot Al heard was the one that finally brought the crazed gunman's shooting spree to an end. They stormed the room and dragged his body down onto the streets below. James Griffiths, a career criminal who had been charged with murder, was dead.

"I suppose if you're going to go, why not go in a blaze of glory," Al thought. *"I wouldn't shoot innocent people and definitely not kids though, just those that were out to get me."*

"I did time at a Borstal not that long ago," Des said.

"Really?" Al said as he turned back to face Des.

Borstals were run by HM Prison Services for convicted adolescents under the age of twenty-three. They had a notorious reputation for both convict on convict violence and prison officer on convict violence. It was a hard, tough regime with the ability to break the weak.

Des went on to tell a few stories of how he became incarcerated and that he chose never to go back to that life, which was why he became a truck driver.

"Al, are you on the run?" Des said calmly.

Al hesitated and then nodded his head.

Des handed him his lunch box full of ham and pickle sandwiches before reaching into his pocket and producing a one-pound note.

"There you go," Des said with a smile. "It's not a lot but it'll help you get by for a while. Good luck and take care of yourself."

Al thanked him and the two parted company shortly after at the Charnock Richard Service Station.

Al could feel a buzz rise up from the pit of his stomach as he looked at the Charnock Richard Service Station sign.

"I'm in England. I can't believe it. I'm really here!" Al thought.

The rain had eased up. Al put his left hand into his pocket to keep warm, while he held his right thumb out to attract a lift. As he stood in the rain, he began to think about his family life and how his da would beat his mammy black and blue and take money that had been put aside to feed the family so he could get drunk in the pub. Al could feel his left fist clench as the images of his da entered his mind.

Al had been fifteen years old and had been awarded a weekend at home through the 'Good Book' system at Thornley Park. He had got himself dressed up in some new clothes and had arranged to meet his friend. By this time his mammy and Da were now divorced and his da had taken up with a new girlfriend. They had moved in together on the same road as his friend. As Al approached his friend's tenement, he saw his Da approaching him.

"What's all this then, you poof?" Da called out.

"This is my new Duke of Windsor tie, everyone is wearing them Da," Al said as he stroked his purple tie proudly.

"Yeah, fashionable for poofs like you," Da said as he stepped up to where Al was standing.

"There's nothing poofy about wearing fashionable clothes," Al said sneering. He looked his da up and down. "Not that you would know anything about that."

Da reached out and grabbed Al by his new tie and yanked him forcefully towards him. Al could smell the rank odour of alcohol and stale nicotine on his breath.

"You're nothing but a little poof!" Da said, tightening the grip on Al's tie.

"Now you've fucking had it," Al thought, *"Your reputation and size do not intimidate me!"*

Al managed to twist his body away to the right. He clenched his fist and threw a powerful punch that lifted his da's chin into the air. He yelled out in pain and his head ricocheted against the brick wall. As he slumped forward Al could see a splatter of blood. He took a step back with both fists tightly clenched and with gritted teeth he was ready let loose years of anger and frustration. Da groaned, and his legs gave way as he slid down the wall.

"You ain't getting away with it that easy, you useless piece of shit!" Al yelled as he fired a vicious kick deep into his Da's stomach. "Poof? Poof? I'll give you fucking poof!"

Al fired three more ferocious body kicks.

"You know fuck all about me or what I'm capable of!" Al said as he lined himself up and launched a brutal kick to his da's face.

His head shot back with the sickening sound of broken bone and shattered teeth. He choked and groaned as blood poured from his nose and mouth.

Al looked down at the bloody, beaten man.

"Now I'll only tell you this once," Al said as he hurled a kick into Da's motionless body. "Don't you ever touch my brothers, sisters or Mammy again or I'll fucking kill you!"

Da coughed and spat a mouthful of blood out on the concrete pavement before releasing a hissing sound, closing his eyes and falling into a state of unconsciousness. Al reached down and emptied his pockets. He silently counted the notes.

"Twenty-nine quid," thought Al. *"Well, that's mine now!"*

***

Al looked up to see a truck with his indicator on. He pushed his shoulders back and forced a smile as the driver stopped and wound down the window.

"Where are you going?" the driver said as he looked Al up and down.

"London," said Al

"Come on then, get out of that rain," the driver said as wound his window back up.

Al climbed into the truck and in no time they were back on the motorway. The driver spoke briefly about the weather and about his trip to London. Then the driver said that he would be travelling to Leeds first and because of the time they would need to sleep in the cab overnight before driving down to London the following morning.

"Leeds? Sleeping in here with you?" Al thought. *"That's not happening. There's something not right about you."*

"No, sorry mate that's not going to work for me," Al said.

"How about I give you ten pounds to have sex with me," the driver said with a crooked grin.

"No chance!" Al said.

The driver looked over at Al through vexed, squinted, eyes.

"Well, best you get out here then," the driver said as he slammed on his brakes and brought the truck to an abrupt halt on the motorway's hard shoulder.

Al looked over at the driver and the rain on the glass window.

"Fuck you then," Al said as he opened the truck door, leapt out and then slammed it shut.

Al was stuck on the side of the motorway. He was worried about a police patrol car passing and concerned that no one would risk stopping to pick him up. However, within a few minutes a Ford Anglia stopped. The driver was a middle-aged woman. Al thought she looked like a school teacher. He smiled, got into the car and thanked her for the lift. The woman fired a series of questions starting with his name, where he was from, where was he going, and what he was doing on the hard shoulder. Al answered with lie after lie, and he could see that the woman was suspicious. She suggested they stop off at the next service station to get a cup of tea.

"Thank you, that will be nice," Al said.

The woman stopped in the service station car park and insisted on paying for Al's food and tea. He sat on the hard wooden chair and nursed the hot beverage.

"I've got to go the ladies' room," the woman said as she stood up. "I won't be long."

Al took a sip of his tea and nodded. All his instincts told him that something was not right, so once she turned the corner he got up, walked over and peeked around the corner. He was right, the woman was talking in the public telephone cubicle.

"She's calling the police," Al thought.

Al walked back to the table, took a last sip of his tea and then shot out through the doors, back into the car park. He walked around the building and slipped into an alleyway that led to the back of the canteen. He slipped down behind a large industrial bin and huddled up tight against the wall.

"What did she call the police for?" Al thought. *"Why didn't she just let me go about my business?"*

The ground was wet, and he could feel the dampness seeping through to the back of his trousers. Al crossed his arms over his knees and leant forward, curling himself into a ball to keep warm. He found himself thinking about Thornley Park Approved School, the masters and the one hundred and twenty kids that had been placed there because they were deemed out of control by the authorities.

A memory of the master, Mr Regan, came to mind. Everyone liked Mr Regan. He was like an apple tree in a field of thorn bushes. Al remembered how Mr Regan had woken him and several other boys late one night and had taken them down to watch the Apollo 11 moon landing. He told them it was an event that they would remember for the rest of their lives. Al and the boys watched in silence as Commander Neil Armstrong and lunar module pilot Buzz Aldrin landed the Apollo Lunar Module Eagle on July 20th, 1969, at 20.17 UTC (Coordinated Universal time). He was spellbound that the human race, who had been, just a few decades before, travelling the country's roads in horse and cart, had blasted out of the Earth's orbit into the vast universe and then landed a man on the moon. Al felt somehow connected to every person on the planet for those few hours. It hadn't been just a magnificent triumph for America but for the entire world.

Al peered out from the industrial waste bin. The car park was still full.

"I can't sit around here in the rain all night," Al thought. *"I need to get to London."*

He scrambled back onto his feet and scampered out of the alleyway, through the car park and stood by the road that led back down onto the motorway. He held out his thumb and waited patiently as car after car drove past.

"I never got to say goodbye to Adam," Al thought. *"I liked Adam; he was alright."*

Al and Adam had become friends. He was unlike any friend Al had had before. He was a deep thinker and would often try to lead Al into discussions and then challenge his thinking and open his mind to an alternative.

"Al, did you know that the Roman Emperor, Constantine, wrote the bible?" Adam said, taking a bite from his Mars bar.

"I've never given it much thought," Al said.

"Christians would have you believe that they are the words of God and that simply isn't true," Adam said as he popped the last piece of the chocolate bar into his mouth. "It was all about control."

"How do you mean?" Al said.

"Constantine was a very powerful ruler with a vast empire. He understood the power of religion and how it could make the most loyal of subjects betray a person because of their religious beliefs," Adam said before swallowing his chocolate and throwing the empty wrapper into the bin.

Al nodded.

"Constantine collated all the religious beliefs and stories from the four corners of the Roman Kingdom and created what we know today as the bible. It was also the birth of the Catholic Church which means 'universal' or 'embracing the whole universe' in Greek. By bringing the empire together under a single religion he was able to lead a single people under one religion directed by a single Emperor," Adam said as he pushed himself back in the armchair. "Did you know that there are tens of religions that all have a prophet born by a virgin, who had twelve followers, died and came back to life?"

"No, that can't be right," Al said.

"It is, Al, and all the information is out there if people could be bothered to look for it in the libraries. Buddha was supposed to have been born to the virgin Maya. The Siamese had a God and saviour who was born to the virgin Codom. The Egyptian people have had several messengers of God

164

all born to a virgin. The list goes on and on, but most people are just blinkered and believe what they are told by some bloke in a uniform, well, a priest's gown, without question," Adam said, sighing heavily. "Religion is nothing more, in my view, than a form of control of the masses and has been responsible for more deaths than every world conflict since time began."

"What is it with you and religion, Adam?" Al asked.

Adam chuckled.

"I suppose I'm driven to question everything and not just take what I'm being told as the truth. I don't trust those in uniforms. We both know that they will take bribes and give you a good hiding just because they can, and safely hide behind a uniform or a badge. Politicians lie, Al, they lie through their teeth. The next time you see one on television being asked a specific question, watch and listen to see if he answers it. I'll have a ten pence bet with you right now that you'll never get a yes or a no answer, and instead they'll direct their answer to something they want to make a point about. Why would anyone ever trust individuals that actively seek power?" Adam said.

"There will always be someone pulling the strings," Al said. "There must always be some kind of leader."

"True, but that doesn't mean we have to believe everything we're being told."

"Adam, why did you rob the same church six times?" Al said.

"I suppose I was making a kind of statement. I gave the old bill grief when they nicked me and then found myself in front of a magistrate. When asked why I did it I just launched into the whole control thing. Anyway, it turned out he was some kind of religious lunatic and had me down as an out-of-control renegade heretic that needed saving. So," Adam said with a sigh, "I found myself shifted off here."

"I'm sorry I didn't get to say goodbye," Al thought as he wiped the rain off his face. *"Most of the time I thought you were a bloody crackpot but every so often you did get me thinking."*

Al was brought back to the present by the sound of air brakes. He looked up to see a driver beckoning him in. Al raced around to the passenger's side and climbed up into the warm cab. The driver didn't talk much but hummed along to *'Sugar Sugar'* by The Archies, *'Build Me Up Buttercup'* by The Foundations and *'I'm Gonna make You Love Me'* by Diana Ross & The Supremes.

Al managed to doze but was kept awake by the thought of finally getting to London. Travelling had been a dream of his forever and he often found himself on the end of a slap from Mammy when he told her that one day he would leave and go to England. Al became increasingly excited as the truck trundled through the streets of London.

"Who knows, maybe I'll get to meet Twiggy or Jean Shrimpton," Al thought.

The driver pulled over at Finsbury Park. Al thanked him and closed the door firmly.

"I can't believe it," Al thought, rubbing his hands enthusiastically and grinning from ear to ear. *"I'm here, right in the heart of London!"*

Al was buzzing like a child on Christmas morning. He looked around him. Cars lined the streets while smartly dressed men and woman bustled along the pavements. The shops were brightly lit and looked inviting.

"I need to get to Carnaby Street," Al thought. "*Maybe the Beatles, The Who or The Rolling Stones will be out shopping for the next big tour. Better still, David Bowie, he is just so cool!*"

"Excuse me," Al said to a passing postman. "How do I get to the West End?"

"Get the Tube," the postman answered bluntly.

"Take the Piccadilly Line," the Postman said as he pointed down the street.

"Right, thank you," Al said.

Al patted his empty pockets and decided to jump the barrier. He read the signs and finally arrived at Tottenham Court Road Tube Station. He crossed over the busy Tottenham Court Road and after asking for directions, he followed Oxford Street, passed by The London College of Business and turned left into Berwick Street, Soho. His heart thumped wildly as he scanned the pavements looking for a pop star or celebrity. He found himself humming *'Dedicated Follower of Fashion'* by The Kinks, a mid-1960s song he was told was all about Carnaby Street. Al turned into Broadwick Street.

"*Come on, Twiggy, Roger Daltry, or even Paul McCartney*," Al thought, "*Show yourselves. This is where you guys are all supposed to hang out.*"

Carnaby Street was the fourth turning on his right. Al looked up at the sign that read 'Carnaby Street Welcomes the World'. He quickly scanned the road and saw four girls in miniskirts chatting outside a blue and white shop. The sign read 'Ravel'.

"*No, that's not Twiggy*," Al thought as he turned his gaze further down the street.

A tall, pretty girl in a short, chocolate brown coloured dress and white knee length boots pushed passed him.

"Sorry," she called back, scurrying off.

"No problem," Al called after her.

"She looked like a model. Maybe she's an actress on her way to a film shoot," Al thought as he looked at the shops.

"Lord John, Lady Jane, I wonder which ones the stars use," Al thought.

Al walked the short length of Carnaby Street then turned back.

"There's no pop stars here, not even a model," Al thought. *"Not even a fucking tree anywhere with fivers hanging off it."*

Convinced that he had arrived too early, Al spent most of the day traipsing through the streets of Soho and returned to Carnaby Street at nightfall. He thought he'd caught a glimpse of Dana, the winner of the Eurovision Song Contest with her chart hit *'All Kinds of Everything'* as she climbed into a black taxicab on Broadwick Street, but he couldn't be sure. Al couldn't hide his disappointment. He looked up at the bright lights, but without the celebrities he'd seen on television or in magazines, it felt empty. Hungry and disillusioned, Al headed slowly back towards Tottenham Court Road. He crossed the busy street and entered Great Portland Street.

"I thought there would be celebrities on every street corner in London," Al thought as he slipped his hands into his trouser pockets, lowered his head and walked aimlessly. At the end of the street, Al spotted Regents Park.

"I'm going to need somewhere to sleep," Al thought, *"This looks as good as anywhere."*

Al looked up at the moon and how its light lit up parts of the park. He spotted a park bench that hadn't been lit up.

"That will do," Al thought.

He had been lying on the bench for less than hour when he spotted a young couple enter the park. They were holding hands and laughing. The young man was in his early twenties and dressed in a smart pair of flared trousers and a blazer. The girl was blonde with hair that shrouded her moon shaped face. She had a songbird sweet voice and appeared to laugh at everything the young man said. The couple passed by the moonlit bench and were heading towards where Al had been lying.

"Oh, come on. The park is full of benches! Why do want mine?" Al thought as he quietly slipped off the bench and scrambled under it.

The girl with the thin, hourglass, figure was the first to sit on the bench.

"Karen, don't you just love the city at night?" the young man said as he sat down on the bench beside her.

"Oh, come on," Al thought.

"It is rather special Daniel," Karen said.

"I think London must be the greatest city in the world," Daniel said.

"It bloody well would be if the stars and celebrities actually hung out in it," Al thought, trying desperately to remain quiet.

"It is," Karen said, "But I think New York might be a close second."

"Have you been, Karen?"

"No, not yet, but Daddy said we're going next year for Christmas. It's something to do with his business and needing an American partner," Karen said.

"That should be nice," Daniel said.

"Why don't you take her to a nightclub or something?" Al thought.

"I think you look really nice tonight," Daniel said softly.

"So do you," whispered Karen.

"Oh no, you're not," Al thought as he lay in complete silence listening to Daniel and Karen kissing passionately on the bench.

"No, I can't do that," Karen whispered.

"Do what?" Al thought.

"But you know how I feel about you, Karen," Daniel mumbled.

"Just that then, you know," Karen purred.

"Just that?" Al thought, hearing the sound of clothing being ruffled. *"He's not, is he?"*

Al could hear the couple kissing and breathing heavily as the sound of clothing continued to rustle.

"I don't believe this," Al thought, *"Why is this happening to me?"*

Karen began to moan, groan and gurgle. It was then that Al heard the distinct sound of a trouser zipper being undone.

"No, no, no! Not that," Al thought as he clenched his eyes shut.

"What are you doing?" Karen whispered.

"Just touch it," Daniel pleaded in a soft voice.

"Maybe just for a bit," Karen murmured.

"She's got it out. I don't believe this," Al thought. *"I'm stuck under this bench on the damp ground, and she's got his thing out!"*

"That's it, just a little faster," Daniel whispered.

"Yeah, get it over and done with and leave me be," Al thought.

The moaning, groaning and heavy breathing continued until Al felt a distinct movement on the bench.

"Daniel," Karen whispered, "What are you doing?"

"I need you," Daniel said.

"No, we can't do it yet," Karen said in a faint voice.

"But I love you Karen," Daniel whispered sweetly.

"You love me?" Karen said.

Al lay in the dark while the couple tugged at each other's clothes, kissing heavily while panting and gasping for breath.

"Oh my God," Karen called out. "I love you Daniel, love you, love you, Daniel!"

The bench began to shake and rock while the couple moaned, groaned and gasped for air.

"No, no this isn't real, it can't be. I'm still stuck in that truck bringing me to London and I'm fast asleep having a bloody nightmare!" Al thought, still clenching his eyelids closed.

The bench began to rock, shake, screech and whine as Daniel and Karen increased the pace of their lovemaking.

"I'm gonna cooome! I'm gonna cooome!" Karen shrieked as the bench shook wildly.

"Oh my God!" Daniel called out.

"Not yet, not yet, not yet," Karen pleaded

"Arghhh!" Daniel roared out to three last violent shakes of the park bench.

"I'll be fucking scarred for life after this," Al thought.

"I'm sorry," Daniel muttered as he got off the bench, pulled up his trousers and did his zipper up.

"That's okay," Karen said to the sounds of clothing being rearranged.

"I do love you, Karen," Daniel whispered.

"I love you too, big boy," Karen chuckled as she stood up from the bench and brushed her skirt down.

"Come here," Daniel said as he made a playful grab for her.

Karen burst into fits of giggles.

"Mummy and Daddy are going away on Friday night for the weekend. Why don't you come over?" Karen said as she kissed Daniel on the cheek.

"That would be fabulous," Daniel said, taking Karen by the hand and leading her back out into the moonlight.

Al watched from under the bench as the couple waltzed across the grass and out of the park. He counted to ten before clambering out, brushing himself down and sitting back on the bench.

"If anyone else comes in I ain't moving, that's it, I'm definitely staying put," Al thought as he carefully spread himself out on the park bench and closed his eyes.

***

The sound of a car tooting its horn woke Al. It was still early and already the traffic had built up.

"I'm hungry, really hungry, and I need something to eat," Al thought.

Al stood up and stretched, gulping in the London air. He wandered out of Regents Park and into one of the side streets where he spotted several bottles of milk on a doorstep and what looked a cake. Cautiously Al opened the black wrought iron gate and scampered up the pathway. He took a bottle of milk and grabbed the cake box.

"Mr Kipling Cherry Bakewell tarts. Mmmm," Al thought as he walked briskly back down the pathway, closed the gate and hurried back to Regents Park where he sat on the bench and gulped down the fresh milk and took large bites of the Bakewell tarts.

Once he finished the box of cakes and guzzled the last of the milk, he put the rubbish in the bin.

"I need to wash and freshen up," Al thought. *"I'm sure I saw a public toilet in Soho Square."*

He crossed over Tottenham Court Road and made his way back to Soho where he found the public toilets. Al was washing himself in the basin when a middle-aged man entered the toilets. He wore a blue pin stripe suit with highly polished black shoes. Al saw him from the corner of his eye but continued to wash himself.

"I say, are you okay?" the gent called over while he used the urinal.

"Me?" Al replied. "Yeah, I'm fine."

"Are you sure?"

"I'm positive," Al said as he splashed the hot water on his face.

"It's just that I don't live too far away from here and you'd be very welcome to come home and use my shower," the gent said.

Al reached down and turned both the hot and cold water taps off.

"Like I said, I'm fine thank you," Al said firmly.

"Okay, I was just being neighbourly," the gent said as he walked up to the basin next to Al's and proceeded to wash his hands.

"I love the feel of warm water on my skin, don't you?" the gent said.

Al ignored him.

"Okay, well you have a nice day," the gent said as he pulled down the white towel on the rail and dried his hands.

"Hey," Al called out as he turned to face the gent. "Have you ever seen the Beatles around here?"

"No," the gent said slowly shaking his head. "I do have some of their records at home though."

"Yeah, course you do," Al thought as he turned his back on the gent. *"Right, well what am I going to do today? Shall I give Carnaby Street one final go?"*

Al spent the day wandering around Soho and then took the Tube down to Regents Park where he walked up and down the side streets. He spotted a bag on the doorstep of a large four storey home.

"There might be something to eat in that," Al thought as he raced up the pathway, grabbed the plastic carrier bag and dashed back out onto the street again.

"It's a chicken," Al thought as he peered into the bag. *"A raw chicken."*

As night fell Al, made up a little fire in the park with sticks, leaves and a tree branch that he managed to break off. Al tore at the raw chicken, drove a sharp stick through the flesh and held it over his homemade fire. The outside appeared to cook quickly. Al took a small bite.

"Damn that's disgusting," Al thought. *"But I'm hungry."*

Later that evening Al was violently sick, he vomited so hard that he literally fell to his knees. It was only after there was no more to be sick that Al managed to fall into a deep sleep on the park bench.

Chapter 14

Al had been sleeping rough in the park for ten days. He lived on bread, milk and fruit that he stole from doorsteps and stalls. Some nights he would sleep on the bench and others on top of the public toilet. Al was determined to make London work for him. He shuddered with dread at the thought of returning to Thornley Park Approved School.

As he sat on the park bench two people passed by chatting to each other. They were men wearing woman's clothes and they wore makeup. Al was stunned. He had never seen or heard of a man dressed as a woman before. Al was convinced that despite the clothes and makeup, he recognised one of them.

"Billy, Billy Fisher is that you?" Al called out.

The two women stopped.

"No!" the taller of the pair said and began to walk away.

She had walked no more than ten steps when she stopped, turned and walked back to Al.

"How do you know that name?" the woman with the platinum blonde hair said.

"I'm Al McIntosh. I was at Thornley Park Approved School in Paisley. It's just that you vaguely resemble a guy called Billy Fisher who left shortly after I arrived. I didn't mean any disrespect," Al said.

"Are you on the run?"

Al nodded.

"I know you, Al, but I don't go by the name Billy Fisher anymore. I'm Mae West and this is my friend Jean Harlow," Mae said.

"It's good to see you again Mae, and nice to meet you, Jean," Al said.

Mae put her hands on her hips and shook her head.

"Are you hungry?"

"When you're as hungry as I am just about anything tastes good," Al thought.

"I'm starving Mae," Al said, rubbing his stomach.

"Come on, let's get you something to eat," Mae said with a broad smile.

Mae and Jean led Al through the park and out to a fish and chip restaurant.

"I'm struggling to get my head around this. I've never seen a man dressed like a woman," Al thought. *"But who gives a flying fuck what they're dressed like? I'm just damn grateful for some food."*

Two medium fish and chips for us and a large one for the boy," Mae said to the owner.

"Coming up Mae," the owner said with a smile.

"The fish and chip bloke didn't bat an eyelid," Al thought.

Al told them how he had escaped from Thornley Park and hitch hiked down to London. The owner put fish and chips on the table.

"That's huge!" Al thought as his eyes lit up.

"Thank you," Al said before pouring salt and vinegar over his meals and steaming in.

Mae and Jean watched as Al pushed the last of his chips into his mouth and ate enthusiastically.

"Are you still hungry?" Mae said.

Al nodded.

Mae raised her hand and ordered a second large portion of fish and chips.

"So, what do you want to do now that you're in London?" Jean asked.

"I honestly didn't think that far ahead. I just wanted out and to get to England," Al said

"Do you want to earn some money?" Mae said as she sat back in her chair and looked him up and down.

"More than anything," Al said, placing the last piece of battered cod into his mouth and putting the knife and fork neatly on the plate.

"Good," Jean said.

"I really don't want to wear a dress or put on make-up," Al muttered.

Both Mae and Jean laughed out loud.

"No, you won't be wearing a dress," Mae said. "You'll be carding for us."

"Carding, what's that?" Al asked.

Mae reached into her pocket and put a card on the table. Al looked down and noticed that the 'Men Only' print was in bold and italics.

"Jean and I are male prostitutes, Al. We sleep with men for money," Mae said with a grin. "We will pay you five pounds for every one hundred cards you leave in telephone boxes around the West End.

"Five pounds?" Al said with a smile.

"Yes, five pounds, Al, but don't try to cheat us, because we'll know," Mae said.

"That's right," Jean said. "We receive ten calls for every one hundred cards delivered so we will know."

"I wouldn't do that," Al said, shaking his head.

"Good," Mae said. Now, can you take care of yourself, because it can get nasty out there?"

"Yeah, no problem," Al said.

"I'd tell you that I could smash seven sorts out of Muhammad Ali for five pounds right now," Al thought.

"We're not the only male prostitutes. Rock Hudson, the bitch, has his own team of carders and they have been known to get violent. That said, if they have a card in a telephone box then I want you to remove it and put one of ours up. Do you think that will be a problem?" Mae said.

Al clenched his fist.

"No problem, Mae.

"Okay, so where are you staying?"

"I've been sleeping rough in the park," Al said.

"We can't be having that," Jean said. "Come on."

Jean held out her hand and flagged down a black taxicab. Mae, Jean and Al climbed into the back.

"Gloucester Drive, Finsbury Park," Mae said.

The taxi sped across the short distance and stopped outside a large three storey, semi-detached house with a bay window. Jean leant forward and paid the fare.

"Come on Al," Jean said as she walked up the path and knocked on the door. As the door opened, Al could hear *'Rock 'n' Roll Suicide'* by David Bowie playing.

"Hello Mae, Jean," a tall man in a white shirt with the two top buttons undone, said.

"Room for one more?" Mae said.

"Sure, come in," the man said, beckoning them in.

"Al, this is Gas Man," Mae said, pointing to Al. "Gas Man this is Al, and he'll be carding for Jean and I."

"Gas Man? What kind of name is that?" Al thought.

Gas Man led Al, Mae and Jean upstairs to a bedroom.

"This one is free," Gas Man said before going back downstairs.

The Bowie song was followed up with *'Starman', also* by David Bowie.

"This must be the Ziggy Stardust & The Spiders from Mars Album," Al thought.

"So what do I owe for rent," Al said.

Jean chuckled.

"You don't Al," Mae said.

"Okay, so what do I have to do?" Al said.

"This is a squat, Al, and the people here are enforcing squatter's rights," Mae said.

Al looked at them both blankly.

"In England the law says that providing you don't break into a property, you are legally within your right to enter and claim squatter's rights. You turn the electric and gas back on and you have a roof over your head and an address to call your own," Jean said.

"You're kidding me," Al said.

"No that's the law, so we're making hay while the sun shines," Mae said.

"Gas Man," Al said curiously. "What kind of name is that?"

"Gas Man is one of several people living here," Jean said. "He is notorious for travelling the country, getting jobs in British Gas showrooms and once he's settled in, he robs the safe and clears out all the electrical appliances. Then he moves on to the next job. No one really knows his name, he's just Gas Man."

"He's a thief, like me," Al thought.

"Do you think you'll be alright here?" Mae said.

"I'll be fine," Al said. "I can't thank you both enough."

"Come on, we'll introduce you to the others here and then we're away. We have work to do," Jean said.

Al followed them downstairs to the sound of *'Five Years'* by David Bowie. They went into the front room and eased past two television sets and a cooker still in their boxes.

"Hello everyone," Mae said. "Al, this is Eddy, Delores, and you already met Gas Man."

"Hello there," Wally said in a broad Scottish accent.

Al had never seen a black person in real life before. Delores was beautiful and had the warmest of smiles.

"Do you like David Bowie?" Eddy said as *'Ziggy Stardust'* began to play.

"I think he's brilliant," Al said with a broad smile.

"Well, that makes all of us," Gas Man said.

"Right, we'll be in in the morning with the cards, Al," Mae said.

"You take care," Jean said.

"Thank Mae, thank you Jean," Al called out as they closed the door.

Over the next few hours, with the Ziggy Stardust Album being played twice, Al learnt that Eddy would go out during the day and buy electrical items on 'tick' (hire purchase) under a pseudonym and have them delivered to squats in the area. Delores and her husband, Stumpy, were Jamaican, and were a genuinely hardworking couple. Stumpy and his brother in-law, George, both worked at British Rail and had no dealings in villainy.

It was just after 9.00pm when there was a knock at the door. Gas Man raced over to the window and peered out.

"It's alright, its only Louis," Gas Man said as he bolted out into the hallway and opened the front door.

Al could hear muffled voices and the Gas Man returned with a heavy-set black guy dressed in a suit.

"Louis, this Al. He'll be staying with us," Gas Man said.

"He looks just like Louis Armstrong," Al thought.

"Nice to meet you Al," Louis said, shaking his hand warmly. "I'm a fence, so anything you get, that's TV's, electrical goods, jewellery, well, just about anything really, just come and talk to me, alright? I'll always make you a fair deal."

"That's right, he does," Gas Man said, nodding his head.

"Thank you, I'll remember that," Al said.

Louis looked over the television sets and cooker and then produced a huge wad of money from his inside jacket pocket. He counted out a bundle of notes and handed them to Gas Man.

"Are you happy with that?" Louis asked.

"Yeah, that's fine," Gas Man said. "Cheers."

Al watched as the two men carried the goods out of the front door and lifted them into the back of a transit van.

"I'm going to go up now," Al said as he got up out of the armchair, waved and left the room.

"Good night," Delores called out after him.

Al went upstairs and lay down on the bed. It was the first time that he had felt the comfort of a mattress in weeks.

"I think I'll be alright here," thought Al. *"I really like Mae and Jean, and this lot here seem like a nice bunch too. I think I might have fallen on my feet."*

While Al lay on his bed in a state of semi-consciousness, he found himself thinking back to Thornley Park and how very different it was when Mr Brown marched the boys down to the church in Paisley on a Sunday morning. Mr Douglas would have the boys singing 'Onward Christian Soldiers' while Mr Brown would sing out 'Who do we hate?' and the boys would yell back 'The Hun'. 'Who is the Hun?' Mr Brown sang out, and the boys, at the very top of their voices sang back 'The Fucking Kaiser!'.

Al turned over and buried his head in the soft pillow. Images of the minister delivering his sermon of hate, with spit dribbling from his lips, filled his mind and then shaking the parishioners warmly by the hand as they left the church but nothing for the boys. Al thought about John McDaid, the lad who had clyped on Al, his brother Brian and Jack.

"Wherever he is, I bet he's shitting himself, because sooner or later he'll come face to face with me again," Al thought before falling into a deep sleep.

***

Al took to carding quickly. He would hunt down telephone boxes in and around the West End and place the *'Men Only'* cards inside. If he found a Rock Hudson card, he'd remove it. Al did have a couple of run-ins with other carding crews. The threat of violence only happened when Rock Hudson had a fall out with either Mae West or Jean Harlow. Al would stand his ground when equally matched and have it away on his toes if he was outnumbered. Day in and day out Al would place the cards in telephone boxes. He wouldn't let Mae or Jean down. While eating a bag of chips he overheard one young lad talking with an older man in a suit.

"So would you like to come back to my place?" the older man said.

"Okay, but it will cost you," the young boy replied.

"How much?"

"Ten pounds," the boy said.

The older man stepped back and appeared to be thinking about the proposition for a moment.

"Okay, ten pounds it is then," the older man said.

"You need to show me your money first," the young boy said defiantly.

"I'll pay you later when we get back to my place," the man said.

"No, not doing that. You show me that you have the money and then we'll go," the boy said.

Reluctantly the older man reached into his pocket and produced a wallet. Quick as a flash the young boy reached out, grabbed the wallet and bolted off down the road. The man was too old and too overweight to give chase. He shouted out, 'Thief!' but the boy was off and down the alleyways. Al loved being in London; he enjoyed carding and had grown to really like Mae West. He looked upon her as a great friend.

***

Al got back to the squat in Gloucester Drive late one night. *'Hot Love'* by T Rex was playing in the front room. He entered the room and found that yet again it was filled with new electrical goods. Both Gas Man and Eddy had been busy.

"Here, Al," Gas Man said. "We have some new guys upstairs."

"Yeah? Are they alright?" Al said as he sat down in the armchair.

Gas man lowered his voice.

"Armed robbers," Gas Man whispered, looking left and right. "The real deal, by all accounts. I heard something about doing over dole offices and one of them, a right mean looking geezer called Black Wally, was carrying a shotgun."

"I'm sure they'll be fine," Al said as he relaxed back into his chair.

"Each to their own," Al thought.

Delores handed Al a plate of Jamaican food, smiled and then changed the vinyl record to *'I'll Be There'* by The Jackson Five. She had taken a mothering shine to Al and would constantly check to see that he'd eaten.

"Thank you, Delores," Al said, tucking into the beef patty.

"Have you ever thought about a parallel universe?" Gas Man asked, lighting his cigarette.

"No, can't say that I have," Al said.

"I believe that this isn't the only Earth, solar system or even galaxy," Gas Man said with a hint of excitement in his voice.

"Really?" Al said as he took a bite of his beef patty.

"Yes, just as you have the Earth here, there is another exactly the same," Gas Man said.

"So, in theory, there could be another you or another me there?" Al said.

"Exactly," Gas Man said as he drew heavily on his marijuana joint. "Only the Al or the Gas Man on that parallel Earth might have made different choices."

"So, Gas Man on the alternate Earth could be, what, a politician?"

"Maybe, or an astronaut, or maybe, just maybe, he's a time traveller," Gas Man said, his eyes lighting up.

"I think that even if I had been born to a wealthy family somewhere, I'd still be a thief. There's nothing quite like that buzz and excitement of nicking something worth having," Al said.

"So, if there's a parallel universe you hope that the Al on Earth number two is doing the same as you here?"

Al nodded.

"That doesn't show much imagination," Gas Man said as he stood up, checked his wristwatch, drew heavily on his joint and then walked over to the window. "Louis must be running late."

"Fancy a game of Dominoes?" Stumpy asked Al as he collected the empty plate.

"That would be great," Al said.

***

Al would meet up with Mae and Jean daily. When they weren't busy, they would have lunch together. It was then that Al was introduced to 'Harry the Poof'. Harry stated that he wasn't gay and that he was a poof. Al learnt that Harry the Poof was a professional blackmailer. Jean would meet with married men who had sought her out for paid sex. She would offer them a drink that had been laced with chloral hydrate which would knock them out cold. Harry the Poof would then come in and take explicit photographs. Once they came around, he'd introduce himself and threaten to send the photographs to the man's wife and family.

Not long after leaving Mae, Jean and Harry the Poof, a middle-aged man dressed in a blue pin striped suit approached him.

"Hello young man," the gent said with a broad smile.

"Yeah, hello," said Al.

"I just bet you love reading comics like the Beano and Topper," the gent said.

Al shrugged his shoulders.

"Why don't you come back to my apartment, it's not far from here, and you can read my collection in comfort," the gent said.

"No, I don't think so," said.

"Are you sure? I have lemonade, sweets and all sorts of chocolate goodies at home," he said.

"I told you no!" Al said firmly.

"Oh, okay, another time maybe," the gent said before turning quick sharp on his heels and walking off.

***

Al had learned that Bernie Silver was the number one crime boss in Soho and had been since the 1950's. His rise to prominence came shortly after taking over the remnants of the Maltese 'Messina Brothers' operation which consisted of a vice ring of male and female prostitutes. He became a legend in Soho after being arrested for living off immoral earnings and then being inexplicably let off by the Judge. Bernie went on to open several adult bookstores and controlled nineteen strip clubs. Mae had told Al how the bookstores would get systematically raided by the Metropolitan police with photographers documenting the event and then, just a few hours later, all the store's stock would be returned. Bernie Silver had them all on his payroll, including Detective Chief

Inspector Bill Moody. Al approached one of the shops for work and was given a job delivering adult 8mm cine porn movies. He would collect the movie, take a tube to the London address and make the delivery. The recipient would usually give Al one or two pounds as a tip and the store manager would give him one pound.

Al arrived back at the squat a little later than usual because the adult bookstore had been unusually busy. *'Band of Gold'* by Freda Payne was playing on a new record player that Eddy had stolen for the house. Al walked into the front room and saw that Gas Man was smoking marijuana.

"Please, not another sci-fi session," Al thought.

"Hello Al," Gas Man mumbled.

Al nodded.

"You'll never believe what those damn Yanks are doing on the dark side of the moon," Gas Man muttered before taking a long drag on the home made joint.

"I've got to go," Al said as he opened the door and took a step out into the hallway. "I'll catch you later."

"Yeah, man, cool," Gas Man said.

Al began to walk up the stairs when a broad, well-built black man carrying a guitar met him half way."

"You must be Al," the black man said in the thickest of Scottish accents.

"Yeah, that's me," Al said.

"I'm Wally," the man said, shaking Al's hand. A few of the lads will be over later for a drink if you fancy popping in."

"Yeah, cheers. I might just do that," Al said.

"I've never heard an accent like that on a black fella, fascinating!" Al thought.

Mae had a room in the squat, and she would generally stay over three times a week. Al was hoping that tonight would be one of those nights. He enjoyed chatting to and spending time with her and found it strange to see her in a suit and without make-up. Al opened his bedroom door and threw himself onto the bed. He had food in his stomach, money in his pocket and friends that he could rely on. London, despite the lack of celebrities, was all he could have hoped for.

Just as he was about to doze off there was a knock at his door.

"Come in," Al called out as he sat up and put his feet on the floor.

The door opened and it was Mae.

"Hi Mae, good to see you," Al said, rubbing his eyes.

"I'd like you to meet someone," Mae said standing to one side.

A young, beautiful, girl with a slender, graceful figure and tapered waist stood before him. Her hair was rouge red and spiralled down over her shoulders. She had a pert nose and blossom-pink lips. Al could feel his mouth go dry as he looked into her lambent, jade green eyes.

"Al, this is Jo," Mae said. "Jo, this is my friend Al. You'll be safe here."

Jo stepped forward. She had bewitching, unicorn-white teeth and an angelic smile.

"Hi Al," Jo said.

"I'll leave you two to get to know each other," Mae said, closing the bedroom door.

Al and Jo talked into the early hours of the morning. Jo had been born out of wedlock and had been given up to the authorities by her mother. She had been moved from one establishment to another and finally sent to a school run by nuns in Southern Ireland. Jo told Al that life in the school was nothing like 'The Sound of Music' movie would have you believe. The girls were stripped naked, ritually beaten and verbally abused. Jo would be ridiculed and constantly told that she had no moral worth, having been born to a slut. She was fifteen and could no longer take the abuse. Al was shocked and saddened by all that she told him. He had believed that nuns were nice people. Jo told him that she had spoken out to the authorities as a last resort, but they simply ignored her pleas for help. It was then that she decided to run away to London and by chance met Mae.

Al told Jo a little about his own background and how London had seemed like the only option. The two youngsters became friends and lovers. Within a few days Al invited Jo out carding with him. The police would often do round ups and while Al and Jo were out in Soho they turned up in force. Jo darted into a shop while Al had to scamper down an alleyway with an officer hot on his tail. He jumped over a fence and ran down a long street. He looked over his shoulder and the police officer was still after him.

"I'm not going back to Thornley Park' Al thought as he darted into a side street that he knew to be full of working girls. He ran up the pathway, through the front door, bolted up the stairs and into a bedroom. A working girl, dressed in just her black stockings and suspenders was putting her makeup on.

"Police!" Al hissed as he fell to the floor and scrambled under her bed.

191

Moments later Al could hear the thunder of feet running up the stairs. His heart was beating so hard he put his hand over his mouth to control his breathing.

"Police, we're looking for a runaway," a police officer said, panting for breath.

"There's no one in here sweetheart," the girl purred.

"Err, okay, thank you," the officer said, slowly pulling her door closed.

Al stayed where he was for several minutes before venturing back out. He thanked the girl and cautiously crept back down the stairs. He looked up and down the street and once he saw there were no police officers he scampered back off towards Soho. He found Mae West, Jean Harlow, Harry the Poof and a young ginger headed kid known as Rusty sitting outside the café drinking coffee. Al joined them and explained what had happened. While he worried about Jo, Mae convinced him to settle down, catch his breath and have a drink because Jo would almost certainly have gone back to the squat in Gloucester Drive.

Al had been told by Mae a few months back that Rusty had been selling himself for sex and made the mistake of getting into a punter's car. He was beaten, raped and dumped back in Soho after the two hour ordeal.

"Do you know that almost ninety per-cent of all the girls that run away have been systematically abused by their stepfathers," Jean said.

"I'd like to cut their bloody Jacobs off," Harry the Poof said.

"Someone should do something," Al said.

"No one really cares Al, which is why you have to take care of yourself and your friends," Mae said.

Al nodded and took a sip of his tea.

"That's him!" Rusty said. "That's the bastard who raped me!"

"Are you sure?" Mae said.

"Damn right I am," Rusty said.

Mae and Jean were up and out of their chairs. They stomped off towards the parked blue Rover P5B. Mae yanked open the driver's door, grabbed the driver and dragged him out onto the road. Mae and Jean punched, kicked and stomped on the rapist while Al, still sitting at the cafe, looked on. He could hear the faint pleas, but the kicking he got was relentless. Harry the Poof swallowed the last of his drink and stood up.

"Mae, Jean, bring him over here," Harry the Poof said, motioning them to bring the rapist over to the shop next door. Mae grabbed him by his hair and dragged him along the pavement. The rapist yelled out in pain, but they were having none of it. There would be no mercy. Al finished up and followed the ensemble into the shop and through a door at the back which led downstairs to a gay bar. Al walked in to see two men kissing passionately while others danced in the darkened bar to *'Tears of a Clown'* by Smokey Robinson. Harry opened a side door that led into a small room. Mae, Jean and Rusty went inside and closed the door firmly.

Al could hear the cries of pain from outside the room. Harry the Poof spoke to the DJ who turned up the music. Al sat outside while the rapist was beaten and tortured. Harry the Poof shot off and returned just minutes later with a camera.

"He'll pay for this," Harry the Poof said as he passed Al.

Mae, Jean and Rusty finally came out of the room. Al peered in to see the man lying in a pool of blood.

"You'd better get off and see if Jo got back," Mae said, wiping blood from her knuckles.

"Yeah, right. I'll see you later," Al said as he got up and left the club.

When he got back to the squat in Gloucester Drive, he discovered that not only was Jo safe, but it was Delores' 41st birthday. Eddy had brought a new gas cooker home that he'd got on tick under a false name and Gas Man had help to fit it. Delores was over the moon and beamed with pride as she looked at her new gas cooker. Wally, the armed robber, had brought home a box full of alcohol and Stumpy had a carrier bag full of ingredients.

"Right," Delores said as she wiped a tear from her eye. "I'll make food for everyone on my new cooker, while you go and put some music on."

Mae and Jean arrived an hour later and joined the party in the garden. *'Reflections of my Life'* by Marmalade pounded through the new stereo speaker system. Al and Jo were happily holding hands while Mae physically lifted Delores up and sat her in a chair because she had been so busy running around after everyone else. The weather was warm, and the sky was red. Mae turned the stereo off.

"Delores, you are a wonderful person and loved by everyone in the house," Mae announced.

Everyone cheered and raised their glasses.

"Happy birthday, Delores, and you look bloody great for twenty-one!"

Everyone burst out laughing and called out 'Delores' before taking large swigs from their glasses.

Mae and Jean stood side by side and as the cheers and clapping came to an end, they sang

'You Don't Have to Say You Love Me' by Dusty Springfield as a duet.

"Happy birthday, Delores," Al thought as he refilled his glass. *"You've been like a second mother to me."*

* * *

Al continued with his carding throughout the summer. There were several clashes with other carding teams when Jean, once again, fell out with Rock Hudson. Mae told Al that Harry the Poof had been sentenced to twelve years. He had met a married man under the pretence of having paid sex with him and had laced the man's drink with chloral hydrate. Once he was unconscious, he took several explicit photographs. When the punter came around, Harry the Poof demanded money. The punter went home, confessed his homosexuality to his wife and then went to the police station and made a statement. Harry the Poof's home was raided and he was found to have scores of illicit photographs of married men engaged in homosexual acts in his possession.

Al had taken to screwing electrical shops with Eddy. They were bringing back television sets and Louis the Fence, paid one hundred pounds for each one. Al thought about Stumpy working a forty-hour week for thirty pounds and here he was now earning three or four hundred pounds every week.

Al and Jo were out carding in the West End. They had jumped the tube down to Covent Garden and put cards in every telephone box on the way back to Soho. Al took out a card and went into a telephone box. He turned to see an enormous guy in a black suit with a huge crucifix hung around his neck. Al tried to open the door, but the man had raised his hand, which had a bible in it, and was leaning against the door.

"This heathen is working for the devil!" he shouted.

Al pushed harder against the door, but it wouldn't budge.

"This boy will rot in the depths of hell for facilitating all the immorality that Soho is!"

"Get out of the fucking way!" Al thought as he kicked and pushed at the door. *"The police will be here at this rate!"*

Jo, seeing what was happening, ran over and kicked the man in the shins with all the strength she could muster. It was enough; Al slammed open the door, nearly knocking the religious preacher off his feet. The two held hands and ran off down the road and into the safety of Soho.

Soho was a massive den of inequity. It was filthy, dirty, nasty and filled with villains and criminals and Al loved it.

The following day Al had been out carding on his own when he was suddenly grabbed by a police officer. He struggled to get away, but the officer had a firm grip and was promptly joined by a second enthusiastic officer.

"Come on let me go," pleaded Al.

The officers bundled him into the back of a waiting police car, and he was driven to West End Central Police Station. When questioned, Al gave a false name, but the police were having none of it. They wanted his address. Al knew he couldn't give up Gloucester Drive because of his friends. Gas Man had warrants out for his arrest all over the UK, and Eddy would most likely have stolen property waiting to be collected by Louis the Fence. Jo could be sent back to the evil nuns in Ireland, and Wally, the armed robber, had a sawn off shotgun in the house. Al kept quiet.

Within a few hours an officer entered the interview room.

"We ran your description, and it appears you're wanted for absconding from Thornley Park Approved School in Paisley," the police officer said with a wry smile.

Al sighed heavily as he thought about not seeing Jo or his friends Mae, Jean, Gas Man, Eddy, Stumpy and the wonderful Delores again. The police officer led him outside to a waiting car where he was driven from London to Glasgow. While Al remained quiet for most of the journey, the police officer bragged several times that he had been the officer to put a gun to John McVicar's head. Al shrugged his shoulders as he had no idea who John McVicar was.

"Well, I did get to see some celebrities in London," Al thought as he stared out of the side window. *"There was that bloke from the TV show 'Softly Softly' who I saw negotiating with a young girl for sex. Those two Irish lads gave him a right kicking when he tried to get the price down. Boy, did he plead for mercy. 'Please, please not my face. I work on television.' And I thought he was a tough copper!"*

Al shook his head as he passed the road sign to Birmingham.

"Yeah," Al thought. *"There was that Jimmy Edwards too from the TV show Whack-O. I watched him disappear with Mae."*

The car slowed down as it drove up towards the entrance of Thornley Park Approved School.

'London will be my life," thought Al. *"I have access to a criminal network and I will be back!"*

***

Al was ritually forced to take a cold shower daily and brought before Wee Garry every Friday for six weeks where he received six lashes across his palms with the leather belt. Al bit his lip and refused to show pain despite being caught across his wrist several times. He remained at Thornley Park until his time was served.

Chapter 15

A condition for Al's release from Thornley Park Approved School was that he had to have a job. He found himself employed by the Citizen Newspaper. Al was positioned outside Glasgow Central Train Station. His job was to receive the newspapers and sell them to travellers. He would also run the parcelled-up newspapers down the platform on the sack barrow. He did so, narrowly missing passengers for the waiting train. The newspapers would be taken off and distributed to the shops. Al was paid a weekly wage of five pounds and thirty-five pence.

The hotel beside the station had a grid system that expelled hot air. Al would, when he wasn't busy running the newspapers to the platform, sit back and dream of his past back in London. He looked up to see an old homeless man rubbing his hands together.

"Are you cold?" Al called out.

The homeless man nodded and rubbed his hands together harder.

"Come on up here," Al said as he climbed off.

"Thank you, thank you."

"Warm yourself up," Al said, looking over at the van as it pulled up. The driver jumped out and ran around to the back. Al ran over to take delivery.

"It's Al, isn't it?" the driver asked.

"Yeah," Al said as he reached in and grabbed a stack of newspapers.

"Do you want to make a few quid?" the driver said with a slight smile.

"Always," Al said with a broad smile.

"I've got an extra bundle of newspapers, interested?"

"Yeah, course," Al said.

"Okay, this is how it works. You take them from me, sell them on and we share the takings," the driver said as he pulled the extra bundle of newspapers forward.

"That works for me," Al said.

***

Al took the extra newspapers and had them all sold within hours. The following day he asked the driver to get two bundles. Within a few weeks Al had young lads from Springburn taking the stolen newspapers and selling them around the town. Al had increased his weekly income to just over thirty pounds from the fiddles. The driver was happy, the young kids from Springburn made a few shillings, and Al was feeling the power of money going back into his pocket.

While sitting back on the warm grid he watched as the train porters ran cases around, Al thought, *"I can do that."*

With a young lad watching the newspaper stand, Al set himself up as a porter and began to help visitors and rich 'Yanks' with their luggage. The Yanks always tipped well. A couple of the porters tried to intimidate Al out of his new money-making enterprise. When he offered to go out to the back with them both, they backed off. Al brought in another couple of lads to help the passengers, and with the newspaper fiddle he was now pulling more than fifty quid a week, almost ten times his wage.

It wasn't long before the station management received complaints that Al had been taking the porters' work and had even threatened strike action if it wasn't brought to a rapid close. Al could see the revenue stream drying up again, and he wasn't about to go back to a measly five pounds a week for an income. He packed up a few items of clothing, bought a train ticket and went back to London.

On the long trip back down south, Al found himself remembering events that led him to where he was today. Images of the older lads lifting him over the turnstiles at the Rangers home games made him smile. He thought about the young runaway lads in Soho that were screwing the one-armed bandits and jackpot machines. Some of the braver lads would wait until they spotted a player pull out his wallet then run over, grab it, and run.

Al turned to face the window and stared out at the scenery. He reflected on his time at Thornley House and the daily provocation, insults, and death threats. The images of the weaker lads who had been beaten, bruised or left with bite marks while others cowered and lived in constant fear, flooded his mind. The masters had strutted around trivialising complaints while bombarding the young boys with insults, calling them stupid, losers or chubby. The relentless character assassination 'you're worse than useless' or 'you're always blubbing' to those that had been bullied.

Al closed his eyes and shook his head.

"What am I supposed to take from that?" Al thought.

Al thought about Mammy and the horrific, extreme violence she had inflicted on both him and his siblings. He remembered begging her not to hurt the twins anymore, but his child-like pleas fell on deaf ears. The images of his da coming home drunk and punching, kicking and throwing Mammy around the living room came back too.

"It was almost as if she took the violence inflicted on her by Da out on the twins," thought Al.

***

Al was back in Gloucester Drive, Finsbury. He had been thinking about Mae West, Jean Harlow, Gas Man, Eddy, Louis the Fence, Wally the armed robber, the wonderful Delores and her Jamaican cooking and... Jo, all the way down on the train.

"I can't be doing carding now," Al thought. *"I'll need to step things up a bit."*

"Is that you Al?" Eddy said as he opened the front door.

"Good to see you, Eddy," Al said.

"It's been, well, years," Eddy said. "Come in, come in."

Eddy beckoned him in. The two men walked through to the front room. Al smiled when he saw several boxes of electrical goods stacked by the window.

"Business still good?" Al said with a grin.

"Yeah, well, you've got to get by," Eddy said as he sat down on the settee. "What happened to you?"

Al explained how he had been caught and sent back to finish his sentence.

"You were missed," Eddy said, shaking his head.

"How is everyone, are they still here?"

Eddy gave a sad look and shook his head slowly.

"Gas Man was nicked. I heard he's doing some serious time. Wally and his boys bolloxed up an armed raid and got them themselves nicked. Delores and George got themselves a place over in South London and Jo, well she hung on for you but eventually left. She didn't say anything, just got up one day and left," Eddy said.

Al could feel his heart sink.

"What about Mae?"

"Oh, Mae still has a room here which she uses two or three times a week," Eddy said.

"Brilliant!" Al thought as a huge grin spread across his face.

"I'm going to need a bit of work and a place to stay, Eddy," Al said, as he sat forward and rested his hands on his knees.

"It's not the same here," Eddy said softly. "They're not, well, proper people here now, do you know what I mean?"

"Have you got a room?" Al said.

"Yeah, there is one here you can use," Eddy said.

"Cheers," Al said. "What about a bit of work?"

Eddy smiled.

"You can do a bit with me if you like. We can make out we're father and son or something," Eddy said

"That works for me," Al said as he sat back in the chair.

"Do you have a drink or something?" Al said with a smile.

***

Al stayed for a couple of evenings. Mae was thrilled to see him, and the two friends spent several hours catching up over drinks. During the day Al and Eddy visited electrical shops around the capital and bought televisions, cookers, washing machines and stereo systems on 'tick' with fake aliases. Louis the Fence made his usual visits and paid cash for everything they managed to get.

On the fourth day Al checked out an empty house across the road. He broke in, changed the locks and used his knowledge to turn the electricity and gas back on. Al now had a full house rather than a room. The house next door, he later learnt, was a brothel, and run by a woman known simply as 'Madge'. There were several pretty working girls in the house. Most had been run-aways looking to make a life in London. Al joked around and had fun with the girls. On one occasion he jokingly suggested that he'd like to go on a date. Madge intervened, smiled, and told him to come back when he was twenty-five years old.

"We need to step up the money-making game," Al. *"Eddy's a good guy and I appreciate the work, but he thinks too small."*

Al remembered a conversation with Eddy during his last stay in Gloucester Drive. He had been scrawling an address in childlike writing on an envelope. When Al had asked him what he was doing, Eddy explained that the post office, believing that the letter had been written by a child, would let the letter go through without an official stamp. Eddy became quite enthusiastic about his money saving scheme and offered to show Al how he did it.

"I'm going to have to take the lead here if we're to make any proper money," Al thought. *"A hundred pounds for a brand new television from Louis is good money, but the risk just doesn't fit the reward."*

Al invested in a three pound lump hammer.

During the day he wandered around the streets of London making a mental note of jewellery shops and what they had in the window display. Eddy was a little resistant at first, but eventually joined Al on their first smash and grab. With one swing of the hammer the glass shattered into a thousand pieces. With thick gloves on their hands and the alarm bell ringing, they grabbed everything they could from the window display. The raid was over in minutes and in no time they were back at Gloucester Drive to see what they had. Al and Eddy emptied their haul of expensive watches, gold rings, bracelets and necklaces onto the carpet.

"Nice, very nice," Louis the Fence said as he checked through the haul. "I'll give you two thousand quid for it all."

Al knew that Louis was fair, reasonable and could be trusted. They shook hands.

With a stash of three pound lump hammers and a trusted fence that would buy everything for cash, Al and Eddy went to work smashing jewellery shop windows and grabbing everything on display.

A month later both Brian, his brother, and friend Jack Payne, turned up at the squat and all four of the men went to work on various criminal enterprises. Al had the smash and grabs organised like a military operation. The four men were clearing seven and eight hundred pounds most weeks. The men all bought smart clothes. Al, Jack and Eddy all bought black leather trench coats while Brian, to be different, bought a white one. Eddy saw the extended team as a wage decrease and hadn't been happy. However, he had been told about an electrical goods shop had taken a large amount of stock in and that the alarm system was down and wouldn't be fixed for a couple of days. The opportunity had been too good to let pass. Al had managed to get his hands on a small truck at short notice. The extra capacity and the alarm being out of order would mean they could empty the entire shop.

The four men arrived at the shop during the early hours of the morning. Al climbed up through the air ventilator and once inside he used a jemmy bar to get the door open. The men were ready to make their escape if the alarm were to suddenly go off. It didn't. They cautiously entered the shop and began to pile up the televisions, cookers and stereos by the door.

"This is a right result," Eddy whispered.

"Louis will love this," Al thought as he humped a boxed television out of the door and onto the back of the truck. *"This haul has got to be good for two or three thousand pounds."*

With the last television sets loaded onto the back of the truck, Al pulled down the roller door and patted the side of the truck, indicating that they should leave. As the truck began to pull away, a police officer ran towards him. Al quickly turned to run but was brought down with a rugby tackle. He landed on the road with a thud. The officer began to throw punches at the side of his face, to the back of his head and his neck.

"Leave it out!" All called out.

"You're fucking nicked!" the officer said as he grabbed Al by the hair and turned him over. A second officer raced over with a set of handcuffs.

Al knew the game was up once the handcuffs were on. He remained quiet in the police car and looked out of the window.

"It was a silent alarm, you fucking idiot," the arresting officer said with a sneer.

Al closed his eyes and slowly shook his head.

"They must have fixed the alarm without Eddy's contact knowing," Al thought.

The custody sergeant had Al's fingerprints taken before putting him in an interview room.

"Right then, I'm Detective Sergeant Skinner. Do you want to tell me what's been going on?"

"I've got nothing to say," Al said as he folded his arms and sat upright in the wooden chair.

"You know we've got you bang to rights," DS Skinner said.

Al shrugged his shoulders.

"What? You want to take the rap for it all?" DS Skinner said as he opened a file. "That wouldn't be fair, would it?"

Al remained silent.

"The best thing you can do is just come clean and I'll speak with the judge and let him know that you've been co-operative and to be lenient. All I'm asking is that you tell me who else was involved."

Al turned his head away.

The door slammed open and the officer that had rugby tackled Al to the ground entered.

"I'm Detective Inspector Young. On your feet!"

Al stood up.

"Cuff him," DI Young said, closing the door.

DS Skinner took out a pair of handcuffs and proceeded to handcuff Al.

"What has he told you?" DI Young said as he took a short step towards Al.

"Nothing Guvnor," DS Skinner said, moving around the desk to join DI Young.

"Nothing? Nothing? I'll give you fucking nothing!" DI Young said before launching a powerful punch into Al's stomach.

Al bent forward and gasped for breath.

"I fucking eat nasty little back street villains like you for breakfast," DI Young said as he kicked Al and knocked him over.

"You wouldn't be so tough if you didn't have that badge to hide behind," Al said.

"Yeah, but I fucking do, don't I?" DI Young said through gritted teeth as he kicked Al again.

Al doubled over from the excruciating pain.

"Get this slag back on his feet," DI Young said.

DS Skinner grabbed Al by the arm and tugged hard until Al staggered up onto one knee and then finally stood up.

"You're no fucking hard man here, slag! Just another villain we'll be putting away," DI Young said, and he turned sharply and left the interview room.

"You shouldn't have upset the Guvnor," DS Skinner said as he took Al firmly by the arm and led him down to the cells.

"Fuck him" Al thought, *"and fuck you too!"*

Al rubbed his stomach before sitting down on the cell floor.

"So what happens now?" Al thought.

Al had some clothes sent in and met with an appointed solicitor shortly before going into court. The judge heard the evidence and sentenced Al to a one year conditional discharge.

"What's that?" Al thought. *"Am I going down or what?"*

The solicitor explained that he would be released with the offence being placed on his criminal record. If he were to get into any kind of trouble again during those twelve months the court had the power to review sentencing.

"I'm free then!" Al thought.

Al beamed and punched the air

"Yes!" hissed Al.

Al was feeling on top of the world.

"Right, I need to find Brian and see what we got from that little haul," he thought.

Al caught sight of DS Skinner and DI Young. They were walking towards him with smiles on their faces.

"McIntosh I'm placing you under arrest for robbery. You do not have to say anything, but it may harm your defence if you do not mention, when questioned, something which you later rely on in court," DI Young said. "Handcuff him."

Al was led through the courthouse and outside to a waiting police car. He was transported back to the police station, processed again by the custody sergeant and taken back to the same interview room where he sat, still handcuffed.

"I bet you thought that you walked clean away from that, didn't you," DI Young said.

Al smirked.

"You're a flash bastard with those clothes, aren't you? I bet you think you're something special," DI Young said as he stood up and walked towards Al.

Al said nothing.

DI Young reached out and grabbed hold of Al's shirt. He tugged hard and ripped the top buttons off.

"Oops," DI Young chuckled before tearing his shirt clean open. The buttons pinged off and shot across the floor.

"He doesn't look so flash now," DI Young said.

"No Guv," DS Skinner said with an exaggerated laugh.

"We know you've been out robbing jewellery shops," DI Young said as he rested his rear against the table.

"How the fuck do they know that?" Al thought.

"I bet you thought you'd walked clean away from that, didn't you? But you left evidence," DI Young said.

"What do they have?" Al thought.

"We have your fingerprints," DI Young said with a smug smile.

"Bollocks you do," Al muttered.

DI Young leapt back onto his feet and kicked Al and the chair over.

"Wearing gloves, were you?" DI Young said as he kicked Al in the side.

Al winced.

"Well, we found one, just one fingerprint left in blood on a single piece of glass, and we have a clear match, so you, McIntosh, are now well and truly fucked!"

"Shit, I remember that cut," Al thought.

DI Young bent down over Al as he lay handcuffed on the floor.

"I don't like you!" DI Young spat the words into his face.

"I don't like you that much either," Al thought.

SMACK!

DI Young fired a punch straight into Al's face.

"I want your confession and I want the names of everyone else involved," DI Young said, punching Al again.

"I've got nothing to say," Al said, spitting blood.

"I've got plenty more of this," DI Young said, holding his clenched fist over Al's face.

"You've made a mistake, it wasn't me," Al spluttered through his bleeding lip.

"We've got you and I want names!" DI Young yelled.

"I've told you. It wasn't me," Al said.

DI Young kicked and punched Al several times before having him taken to a cell.

***

Al was remanded in custody and taken to Latchmere House, a large Victorian house and Detention Centre, in Ham, South London. Six weeks later he was taken before a judge.

Al sat with his solicitor in the court room and listened to DI Young tell the judge how they suspected the accused was responsible for eleven smash-and-grab raids on jewellers and had stolen over eighty thousand pounds in goods. DI Young bleated on and on about the value of the robberies and that a three-pound lump hammer had been found at the scene of each crime.

"Detective Inspector Young," the judge said.

"Yes, sir," DI Young answered.

"You have brought Mr McIntosh here with a charge of one single robbery, is that correct?"

"Yes, sir," DI Young said. "But we suspect that he's responsible for at least eleven robberies."

"Do you have any evidence that you show the court?"

"No, but…"

"Detective Inspector, I shouldn't have to remind you that unless you can demonstrate unmistakable evidence, everything else is hearsay or circumstantial and not admissible," the judge said peering down over his glasses at DI Young.

"Yes, sir." DI Young said with his head lowered.

Al managed a wry grin.

"Mr McIntosh," the judge said.

"Yes, sir," Al said as he stood up.

"You are sentenced to six months," the judge said firmly. "Take him down."

"Fuck!" Al thought as the officer took him by the arm and led him down to the cells under the courthouse.

Al was handcuffed and bundled into a prison service van and driven through London and down to Goudhurst in Kent. The prison van stopped outside Blantyre Detention Centre. Once Al had been processed and given his prison clothing he was taken through to his cell.

Al had seen and experienced first-hand how the 'system' treated young offenders and wasn't surprised when he saw two uniformed officers making a young lad 'bunny hop' in a fully crouched position along the corridor without the use of his hands or arms to steady himself.

"Move it lad!" the screw yelled.

Al joined the queue to buy goods from the internal shop when a well-built black lad with a shaven head pushed past the lads and handed Al a folded-up piece of paper. Al unfolded the paper and read:

- Toothpaste
- Tobacco
- Sweets
- Custard Creams

It suddenly dawned on Al that this was what the lad expected Al to buy for him. Al could feel the anger of being beaten up by the police, re-arrested and being sentenced to six months build in his stomach. The hate and anger raced through his veins until he screwed up the piece of paper and looked the bully boy in the face.

"Custard Creams? I'll give you Custard Creams, you cunt!"

SMACK!

SMACK!

SMACK!

Al threw a wicked right hook, left uppercut and then jabbed the con hard on the chin.

The big lad stumbled but didn't go over. He fired a clumsy punch which Al ducked to the side to miss. The bully had left himself open. Al steamed in with a series of left hooks, right hooks and a right cross that put him down on one knee. The rage raced through his body, and he wanted blood. Al kicked the bully, knocking him over, and kicked him again in the face. The lad yelled out as his nose cracked and broke. Al looked down at the blood pouring down the lad's mouth and chin.

"Fucking Custard Creams!" Al thought as he continued to kick the boy with relentless fury.

"Leave it out,'" the bully whimpered.

Al stopped and looked at the young men around him before raising his right foot and stomping it down hard on the bully's face. He was finished and lay motionless on the hardwood floor.

Al and the other inmates scarpered off in different directions, leaving the bully to be found by the screws.

"That was Toby," one of the inmates said.

"I couldn't give a flying fuck who it was," Al said.

"Yeah, I think we could all see that," chuckled the lad. "I'm Peterson."

"McIntosh," Al said.

"Toby's a right hard nut here and a proper nasty bastard too. He'd bully the new kids and he was at it as well."

"What do you mean? Noncing the younger, weaker, kids?" Al said.

"Yeah, the screws turn a blind eye. You know how it works," Peterson said.

"Yeah, I know. There's more crimes done to us in places like this by the screws than we have ever perpetrated on society," Al said.

"Well, it's good to meet you," Peterson said, holding out his hand.

The screws had Toby gathered up off the floor and taken him down to the medical centre. He didn't make a statement and was adamant that he slipped on the wet floor.

Al had been in the detention centre just a few hours and had secured a reputation for being no mug.

The following day Prison Officer Slater cornered Al outside the canteen.

"I know who you are, McIntosh, and I have my eye on you," Officer Slater said as he dug his index finger into Al's chest.

"Yes, sir," Al said with a hint of sarcasm.

"Don't you be coming in here and trying to cause trouble, we run this nick, not you, alright?" Slater said stabbing his finger into Al's chest again.

"I just want to do my time and get out of here, sir," Al said.

"Good," Slater said leaning forward. "You just keeping your fucking head down or we'll smash the living shit out of you, understand?"

"Yes, sir."

"Good, now get yourself out in the yard," Slater said.

Al turned and began to slowly walk away.

"Move McIntosh!" Slater yelled.

It was customary for all new arrivals to spend the first three weeks marching around the grounds through all kinds of weather before joining the general population. Al would smile when he caught a glimpse of Abba performing their number one hit *'Waterloo'* when they marched past the television room.

On Sundays, the cons were marched down to the chaplain where they were systematically told that women were the root of all evil with their short skirts and high heel shoes and that they were no good scum who were destined to father the devil's children.

Al had taken an instant dislike to him.

"How can all women be evil and avoided at all costs?" Al wondered. *"The human race would come to an end tomorrow. Sure, there are bad women in the world and bad men too, but who are you to judge anyone?"*

* * *

The inmates were encouraged to play 'Murder Ball' as exercise every other week. Two teams of thirty young offenders would stand on either end of the sports hall. Slater would then throw the ball into the middle and all hell would be let loose. The boys would steam into each other, punching, kicking, biting and pulling hair in a bid to grab the ball while the two prison officers sat looking on, drinking coffee from a flask. Cons would fall to the floor with fractured and broken bones, but still the game continued without any interference from the officers. Al took great pride in being amongst the last of the lads to still be standing when the final whistle was blown.

Al was fortunate to have got a job in the canteen. It was warm and there were fiddles to be had. He preferred it to working in the gym, which was looked upon by most of the inmates as a punishment. Al kept his head down, avoided unnecessary conflict and now had just three weeks of his sentence left before release when Officer Slater led Al to the Guvnor's office.

"Well, hello McIntosh," Detective Inspector Young said.

"Fancy seeing you here," Detective Sergeant Skinner said with a broad grin.

Al closed his eyes and sighed heavily.

"What do you two want?"

"You're nicked for robbery, McIntosh," DI Young said.

"How could it be me? I've been banged up here for nearly six months," Al said.

"Do you know Henry Ball?" DI Young asked.

Al didn't answer.

"Of course you do. You did several smash and grab jobs with him," DS Skinner said with a self-congratulatory smile.

"Yeah, we know that because he named you for the job in Piccadilly. Do you remember the electrical shop and all the stereos, nearly two thousand pounds worth of high quality equipment, according to Henry?" DI Young said.

"I've got nothing to say," Al said.

"I don't fucking believe this," Al thought. *"I've only got three weeks of this shit hole left!"*

"Give us the name of your fence and we'll walk away," DI Young said.

Al turned to see that Slater was standing by the door with his arms crossed. He returned a hardened stare to both the police officers.

"Fuck the pair of you!"

Al was formally arrested and taken to court where he was sentenced to an additional six months to be served at Blantyre Detention Centre.

***

It was summer, and Al and two other inmates were given the task of cleaning the swimming pool that was used by the prison officers and their families. He was surprised and delighted to see that four girls were happily using the pool. They were laughing, giggling and splashing water at each other when the young men arrived.

"We've had a right result here," Peterson said.

"Girls," Al said, as his jaw dropped open.

One of the girls stopped splashing, turned and smiled.

"Hello," Al said as he approached the pool.

The four girls got out of the swimming pool and wrapped their towels around them to dry off. Al made several jokey gestures which soon had the girls laughing. Peterson made a great partner as he was immediately comfortable in the girls' company and helped to keep the conversation flowing. The third inmate kept his head down and carried out the duties they had all been instructed to do.

"What's going on here?" Officer Slater yelled.

"We're just chatting with the girls," Al said with a smile.

"Well get away from them, now!" Officer Slater shouted.

Al and Peterson stood to attention.

"That's my fucking daughter you horrible little Herbert!" Slater hissed.

Al and Peterson remained quiet, their eyes facing the front.

"If you talk to my daughter again, I'll take you around the back and beat you to within an inch of your life!" Slater said.

Al, who, still angry, frustrated and on the edge for being sentenced to another six months with only three weeks until release, felt something snap inside.

"Go around the back, you cunt, let's have it out right here and right now," Al said as he clenched and brought both fists up to his chest.

Al could see the immediate change in Slater's expression.

"Never had someone come back at you, have you?" Al thought, *"I can see fear in your eyes."*

"Right," Slater said, taking a deep breath. "McIntosh and Peterson, get yourselves back inside."

"Yes sir," Peterson said.

Al hesitated for a moment. Slater hadn't held his usual glare.

"Yes sir," Al said with a triumphant smile.

The two lads marched back around to the main building.

"He'll not let that go," Peterson said.

"Yeah, he will," Al said.

* * *

During the following weeks there was an outbreak of scabies.

Scabies is a contagious skin infestation by the mite, Sarcoptes Scabiei, resulting in severe itching and a rash to the infected areas of the body. Al had picked it up along with most of the inmates. However, he had been embarrassed by the condition, kept his body covered and avoided scratching whenever he was around people.

When he was in his bed he would scratch the infected areas on his chest, stomach and right thigh.

"Fucking hell, McIntosh, do you have to?" the lad in the next bed called out in the dark.

"What?" answered Al.

"You know what."

"No, I don't," Al answered. He was a little confused.

"Wanking, McIntosh. Every bloody night you're bashing one out under the covers and I'm sick of hearing it."

Al burst out laughing.

"You silly bastard," Al said still laughing. "I'm not wanking, I've got scabies on my stomach and thighs and they're itching like mad."

The two inmates burst into fits of laughter.

"What? You think I was…?" Al chuckled.

"Yeah, I mean everyone does it, but I thought you were at it every night and for hours at a time!"

With medication the scabies were treated within a few weeks. However, it took over a month to rid the entire population of the mite.

Al's six month sentence had come to an end. He would no longer have to watch prison officers routinely punch and beat inmates or witness them turn a blind eye to the bullies forcing themselves sexually on the weaker inmates. The Master, the inmates referred to as 'Bible Basher' had been assigned to take Al and two other inmates due for release down to the train station.

Bible Basher was the most disliked of all the screws. Al had often wondered how on earth a religious fanatic could land a job in an institution like Blantyre. There were mornings when Al would roll over, open his eyes and find Bible Basher standing over him with his bible:

"Women are the scourge of the human race and don't you ever forget that McIntosh!" Bible Basher said as he slammed his bible shut.

"If you say so sir," Al said.

"I'd like to tell you to fuck the hell off but I'm not losing a day over a religious nut job like you," Al thought.

"I do say so. You take my advice and never get married or have children because they'll have the devil's blood. You mark my words!" Bible Basher said as he stepped away and then quickly turned back.

"Jesus died for my sins," Bible Basher said.

"It's a shame he couldn't do my time for me then sir," Al said sarcastically.

Bible Basher squinted his eyes in horror at Al's remark.

"I'm starting a bible class, I expect to see you there," Bible Basher said as he stomped off out of the dorm. "And you Peterson!"

The inmates would crowd into the television room for Top of the Pops on a Thursday night. Once the Wombles of Wimbledon Common stopped performing, Noel Edmunds, with a group of girls surrounding him, introduced *'Homely Girl'* by the Chi-Lites. The lads all shouted 'whoo-hoo' as Pan's People came onto the screen.

"I love that blonde bird," Peterson said, crossing his arms, clenching his fist, and thrusting his arm up.

"You mean Babs, Babs Lord," Al said.

"Right, nice bit of stuff," Peterson said.

The camera moved from Pan's People's Cherry Gillespie dressed in green overalls to Babs Lord dancing seductively in a short white flimsy nightdress with white fur on the hem.

"Whoo-hoo!" the lads yelled as she slowly danced around.

"Here Al, you know what that fur on her hem is for?" Peterson said.

"No," Al said, shaking his head.

"It's to keep her neck warm mate!" Peterson said, launching into fits of laughter

"Look at the legs on that," another inmate called out.

"They'd keep your ears warm in the winter," another yelled.

"Babs, I love you!" a third inmate yelled.

"Fuck off, she's mine," Peterson said, throwing the newspaper at him.

"What is all this?"

The lads turned to see Bible Basher at the door.

"Oh, give it a rest will you," Al thought. *"At least wait until Pan's People have done their turn."*

Babs Lord, Louise Clarke, Ruth Pearson, Dee Dee Wilde, and Cherry Gillespie danced together in their matching white nightdresses with the cameraman lowering the lens as the girls turned.

"This is exactly what I've been telling you boys. Women, and that's all women, are Jezebels. Look at the way she's tossing her hair back. See that? She's trying to seduce young men into thinking immoral thoughts!" Bible Basher said.

"Her hair's not the only thing I'd like to see her tossing," Al thought, chuckling to himself.

"Women will lead you into temptation with their evil, bewitching charms," Bible Basher said.

"That works for me," Al thought.

Finally, Pan's People finished their routine and Bible Basher stomped off down the corridor.

***

Each of the released inmates had been given three pounds. Al had been given a letter of introduction to a brick manufacturing company in the hope that he would gain full time employment. Throughout the journey through the town and down to the train station 'Bible Basher' had continually warned them of the evils of women, sins against God and how

223

the devil was waiting in the wings to take them down to the fiery pits of hell.

Al stood on the train platform and drank in the fresh, clean, air of freedom.

"You have to ask yourself what all that was about," Al thought. *"Rehabilitation? What? Kicking the shit out of you, marching you about for hours at a time, abusing and encouraging abuse of the weak. What the hell am I supposed to take from the last twelve months?"*

"Sir, can I go to the toilet, please?" one of the cons said.

"Why the fuck are you asking this cunt of a screw for permission to take a leak?" Al said sharply. "You're a free man, so fuck him! I don't know about the rest of you but I'm going to the platform café to buy a beer."

"You'll do no such thing!" Bible Basher shrieked.

"Who the fuck do you think you're talking to, you long streak of piss?" Al hissed. "I've done my time and you have no control over me anymore so back the fuck off!"

Bible Basher opened his mouth and then thought better of it when his eyes met Al's glare.

Al left the two ex-cons and Bible Basher on the platform, strutted down to the platform café and bought a tin of beer. He returned, ripped the top open and swallowed the contents in just three gulps.

"I'll tell you what, you bible bashing bastard," Al said as he reached into his pocket for the letter of introduction. "You can take this letter and shove it right up your arse along with all that Jezebel bollocks you constantly rattle on about. What gives you the right to tell any of us not to have kids because they'll be stained with the devil's blood? Fuck your detention centre, fuck the system, and fuck you!

Chapter 16

Al had used the five hours travelling from Glasgow to Euston to think about what he would be doing in London. After each stop, his spirits brightened. He needed somewhere to stay, to meet with old contacts and to have a sustainable cashflow. As the train rattled through London and came to a final stop in Euston, Al took a deep breath. He could feel a surge of happiness at being back in London, the greatest capital in the world. Al jumped off the train and walked briskly along the platform, smiled at the guard, and headed over to Gloucester Drive in Finsbury Park. As he turned into Gloucester Drive and spotted the house he had previously squatted in, he could hardly contain his happiness. Al knocked on the door, but there was no answer. He spotted two young boys standing in their off-white vests at the cracked glass window.

"I'm not sure I fancy it here, anyway," Al thought as he turned and crossed the street. He knocked on a glossy black door with a shiny brass door knocker and letter plate. The door opened.

"Can I help you?"

Al looked up to see a slim, hourglass, figure. He raised his head further and saw a pretty girl with long, ebony black hair that toppled over her shoulders. Al smiled when his eyes met her alluring galaxy blue eyes.

"Yes, sorry," Al said, desperately trying to hide his delight. "I'm Al and I stayed over the road for a while, some time back, and I'm looking for a place to stay. Do you have any room here?"

The girl looked him up and down and then parted her blossom pink lips with a smile that revealed her porcelain white teeth.

"Sure," the woman said as she opened the door and beckoned him in. "I'm Kate."

"It's nice to meet you Kate," Al said, holding out his hand.

"Nice to meet you too," Kate said. She gently shook Al's hand. "Come through to the lounge. I've just boiled the kettle and was about to make coffee. Would you like one?"

"That would be great, thank you," Al said, stepping into the lounge.

The lounge had a brown fitted carpet with a cream-coloured rug in front of the open fire. The suite was leather with an ox-blood finish. The gold velvet curtains hung from the ceiling right down to the floor.

"This is very nice," Al said.

"Yes, it is."

Al turned to a see a second pretty girl with lavish, moon gleam, blonde hair that framed her angular face.

"I'm sorry, I didn't see you there," Al said with an awkward smile. "I'm Al. I've just been telling Kate that I used to stay across the road and needed somewhere to stay and she invited me in."

"Take a seat, Al. I'm Kim. What brings you to Finsbury Park?"

Kate returned with three coffees and the trio spent the next couple of hours getting to know each other. Al told them how he had stayed in Finsbury Park before, did 'carding' when he was a teenager and had been known to acquire things from time to time to sell on. Kate and Kim confessed to being professional shoplifters and were stealing goods more to order these days.

"I've fallen on my feet here," Al thought. *"Two pretty girls to share with and they're both into a bit of villainy, so I'm safe doing whatever comes my way."*

Al met up with his good friends Mae West and Jean Harlow in Soho. They still had lads out 'carding' for them and Jean had again fallen out with Rock Hudson over a regular client. Mae told him that Eddy had been arrested and was put away for five years. Louis was still on the manor buying stolen gear and she gave Al his new telephone number. Al was introduced to a guy in his early thirties called Colin. He learned that Colin was an active thief, and it wasn't long before the two teamed up.

Al stopped off at a pub in Islington for a couple of pints with Colin, having just moved several stereos and television sets to Louis the Fence.

"Slow down Colin, there's no rush," Al said with a chuckle as he watched Colin order his fourth pint and whiskey chaser.

"You know what it's like Al, once you get the taste for it," Colin said before he sank the pint in four large gulps, put the glass back on the bar and swallowed the whiskey in one.

"Same again Landlord," Colin said as he reached into his pocket and pulled out a large wad of notes.

"Oi, put it away," whispered Al. "This ain't the kind of place to be flashing your money about."

"I'm wedged up and ready to party, mate," Colin said, reaching for his fifth pint. "What about we have another couple here and then get over to that brothel over on Wilberforce Road? My mate reckons they've got a couple of Asian birds in there. Right nice little things by all accounts, and for the right sort of money they'll do a turn together. What do you reckon?"

"No Colin, I can't."

"Come on Al, be a mate. I don't want to go to a brothel on my own," Colin said.

"What? Do you want me to hold your hand or something?" Al chuckled.

"You ain't holding my hand or anything else," Colin said, bursting into laughter.

"Mate," Colin said as he raised his pint glass. "Whatever you have to do it can't be as important as getting laid. I'll even share one of the Asian birds with you if you like, even swap over at half time."

"That's not for me and I'm committed," Al said as he put his empty glass on the bar.

"Committed?"

"Yeah, look you didn't know this but Kate, you know Kate back at the squat?"

"Yeah," slurred Colin.

"Well, we've been kind of seeing each other and I promised to take her out tonight," Al said.

"Oh, right. Well, she's a cracking bird, Al. I don't suppose you could put a good word in for me with her mate Kim? I'll sack the whole brothel thing and tag along with you lot tonight if you like," Colin said.

"Nah, you're alright. I'm meeting Kate on her own, but I'll meet with you tomorrow for a bit of egg and bacon at the usual place around eleven, alright?" Al said as he patted Colin on the back, turned and walked towards the pub's door.

"Right, its back to plan A then with the two Asian birds," Colin muttered.

***

Al returned to Gloucester Drive to find twenty-five brand new, boxed up, stereo systems in the front room.

"What's all this then?" Al said, kissing Kate on the cheek.

"A friend had them away and doesn't know where to shift them," Kate said.

"They must be worth a few quid," Kim said, pouring herself a large gin and tonic. "Do you know anyone we could get rid of them to?"

Al smiled.

"Sure I do, but we have a restaurant booked for 8.30pm," Al said.

"I don't mind giving it a miss if you don't," Kate said with a broad grin. "It'll be worth your while too."

Al and Kate took a taxi down to Louis the Fence's lock up. He paid the driver and then knocked on the door three times.

"Who is it?" a voice called out from behind the locked door.

"It's Al."

"Oh, alright Al."

Al waited while several locks and bars were undone and removed. Finally, the door opened.

"What do you want mate?" the man known only as 'One Shoe' said.

Al had asked Louis about the name when they were first introduced. Louis explained that his assistant, who was still a teenager then, was seeing a mature married woman just off the Seven Sisters Road. 'One Shoe' had been at the woman's home during a weekday while her husband, a burly scaffolder, was at work. One thing led to another, and they ended up in bed. During the spontaneous, passionate, lovemaking 'One Shoe' heard the front door open downstairs. The woman panicked and told him to hide. One Shoe clambered out of bed and lay flat on the carpet. He was completely naked other than a single shoe. The woman slipped on her nightie and slippers and skipped off downstairs. One Shoe could hear the kettle go on and the couple talking. The husband had been passing and decided to drop in for a quick cup of tea and pick up a sandwich as he would be working late. Once he finally left, 'One Shoe', now fully dressed, made his excuses and left. He relayed the story back to Louis the Fence who christened him 'One Shoe' and from that day on he was only ever known by the chaps as 'One Shoe.'

"I need to see Louis, One Shoe. We've got twenty stereo systems and I just know he'll want them," Al said, rubbing his hands together.

One Shoe looked at Al and then at Kate.

"Oh, this is Kate. She's with me," Al said.

"He's not here, Al," One Shoe said.

"What time will he be back? We'll wait." Al said.

"You'll be waiting a fucking long time, Al, he's in Africa," One Shoe said.

"Africa? You're joking with me," Al said.

One Shoe shook his head.

"No mate, he left shortly after he wedged you and Colin out this afternoon. I had to drop him over to Heathrow," One Shoe said.

"So what do we do now?" Al said. "There's a right nice earner here for Louis."

"He's probably on a plane as we speak," One Shoe said, slowly scratching his head. "I don't have any authority to buy anything. You know what Louis is like. He needs to see everything himself before parting with any money."

"So, while Louis is sunning himself in Africa all business here comes to a halt?" Al said with a hint of sarcasm.

"That's about it. I've got stuff here waiting to go and that's about it until Louis gets back," One Shoe said.

"Aw fuck it!" Al thought.

Suddenly Al had a flashback to his days at Blantyre House, the Detention Centre in Kent. He remembered meeting a guy called Ollie Duffy. The lad only had a few weeks left of his sentence but the two became instant friends. Ollie told him he lived near Kings Cross and if he was ever back in London to drop in to the 'Earl Russell' pub. Ollie told him the pub was full of armed robbers, safe crackers, enforcers, fraudsters, working girls and fences. He had assured Al that the locals were staunch and could sell just about everything. Ollie told Al that he only had to mention his name and he'd be alright.

"Alright, One Shoe. Let Louis know I was here," Al said as held out his hand to a passing black taxicab.

"Will do," One Shoe said before slamming the high security door shut.

"Where are we going?" Kate said as she stepped into the taxicab.

"I have an idea," Al said with a grin. "Do you know the Earl Russell in St Pancras?" Al asked the cabbie.

"Yes Guvnor," the cabbie called, as he turned on the meter and sped off towards Kings Cross.

"It looks a bit grim around here," Kate said, looking out the side window.

"Yeah, my mate said it was bit run down," Al said.

"Run down? It wants pulling down," Kate muttered.

The taxi stopped outside a Victorian style building with a large sign over the door reading 'Earl Russell'.

"What a dump," Kate muttered.

"Do you want to get these stereos sold or what?" Al said, handing the fare to the driver.

Kate nodded.

"Right then, follow me," Al said as he stepped forward and opened the pub door. It was packed with people lining the bar. Al looked around for his friend, Ollie, and a table to seat Kate at. He couldn't find either Ollie or a table. Al took Kate by the hand and led her up to the bar. The thick cigarette smoke hung from the ceiling like a blanket. The landlord and barman continued to serve people at the bar and avoided eye contact with Al.

"This place is proper," Al thought as the excitement of being in a pub full of hardened criminals and working girls engulfed him. *"I can feel the villainy in the air."*

"Are you alright mate? Lost or something?" A man with a glass eye and a mop of brown hair combed into a middle parting said while raising his hand to the barman.

"I'm a friend of Ollie, Ollie Duffy. Do you know him?"

The man smiled.

"Yeah, I know Ollie, we all know Ollie."

"Do you know where he is or if he's coming in later?" Al said.

The man motioned the barman to bring him a pint.

"Ollie's not been in for a few days. I'm not sure when he'll be back. What is it you want him for, a bit of business?"

"Yeah, I'm Al and I've got twenty-five brand new stereo systems I was hoping Ollie would get shifted for me," Al said softly.

"It's alright to talk business in here, Al. We sniff out old bill and snuff them out. Know what I mean?"

Al nodded and looked around the pub. He caught a glimpse of what looked like a hand axe hanging in a holster under one guy's jacket.

"The name is Cockney Ron. I can help you get them shifted, if you want."

Al hesitated.

"Do you have them with you?" Cockney Ron said before taking a sip from his pint glass.

"No, but they're close by," Al said. He was feeling a little drunk on the pub's atmosphere.

"Alright, meet me on the Caledonian Road at 10.00pm, and if they're what you say they are, we'll have a deal," Cockney Ron said calmly, taking a second, short, sip from his glass.

"I'll be there," Al said maintaining eye contact.

Al took a taxicab back to Gloucester Drive where he borrowed a van, loaded the stereos and drove down to Caledonian Road. The adrenaline raced through Al's veins when he spotted Cockney Ron standing by a blue transit van. He had considered Cockney Ron turning up mob handed but something inside told him that he was where he should be at this moment in time and that the Earl Russell was his kind of pub and its clientele were his kind of people.

"If it gets nasty, I'll fight until my last breath," Al thought.

Cockney Ron signalled Al to follow him, which he did. They stopped the vans in Northdown Street just a few roads up. Cockney Ron was alone. Al opened the rear doors of the van and Cockney Ron looked over the stereo systems. He paid what Al believed to be a very fair price.

"The next time you drop by the Earl Russell come and find me, Al. We don't take too kindly to strangers, but you know me and Ollie now."

The two men shook hands and parted company. Kate was thrilled with the money Al brought back and gave him a handsome seller's fee.

Later that night while Al lay on his bed, he thought about the Earl Russell pub, its dubious reputation and the nefarious characters that frequented the place. He felt an overwhelming sense of belonging despite only being in the pub for a few minutes.

Al had tremendous admiration for the working girls and how they risked their lives every time they got into a punter's car. He had known of girls getting raped, beaten up and one young girl was murdered. He would shake his head when television documentaries reported that the girls were being forced into performing sexual acts for money by violent pimps. Al knew scores of girls in central London, and none had a pimp. Most had boyfriends or husbands but were working the streets to get money to put food on the table and clothe their children. Poverty had forced the life of a working girl upon them, not the evil, manipulative, pimp that the media would have you believe.

Al and Colin were active thieves and were pulling in decent money. Louis the Fence featured less and less in their dealings as Al preferred to move the stolen gear through his growing circle of new friends at the Earl Russell pub. Al had purposely avoided taking Colin into the pub. He was a friend and good earner, but he liked to drink and had a tendency to get loud. Al had been in the Earl Russell moving on the latest haul of electrical goods but left early to meet Colin at a pub in Islington to give him his share.

"There you go," Al whispered as he discreetly handed over a large bundle of folded notes.

"Nice one, cheers Al," Colin said with a mild slur. "Here, landlord, can I get another couple of pints and a large whiskey chaser."

The landlord was busy pouring drinks for a group of men at the far end of the bar. He looked up and nodded before continuing to pull their pints.

"I've seen a place just ripe for screwing," Colin said. "It should be a right nice earner."

"Yeah, alright, keep it down, Colin, we don't want to talk business in here."

Yeah, I suppose," Colin muttered. "Here, Landlord get a move on. I'm dying of thirst over here!"

The landlord finished serving the others, took payment for the drinks and then traipsed up the bar, took a glass and began to pour Colin's pint.

"About time," Colin muttered.

The landlord put the last of Colin's order on the bar.

"That's one pound and forty pence," the landlord said holding out his hand.

"Fuck me, one pound and forty pence!" Colin said. "That's a right liberty. You know what? You should change the name of this pub to 'The Light Brigade' because you certainly know how to charge!"

"If you don't like it, drink up and leave," the landlord said sternly.

"Here, calm down!" Colin yelled and then threw the contents of his full pint into the landlord's face.

The four men at the end of the bar saw what happened and charged over. One man pulled out a huge meat cleaver from inside his jacket, while another produced a large fishing knife.

"Fuck, this place is protected," Al thought as he narrowly missed being stabbed in the chest.

Al reached down, picked up a pub chair and swung it with all the power he could muster.

SMACK!

The knife wielding 'heavy' caught the full brunt of the chair around the side of the head. He dropped the knife and went down. Al looked up to see Colin grab a bottle of light ale, smash it on the side of the bar and plunge it straight into one of the heavy's faces. Al kicked the man on the floor over and over and then stamped his foot down hard on the heavy's leg.

CRACK!

Al threw punch after punch before being kicked over a table, spilling several drinks. From the floor he could see the heavy that Colin had slammed the broken beer bottle into, kneeling down and cradling his face. The blood poured through his fingers and onto the beer-stained carpet. Al clambered back up onto his feet as the heavy slung the table to one side. He was holding a knife. He jabbed the knife several times and missed before Al found an opening and fired a hefty right hander that caught the attacker's jaw. He dropped down on to one knee and before Al could finish him off, he plunged the knife into Al's knee.

"You're fucking dead now," Al yelled, before grabbing a fallen chair and with Herculean might he brought the chair down over the heavy's head.

"Arghh!" Colin screamed.

The meat cleaver wielding heavy had sliced into Colin's stomach. It was then that the pub's doors slammed open and several uniformed police, wielding truncheons, waded in.

Al, Colin and the four heavies were all arrested and taken to hospital by ambulance. Al learnt that one of the heavies had lost an eye while the other had a broken leg and a severed toe. Al received several stitches in his leg and Colin was kept in overnight for surgery. No charges were brought against anyone caught up in the riot and so, those that could, left the hospital.

"You've gone and fucking done it now, Colin!" Al thought as he limped along the road back towards Finsbury Park. *"That pub was protected, which means behind those tooled up goons is a serious player, a gangster. I've got two choices now. I either fuck off back to Glasgow and keep my head down or go back and front it out."*

Al shook his head vehemently.

"I've never run from anything in my life and I ain't about to start now. Those lairy cunts never had the upbringing I've had. None of them were beaten red raw with a heavy dog chain as a child. I'm an animal; a fucking, fearless, savage beast that feels no pain and runs from no man," Al thought.

***

The following evening, Al, with his strapped-up leg, returned to the pub in Islington. As he opened the door and stepped in, he felt as if the whole pub suddenly went quiet. He looked to his left and saw a heavy set, smartly dressed, man wearing a blue pin stripe suit.

"That must be the gangster," Al thought as he looked over briefly at the several hard-faced men sat by him.

Al strode over to bar.

"I'll have a pint when you're ready, landlord," Al said calmly.

"I'm not serving you," the landlord said firmly, looking over at the gangster and his mob.

Al smiled before turning and walking several steps to the end of the bar. He opened the latch and stepped behind it. He could see the landlord was shaken and had taken several steps back. Al reached up for a glass and began to pour his own pint. Out of the corner of his eye, he saw a huge, six-foot four-inch giant of a man weighing in at twenty stone. Al put the half full pint glass on the bar and turned to face him.

The giant reached into the top of his trousers, produced a handgun and rammed it into Al's stomach.

"Bear, hold it," the gangster called in a relaxed, unruffled, tone.

"Yes, Boss," Bear said, putting his finger over the trigger.

"Bring him over here, I want a word," the gangster said, casually beckoning him over.

Al and Bear stepped back into the bar. The gangster stood up and brushed himself down.

"You have guts," the gangster said, looking Al slowly up and down. "I mean, coming in here on your own."

"I'm pleased you're impressed," Al said curtly.

"Oh, I'm not impressed," the gangster said with an iniquitous chuckle. "You could be dead in the next five minutes. Only mugs or superheroes are doing what you're doing. So, which one are you?"

"A mug," said Al.

"Why are you in here?" the gangster said, his eyes burning into Al's face.

"I live around here, and I'm not frightened by you or your men," Al said meeting the gangster's glare head on.

The gangster's lower lip slowly curled into a smile.

"You have balls and I give you that, but balls get licked all the time," the gangster said. "I like you. Do you want to work for me?"

"No," Al said adamantly.

"Why not?" the gangster asked, hunching his shoulders.

"Because I wipe clean no man's arse," Al said.

"You're a game chicken, so I'll tell you how this will go. Don't you fuck with any of my interests, and I'll live with you and that's it. You can walk away if you agree," the gangster said.

"I agree on one condition," Al said in a resolute tone.

"Yeah, and what's that?"

"That cunt you call the Bear, the mug who stuck a shooter in my stomach but didn't have the balls to pull the trigger?" Al said.

"Yeah, that's the Bear," the gangster said looking to his right.

The colossal giant of a man grunted loudly.

"Fucking Bear, my arse," Al said, shaking his head. "The only animal you can call that cunt after is a rat. Stand aside and I'll prove it."

The gangster took a short step back.

"Here, Bear, this kid reckons you're a rat!"

The Bear, wide eyed and with gritted teeth, began to charge. Al quickly kicked a bar stool in his way. The giant tripped and fell clumsily to the floor. Al bounded over and fired a vicious, relentless, torrent of heavy punches into Bear's face and head.

SMACK! – THUD! – CLUMP! - CRACK! – THWACK! – BAM! – CRUNCH!

While Bear lay motionless, Al battered him repeatedly. Finally, as the rage and fury began to subside, he stood up, looked around the bar, and shook out his heavily blood-stained fists.

"Yeah, that's right, you lot saw it. I am the fucking man!" Al thought. Although Al never worked for the boss of the London Crime Family, they became good friends.

Chapter 17

Al and Colin were bang at it and celebrating another good week at the Albion Pub in Kings Cross. Colin had checked his watch before swallowing the last of his pint. He was meeting with a girl he'd been chatting to at the café where he and Al would meet for breakfast.

"Do you want another gin in there, Helen?" Al said, motioning the barman over to take his order.

"Go on then, Sweetie," the eighty-year-old said, raising her glass.

Helen was a regular at most of the pubs Al had taken to drinking at. All the locals called her 'Old Helen' and would include her when they bought a round of drinks. Old Helen was an alcoholic and would boast that she would consume at least one full bottle of gin each and every day.

Al would always take time to listen to her stories from the 1940's, and admired the way she would always wear smart, dresses from the same era. She made them herself and come rain or shine, she would always have a fox stole around her neck. She told Al that back in the day she had been a talented seamstress with rich clients all over the capital. During one afternoon session, Old Helen confided in Al that she had once been a madam with a high-class brothel with just the prettiest of working girls. She spoke of the glamorous life she had enjoyed, the money, and how the famous television and movie stars would party at her establishment into the early hours of the morning.

Al recalled a conversation they had a few days before when he'd bought her a drink:

'I was connected, Al, everyone who was anyone knew of me. Then there were my girls. They were beautiful, well dressed, and beyond just regular

sexy, and that's why my customers kept on coming back to me despite all the competition in London back then.'

"Did I ever tell you about my friend, Belfast Mary?" Old Helen said, as she took a step closer to the bar.

"No, who was that then?" Al said.

"Of course I've heard it before. You must have told me a hundred times, but go on, knock yourself out and tell me again." Al thought.

"She was the best friend a girl could have," Old Helen said with a broad smile. "We would talk for hours about how we were going to make a name for ourselves in London. That was until that evil bastard Archibald Hall got his hands on her."

Archibald Hall, born in Glasgow in 1924, graduated from petty theft to building a career as a respectable butler to the rich and famous of London. However, this was a respectable front to hide his more elaborate crimes.

"I never liked him, Al. I told Mary, I said to her 'Mary you're a working girl, just take the man's money and move on' but she didn't listen to me. She would have this on and off relationship with him. Maybe it was the money and a taste of the good life that kept her going back. I don't know," Old Helen said.

Belfast Mary was born Mary Coggle.

"He would strut about like an aristocrat after he'd swindled some well to do family somewhere, nah, I never like him," Old Mary said.

"What happened to Belfast Mary?" Al asked.

"That bastard murdered her," Old Helen hissed. "Butler, that's what we girls called him, had her involved in all sorts and then did her in."

"I'm sorry to hear that," Al said.

"We were good friends, you know. I miss her Al, and I'm scared that one day I might end up dead like her," Old Helen said, drinking the last of her gin.

"Al, mate," a voice called.

Al looked over to a see a fellow villain from the Earl Russell.

"Yeah," Al called back.

"Your brother Brian and a few of your Glasgow pals were asking for you at that pub up on the Holloway Road."

Hearing Brian's name made Al feel like he'd just been jump started with an electrical current.

"Cheers!"

"Brian and some pals. I wonder who could be there?" Al thought. "Right, I'm off."

Al called the barman over and ordered another double gin for Old Helen.

"Here, do me a favour, would you make sure that she gets a taxicab home?" Al said softly, handing him a five-pound note

"Sure Al, consider it done."

"It's nearly closing time." Al thought looking down at his watch. *"I better get a move on."*

"I've got to go Helen. I've just heard that my brother's in London. There's a drink behind the bar for you and I'll see you soon," Al said, emptying the last few drops in his glass.

"You're a sweetie," Old Helen mumbled.

Al bolted out of the pub, flagged a taxi and gave him the location.

"Step on it please. I want to see my brother before they call last orders," Al said.

The cabbie shot up through the back roads and had Al at the pub with time to spare.

"Cheers," Al said handing over a note. "Keep the change."

Al entered the pub and was warmly greeted by his brothers Brian, Wullie and his close friends Big Irene and Little Irene.

"That is so typical of you Brian. We all go out and buy ourselves black leather trench coats and you have to be different and stand out with a white one," Al thought.

Standing by the bar was his friend Paul Lee. A few days earlier, after a heavy drinking session, Paul had produced a blade and suggested they became blood brothers. Al cut his palm first while Paul looked on as the blood seeped from the wound. Paul then cut his palm and the two clasped hands and announced that they were now blood brothers.

Al was conscious that it was nearly closing time, so he ordered a pint and then joined his family and friends at their table.

"Bloody good to see you all," Al said with broad grin.

"Come along drink up."

Al looked up to see the landlord standing over him.

"What you on about? You've just sold me the bloody drink. I've not even taken a sip yet," Al said.

"Just drink up, its closing time!" the landlord said, banging on the table with his clenched fist.

Al looked up slowly.

"Why don't you just fuck off!"

Before the landlord could answer, Al was up on his feet and swung a punch. Big Irene leapt up and grabbed the landlord by the hair with her left hand and smashed him in the face with her right fist.

"Fight!"

Al looked over to see several Irish lads sitting at a table. One shot up like a coiled spring and threw an almighty punch at one of a group of lads on the next table. The whole pub erupted into a riot with head butts, punches and work boots flying. The landlord's wife came hurtling across the bar wielding a metal bar. Big Irene sidestepped her swing, grabbed her by the hair and smashed her face into the beer-soaked table, Little Irene kicked at the landlady's legs until they buckled. Tables were being knocked over while innocent drinkers scrambled for the door.

Al could hear a police siren in the distance but still the fight continued in the pub.

"I've got to get out of here," Al thought. *"I can't afford to get nicked again."*

Al made a dash for the pub's door. The sound of the siren became louder. Once outside, a man in jeans and a leather jacket grabbed Al's arm.

"What's going on in there?"

Al looked down at the man's hand on his arm.

"I don't know. I'm just trying to get away," Al said, looking up the road towards the sound of the police siren.

"I'm making a formal citizen's arrest," announced the man as he tightened his grip on Al's arm.

"Take your hands off me," Al hissed.

"If you have nothing to hide then you won't mind waiting for the police to arrive, will you?" the man said.

"Take your fucking hands off me," Al said in a deeper, menacing tone.

"I'll have you know that I am a semi-professional wrestler, so you best not try anything with me."

Al clenched his right fist and then tugged against the guy's grip before turning back sharply and firing a thunderous punch that caught the wrestler clean on the chin.

CRACK!

The wrestler slumped back against the pub wall then made a lunge for Al's leg as he fell on the cold pavement.

"You're under arrest," the wrestler muttered.

"I fucking warned you, didn't I?" Al said as he fired out one kick after another into the wrestler's body.

Al looked over his shoulder. The police were now close, very close.

Al dropped down and began to punch the wrestler in the face and head repeatedly. A final pile-driver of a punch to the wrestler's ear made the wrestler finally release his grip on Al's leg.

"Have that, and that!" Al yelled, as he kicked out and stomped on the wrestler's arm and legs.

With the wrestler now lying across the pavement outside the pub's door, Al looked up and darted away down a side street, through an alleyway, and off to Gloucester Drive in Finsbury Park.

The following day Al met with his brother Brian at the house. He had been arrested for affray but was released on bail. Brian shrugged it off as no big deal.

"There was a robbery, Al," Brian said.

"Where?"

"At the pub. While it was all kicking off downstairs in the bar, three blokes in balaclavas, grabbed the landlord, dragged him upstairs and forced him at gunpoint to open his safe," Brian said.

"You're kidding me?" Al said.

"No, they had it away with over twenty thousand pounds and the landlord put you in the frame," Brian said.

"He doesn't know me. That's not one of my regulars," Al said.

"It was your mate, Paul Lee. The coppers told me that Paul Lee told them he had told you about the safe. You're in the frame good and proper, Al. They were talking about three charges of Grievous Bodily Harm, two of Actual Bodily Harm, causing affray, possession of a lethal weapon, and robbing the place of twenty thousand quid," Brian said.

"Paul Lee, you grass, you fucking grass. You're supposed to be my blood brother and you named me for something I didn't do!" Al thought.

"I didn't do it, Brian," Al said.

"I know that, and you know that, but as far as the police are concerned, they have you bang to rights," Brian said.

"The wrestler you battered the fuck out of is in hospital and in a bad way with a broken leg, arm and head injuries, but he's still talking and has given the cops a description of you. The landlord said he recognised your voice."

"He recognised my voice? The pub was full of Scots and Paddies. How would he know me from anyone else?"

You know how it works Al. If the bits don't fit, the police make them fit.

"Well, that's it then," Al thought. *"I'll have to get out of London."*

Al shook his brother by the hand and then took a taxicab to Euston Train Station where he bought a single ticket to Glasgow.

Chapter 18

Al was back in Springburn, Glasgow. It was 1976 and one of the driest, sunniest and warmest summers in Glasgow since 1868. The area is an inner-city district in the North and made up predominantly of working-class households and strong links to heavy industry which included the manufacture of railways, locomotives, and equipment. The area was being redeveloped with a great number of the houses being vacated, ready for demolition. Al saw that as the perfect opportunity to move in and squat in one of the empty homes. He used the skills his Uncle Tommy had taught him to turn the electricity and gas back on.

There were two local pubs in Cowlairs Road. Al knew that his sisters Sandra and Beth drank at the Highland Fling - known just as the 'Fling' by the locals. Almost opposite was the 'Vulcan Bar' in Vulcan Street. Al got ready and wandered down to the 'Fling' for a drink.

"I can't be going in there and have myself introduced as Al McIntosh or word will be out and the police will be on to me. I'm on the run from London so I can't take any risks," Al thought. *"I need another name. Something that doesn't stand out, fits in and doesn't attract attention."*

Al stopped outside the pub for a moment. Then the movie, *'Shane'* with Alan Ladd came to mind. He found himself pondering over the characters but was drawn to Jack Palance, one of his favourite actors, and his character 'Jack Wilson' the hired gunfighter.

"That's it, Jack Wilson. I'll be Jack Wilson," Al thought. He took a deep breath and entered the pub. It was still light outside but already the pub was buzzing with activity. The juke box had several girls standing around it chatting while *'Afternoon Delight'* by Starland Vocal Band was playing. Al strode over to the bar and ordered a whiskey. He picked the glass up,

turned, and looked around the pub. He spotted his sisters, Sandra and Beth, immediately. They looked up from the table they were sharing with friends, smiled and hurried over to Al.

"It's good to have you back, Al," Sandra said, giving him a kiss on his cheek.

"We've missed you," Beth said with a smile that could have lit up the dimly lit pub.

Al swallowed his whiskey.

"It's good to see you too. But look," Al said quietly, "I'm on the run, so I can't risk being called by my real name."

"Okay, so what do we call you?" Sandra said.

Al smiled.

"Jack, Jack Wilson."

"I like it," Beth said, nodding her head in approval of his name choice.

Al caught the landlord's attention and ordered another whiskey.

"Come and join us," Sandra said, grabbing him by the hand and leading him over to their table.

"Listen, this is a relative of ours. He's just moved here."

"Alright, I'm Davey Campbell. Good to meet you," Davey said.

Al reached out and shook his hand.

"I'm Jack, Jack Wilson," Al said as he pulled up a wooden chair and sat at the table.

"This is Rommel," Davey said, pointing to a stocky guy with a mop of blonde hair.

"Rommel?" Al said with a quizzical expression.

"Yeah, we call him Rommel because his da was a desert rat during the war," Davey said as he raised his glass of ale and took a long sip.

Al nodded and Rommel grinned and nodded back.

"We all have a theory that Rommel here secretly wanted the Germans to win the war," Davey said with a chuckle.

"Did I fuck," Rommel said.

Everyone around the table laughed.

"This is Billy Jones," Davey said, nodding towards a skinny lad wearing an off-white T-shirt.

"Alright," Billy said, raising his glass.

Al drank and chatted with his sisters and their friends. Davey could see that Al was watching the pool table from the corner of his eye.

"Hey Jack, do you fancy a game of pool?" Davey said when he saw that the two lads had finished their game.

"Jack? Fuck, that's me," Al thought.

"Yeah, sure," Al said as he stood up and followed Davey over to the worn pool table.

Davey placed the triangle on the green felt and began to place the pool balls inside it. Al fingered his way through the six odd sized pool cues. He looked at the tips and shook his head.

"I think these may have seen better days," Al chuckled as he took his position at the head of the table.

Davey took a coin from his pocket and placed it on his bent thumb and finger.

"Heads or tails," Davey said.

"Heads," Al replied.

The coin was tossed in the air and landed on the table.

"Heads it is," Davey said.

Al held the cue at the base with his right hand and then placed his index finger in a curved position at the top of the cue. He had learnt from playing in London that this gave him full control of the cue. He lined the white ball up, tuned out the sounds of the pub and *'Get Up & Boogie'* by Silver Connection pounding out from the jukebox, and took his shot with focus, hitting the cue ball straight and with power. The balls scattered, with a red flying down the far right pocket and a second red positioned over the centre right pocket.

"Nice shot. You've done this before," Davey said with a smile.

"Once or twice," Al replied with a smirk.

Al had taken an instant liking to Davey. As the game continued Al noticed a group of twelve lads in the far corner of the pub. They were getting increasingly louder.

"Here, Davey, what's with the mob over there?" Al said as he put his cue in his left hand and took a sip from his drink.

Davey looked over at the loud, boisterous, lads and lowered his voice.

"Those, Jack, are the Springburn Pegs."

"Springburn Pegs?" Al replied.

"Yeah, they're known as the 'Pegs'. Nasty set of lads, very territorial and dangerous, very dangerous. Everyone one of them is known for carrying knives and one of them, Woody, carries a small axe. There were sixteen of them but two are away for murder, another for GBH and one is on remand for beating the shit out of his girlfriend. Apparently she told him to make his own breakfast, so he took a carving knife to the wee thing," Davey said softly.

Al glanced over to the lads and then back to Davey.

"They are not to be fucked with," Davey said firmly.

"So, what's their game? You know, what are they into?" Al said as he lined up his cue on the black ball.

"You mean villainy?" Davey said.

Al took aim, fired the white ball down the table and sent the red ball hurtling into the right pocket.

"What else?" Al said with a chuckle.

"No, they ain't like that. With the Pegs it's just a violence thing. They will beat the living shit out of anyone who shouldn't be in Springburn and there's been times when they mob up and just hit gangs from other areas," Davey said.

"All that violence and no money in it," Al said, placing the cue back in the rack.

Davey shrugged his shoulders.

"They're Rangers though," Al said.

"Fucking right they are," Davey said. "The Fling and the Vulcan are both Ranger strongholds. We ain't having no Celtic fans drinking in here."

The bitter rivalry between Celtic and Rangers runs deep with both religious and political divides. The Rangers fans have long been protestant and support the union with Britain. However, the Celtic fans are mainly republicans and Catholic. Sectarianism has a long, bloody, history in Scotland.

"I take it you're Rangers?" Davey said, still holding his cue.

"Loyalist through and through," Al said bluntly.

"Have you been to many games?" Davey asked.

"Not so much recently, but when I was younger, I loved going to the games with my mates," Al said.

Al had a flash back to 1971. He had been just fifteen and snuck into a pub with his older mates. In the build up to the match he had sunk three pints of ale and was feeling a little pissed. He began to slur his words and found almost everything amusing. He joined the hordes of Rangers fans making their way down to the Ibrox stadium for the 'old firm' fixture.

While he waited in the queue, a police officer looked him up and down suspiciously. Having challenged Al about drinking alcohol he refused to let him in. Al went to another stairway and later waited outside the stadium by stairway thirteen for his friends. It was only later, on the bus going home, that he learnt of the disaster that resulted in the deaths of sixty-six people. He had never forgotten how Mammy had run over and hugged him when he got home. She had smelt the beer on his breath and shot him a look. Al believed that being refused entry for having that first drink had probably saved his life.

"Gers are playing top football this season," Davey said. "We should catch a game some time."

"Maybe," Al said, patting his empty pockets. "I'll need to get a bit of work first."

"What kind of work are you looking for?" Davey said.

"Nothing too heavy if you get my drift," Al said softly.

Davey paused for a moment.

"I have something, it ain't heavy and it pays well. I could probably do with another pair of hands if you want in."

"You have my attention," Al said with a broad grin.

"Me and the lads, that's Rommel and Billy, do a bit of leading after dark."

"What's that? Nicking the lead off the roofs?" Al said, putting his empty whiskey glass on the table.

"Yeah, but I've got it all sorted if you fancy it?" Davey said.

"I'm in, when do we start?" Al asked.

"Tonight," Davey said.

"Excellent, can I get you a drink?" Al said.

"I'm earning," Davey said, pulling out a small bundle of notes from his trouser pocket. "I'll get you one."

When Joe, the landlord, called last orders Al, Davey, Rommel and Billy Jones met up at the end of the road. Al watched as Rommel kissed a girl he'd been chatting to goodnight, while Billy Jones lit a second cigarette from the butt of the one he'd just smoked. Once the streets emptied,

Davey led the lads through Springburn to the row upon row of tenement buildings due for demolition. The lads took a final look around for police or rival crews before Davey wedged the front door open with a jemmy bar. The lads quickly filed in, sprinted up the stairs and up through the skylight onto the roof. Davey handed Al a Stanley knife.

"You got to slide down there, lean over and peel the lead back before cutting it away from around the window. Then lift it up onto the roof. Can you do that?"

"Piece of piss," Al said as he began to slide down the roof tiles.

"Fuck me it's dark. One slip and I'll be over the side," Al thought.

"Be careful. I heard that one lad, on his first time leading, slipped and went straight over the side of the roof and wound up dead," Davey said.

"Cheers mate, that's just what I needed to hear," Al thought.

Al slid down the roof, leant over the side and began to cut and peel back the lead just as Davey had said. It was hard work, but Al found it strangely satisfying. He piled the lead up on the roof and once he had enough, he carried it up the roof, down the other side and piled it up. The lads grafted through the night. As the sun began to rise, Al looked down at his filthy hands. It had been the closest thing he had ever done to a real, physically demanding job, and he'd thoroughly enjoyed it. Al carried the last of his lead up and over the roof. There were two piles of lead, each one almost six foot high.

The four men looked at their haul.

"What's next?" Al said as he sat down on the tiles.

"This," Davey said with a manic grin.

257

Davey kicked the base of the lead with his right foot and the pile toppled over. It hit the concrete base with such force that it sounded like a bomb had gone off. Al flinched and covered his ears. He panicked and began scanning the area from the roof for police.

Davey let out a laugh and kicked the second pile of lead off the building.

BANG!

Once again the morning silence was broken.

"Come on," Davey called, as he led the lads back up through the roof, down the skylight and stairs and into the fractured and broken concrete back yard. The lads carried the lead back to Davey's home just a few streets away. It was just before 6.00am and Davey's wife was awake and standing in the front room with her hands on her hips. Al could see she wasn't happy.

"Look at the bloody state of you lot, traipsing all that shit and dirt into the house!"

Al turned to see his reflection in the hallway mirror. He was black from head to toe with dirt and grime from the night's leading.

"Don't you think I have enough to do around here with a young bairn?" Davey's wife said, still standing firm.

"Give it a rest hen, we've been grafting, alright?" Davey said as he looked down at his watch.

"Why can't you find somewhere else to store it?" Davey's wife asked.

"Oh yeah, that would be really smart wouldn't it. Put all our hard graft and ill-gotten gains somewhere that could just be robbed. No," Davey said shaking his head slowly, "I've got a better idea. Why don't you shut the fuck up, keep your nose out of our business and go and put the kettle on!"

"One of these days!" Davey's wife hissed as she stomped off into the kitchen.

"Alright, he's here lads," Davey said as he peeled back the curtain and looked out onto the street outside.

Davey led Al and the lads into the back yard where they had stored the lead. Out front the scrap-man had arrived in a transit pick-up truck. He reversed down the lane and in between Davey's home and a wall. The lads picked up two scaffold boards and placed them between the wall and the bed of the transit van and then slid the lead down onto the van's bed. Al watched as the scrap-man weighed the lead and then handed Davey a bundle of notes. The lads pulled the scaffold boards back over the wall and stood in a circle on the crumbling concrete.

"You, Jack Wilson, are a good omen," Davey chuckled. "This is our best night ever!"

Davey counted out four hundred and forty pounds and then split it into four equal amounts. Al held one hundred and ten pounds in his hand and all for just a few hours of graft.

"There are mugs out there that graft for forty hours and only take home thirty or forty pounds and I've more than tripled that in one night," Al thought. *"I'm having some of this and more... a whole lot more!"*

Will your wife stand for this, Davey?" Al said as he put the money in his pocket.

"If she wasn't bitching about this, it would something else," Davey said. "She likes the money that leading brings in. So what if you get a bit of dirt on the mirrors or something when you're washing, when she can go down to the shops and buy whatever she wants. Yeah, she'll stand for it Al. It's either that or she can fuck off back to her Mammy and Da's because this is one gravy train that has a long way to go yet."

***

Over the following weeks Al slowly but surely took charge of the leading operation. Davey gave no resistance and fell into line. Al met with the scrap-man at his yard and checked the weighing machine for magnets. The scrappy assured them that he was straight and wouldn't spoil what they all had going by trying to cheat the lads out of a few quid. Al ran the enterprise like a military operation. He had learnt from his younger days on the thieve, to smash through the walls into the next home to avoid going downstairs, into the adjoining house and clambering onto the roof. One hole and the lads just stepped through. The lads were working seven nights a week with an average of one thousand pounds for each of them. Al had come up with the idea of using a rope wrapped around the chimney to haul the lead up and down the roof. It had all saved time and resulted in more money.

With more money in his pocket Al had been out shopping and treated himself to a new wardrobe of clothes. He looked in the mirror and smiled. He looked good, smelt good and felt good with a pocket full of money. He collected his keys, loose change and left the squat for a night out in the 'Fling' with his mates.

Al felt like a million dollars as he entered the pub. It was Friday night and 'Heaven Must Be Missing an Angel' by Tavares was pounding out from the jukebox. News of the fun-loving lads spending had brought a number of new, pretty girls in short summery skirts and high heels to the pub. Al bounded over to the bar amidst several waves and verbal acknowledgements.

"Evening Joe, I'll have a whiskey please, and send a round of drinks over to Sandra, Beth and her mates. And have one yourself. Cheers." Al said as he placed a new, crisp, ten-pound note on the bar.

Joe nodded and began to pour the drinks. Davey patted Al on the back.

"Hello mate," Al said. "What are you drinking?"

"Whiskey, please. Cheers, Jack." Davey said as he put his hands on the bar.

Al turned and looked him up and down.

"Alright Davey, what's up?" Al said before knocking the first whiskey straight back in one gulp and then holding the empty glass up for Joe to refill.

"Err, nothing," Davey replied.

"What's nothing?" Al said firmly.

Davey looked around him and then lowered his voice.

"I've been hearing things," Davey said.

"What kind of things?" Al said as he waved to Sandra after she raised her glass to him.

"It's the Pegs," Davey said in a whisper.

"What about them?"

"I've heard that they've been waiting for leading crews to finish up and then they're robbing them. I heard that one poor fucker got striped," Davey said.

"So?" Al said calmly.

"Well, what if they come for us?" Davey whispered before he gulped the whiskey down in one.

"Fuck them," Al said.

"Fuck them? But they're the Pegs," Davey whimpered.

"I couldn't give a flying fuck who they are! I'm telling you now, Davey, they'll come mighty unstuck if they try any of that old bollocks with us," Al said. "No one will take a penny from our bit of graft."

"Okay, I'm just saying," Davey said.

"Have another drink and stop fretting. You've made over a thousand pounds this week so just relax and enjoy yourself and we'll take care of business as and when it happens."

"Alright, sorry," Davey said.

Al picked up his drink and walked down to join Sandra, Beth and the friends he'd made over the last few weeks. There were two sisters, both called Irene. They shared the same father but two different mothers. Little Irene had a slender build and was just over five foot tall with long coral black hair that tumbled over her shoulders. Big Irene was over six foot tall and was built like a rugby union player. She had short black hair and could sink a pint of ale quicker than most of the men in the pub. Her party trick was to put a pound note on the table and challenge men to an arm wrestle. Big Irene was a powerful woman that rarely lost her money.

Davey cautiously approached the table.

"Take a seat then, Davey," Al said, motioning him to sit at the chair next to him.

Joe, the landlord, arrived at their table carrying a tray of drinks that Davey had ordered for everyone.

"Cheers, Davey," Al said, raising his glass.

"Cheers," the others said one by one.

"Al," whispered Davey, "I know what you said earlier, but Billy's just said that he's out."

"Billy's out?"

"Yeah, he doesn't want any trouble with the 'Pegs," Davey whispered.

"Well, that's his loss then. What about Rommel, or has he shit himself as well?" Al said sarcastically.

"No, he's a bit shaken but he's still in," Davey said.

"What about you, Davey?" Al said as he turned and faced his friend.

"I've got a wife, bairn and bills to pay so I'm still in," Davey said.

"Good," Al said as he turned towards the large group of Springburn Pegs standing around the pool table.

Al stood up, took some coins out of his pocket and sauntered over to the jukebox. *"A Glass of Champagne'* by Sailor was just finishing. He slipped the coins into the machine and made his selection. As the opening of *'Golden Years'* by David Bowie began he smiled, turned and walked back to his table.

"You've got to love a bit of Bowie," Al thought. *"The man is a genius."*

As he sat back down, he turned back to see a group of six girls dancing together by the jukebox. Al raised his hand and Joe, the landlord, immediately turned towards him.

"Joe, send those girls a drink from me would you, and take one for yourself."

Al looked on as Joe spoke with the girls and then returned with a tray of drinks. One girl in particular had grabbed his attention. She had ringlets of tawny brown hair veiled over a heart shaped face. She took the drink from the tray then turned to face Al, raised her glass, and smiled before silently mouthing 'thank you."

Al silently mouthed back 'You're welcome,".

"She's a pretty girl," Al thought.

The pub door opened, and Al saw a familiar face. It was his brother, Brian. He immediately stood up and waved him over. Brian beamed when he saw Al sitting with his sisters Sandra and Beth.

"What the fuck are you doing here?" Al said as he warmly shook his brother's hand.

"First things first, can I get a drink?" Brian said.

Al turned to Joe and called, "Joe, send us over a couple of whiskeys would you, and make them doubles," Al said.

Brian walked straight over to the table and hugged both his sisters. Al handed him the drink and then introduced Brian to all those at the table. Brian took a small sip and then swallowed the rest of the drink in one.

"I needed that," Brian said as he slammed the empty glass down on the table.

Al motioned Joe to bring them another round and then led Brian out of earshot of those around the table.

"So, what the fuck are you doing here?" Al said.

"Oh, fuck them. I had it on my toes after they gave me bail."

"Well, it's good to see you, Brian. How are you for money?"

Brian shrugged his shoulders, smiled and pulled out the insides of his empty pockets.

"Don't worry about that. I've got a lovely little bit of work on the go, and I've just had a lad drop out if you want in," Al said.

"Good money, is it?"

"Thousand quid a week and its nothing heavy," Al said.

Brian's eyes lit up.

"Thousand quid, fucking right I'm in," Brian said, patting his brother on the shoulder.

"Listen, right. No one knows me as Al in here. It's Jack, Jack Wilson alright?"

"Nice one, Al. I mean Jack," Brian said with a chuckle. "Shall I change my name as well?"

"You're a bit fucking late for that," Al said with a broad grin. "You've just introduced yourself to all those lot as Brian.

"Oh yeah," Brian said with a chortle. "Here, how come you had a guy drop out for that kind of money?"

"Well," Al said, as he turned to face the Springburn Peg lads standing around the pool table. "See that little lot?"

"Yeah."

"They're supposed to be a proper serious mob with a reputation for cutting people up and they've been robbing a few crews of their hard-earned graft," Al said as he handed Brian another whiskey.

"Cheeky bastards," Brian said. "They don't look that much to me."

"Here," said Al as he pulled a wad of notes out of his pocket and handed them to Brian. This is a bit of walking around money. You can kip down at my place if you want. It's a nice little squat with running water, gas and electricity. I've got plenty of room but it's up to you."

"Cheers, sounds perfect. When do we go to work?" Brian said as he counted out the money and put it in his pocket. "I'll pay you back."

"Don't worry about it," Al said shaking his head. "Tonight we're having fun and I've got my eye on this cracking little bird so it'll be tomorrow night now and I'll fill you in with all the details in the morning."

"Cheers, Al, I mean Jack," Brian said.

"As one door closes another opens, Billy Jones, my son," Al thought. *"Your loss is Brian's gain."*

Brian stood by the bar and watched as his brother strode over to the jukebox. Moments later *'The Boys are Back in Town'* by Thin Lizzie thumped out of the ageing speakers.

Al turned to Brian, raised his glass, and took a sip of his drink before introducing himself as Jack Wilson to the brunette he'd bought a drink for earlier.

***

The following morning Al and Brian walked down to the café for breakfast. Al explained how the leading operation worked and how the

266

police were not that interested, which meant they could still earn and keep a low profile.

"Who was the girl you were talking to last night?" Brian asked.

"She calls herself 'Babs'. I suppose that must be short for Barbara," Al said.

"Pretty girl," Brian said.

"Yeah, and she's interesting to talk to as well," Al said.

"Now there's a rare combination," Brian said with a chuckle. "Will you be seeing her again?"

"Probably. She's started using both the Fling and the Vulcan," Al said. "What about that bird I saw you talking to?"

"Nah, that didn't go down too well," Brian said.

"Why's that?" Al asked.

"It was all smiles until I asked her what she did and how much she charged. She got the right raving hump and stormed off," Brian said as he shrugged his shoulders.

"What, you thought she was on the game?"

"Yeah, well, with that little skirt and her tits falling out over her top I thought it best to be rather safe than sorry and find out up front what she wanted and what was on offer," Brian said.

"Not all women are on the game, Brian," Al said.

"True, but you end up paying for it one way or another, so I was just cutting to the chase," Brian said as they stopped outside the café.

"Do you want me to ask Babs if she has a nice friend?" Al said as he reached for the door handle.

"No. I can pull my own birds, thank you very much, Al, Jack, or whatever your fucking name is," Brian said firmly.

"Don't get fucking lippy Brian. I was just offering some help, that's all, so wind your fucking neck back in," Al said, holding the café's door handle.

"Yeah, well I'm alright," Brian said.

"No one said you weren't. Now do you want something to eat or not?"

***

That evening, after the 'Fling' had closed, Al, Brian, Davey, and Rommel went to work leading. Al had showed Brian the ropes and he took to it as easily as he had. They grafted through the night. As the sun rose, Al sat on the roof looking out over an old Victorian building, Petershill High School. He was tired and covered in filth and grime from his night's toil when memories of his first year at the secondary school came flooding back and how everyone would call school 'Peasy'.

It was customary for the boys to play a game called 'Run the Gauntlet' during break times. A dozen hardened street kids would line up on either side of the playground while one single lad would have to make his way through them as they punched, kicked and spat. Al had battled his way through. He punched and kicked back and managed to get through the hoard of street thugs intent on causing as much bodily harm as they could. Al watched as one lad, who had tried to bottle it, was thrown into the corner of the school playground, while the kids screamed out 'Mincer, mincer!' and booted the life out of him. When tensions dissipated Al saw the lad curled up in a tight ball on the concrete. For Al and the other lads, it was an initiation and all part of school life. The girls in the playground next door had their own type of initiation. One by one they were forcibly stripped naked. There were times when articles of clothing, mainly underwear and stockings, would be thrown over the wall into the boys' playground. Some of the lads would clamber up onto the wall and cheer as the girls fought to retain their clothes and their dignity. Al never looked; he didn't agree with what the girls did to each other.

With all the lead shifted and then sold from Davey's, the four lads walked out onto the street outside. Al couldn't help but notice the expression on the face of an older man walking his dog on the opposite side of the road. His legs almost buckled when he saw the four heavily blackened faces, like television extras from the black & white minstrel show emerge from behind the wall that led through to the rear of Davey's home. Al stared back and smiled as the dog walker picked up his pace and bolted along with the dog who was trying desperately to stop, sniff and use the lamppost.

Davey disappeared back indoors while Al, Brian, and Rommel walked back towards their homes. It just after 6.30am when they saw a bunch of lads standing around a Ford Anglia. Al immediately recognised them as the 'Springburn Pegs'. As they got closer the seven lads crossed the road to block their path.

"It's Jack, isn't it?" one of the lads said.

"Might be, what the fuck's it got to do with you?" Al said, clenching his fists.

"You boys have been busy little bees and now you have to pay your dues to the Springburn Pegs," the lad said as he put his left hand on the handle of a large knife he had protruding from the top of his trousers.

"You can fuck off!" Al said belligerently.

The Springburn Peg lad began to get agitated. Al could sense that this was not how robberies normally went for them.

"I'll fight each and every one of you before you get a brass farthing from any of us," Al said.

Brian stepped forward so that he stood shoulder to shoulder with his brother. Reluctantly Rommel did the same.

"Now fucking do something about it or fuck off," Brian said as he took two steps forward.

The lads were shaken. There were a few moment's silence.

"We'll let it go this time, but we'll be back," the lad with the blade said.

"We'll be ready," Al said as he began to walk towards the crew of lads.

The Springburn Pegs slowly parted as Al, Brian, and Rommel walked through them and continued to walk back to their homes.

"You've hit a brick wall when it comes to me and Brian," Al thought.

Chapter 19

Brian had become a key part of Al's leading operation. Al had Rommel running around the houses taking off the brass door handles, which were bringing four pounds each as scrap. Al had also found another revenue stream by stripping out the lead window top lights. The scrap-man had agreed to pay Al and his firm twelve pounds for each one. The firm were bringing in some serious money now with a thousand pounds being a poor week. Al had become friendly with Babs. They shared fun and laughter at both the local pubs and on one occasion Al had taken her to celebrate a particularly good week at the Burns Howff Club on West Regent Street in the city.

Wullie, Al's brother, had returned to Springburn from his job as a gamekeeper in Aberdeenshire. He had walked into the Vulcan Bar carrying his shotgun in a leather bag. Several of the lads at the bar had ducked, believing it was a hit on the pub. Al knew that Wullie was as game as both Brian and himself if trouble were to start, so he offered him a place on his leading firm until he had to return to Aberdeenshire. Wullie stayed with Al and Brian. The brothers had taunted him about his shotgun. He took the weapon out of the case, loaded it with bird seed filled cartridges and asked Brian to place the two editions of the yellow pages telephone directory against the wall, one over the other. Wullie then loaded the cartridges, took aim and fired. Both Al and Brian had winced at the noise. Brian picked up the directories and held them both up so Al and Wullie could see that the cartridges had blasted a hole clean through them both.

It was Saturday night and all three of the brothers were dressed in their going out gear. With pockets full of money, they ambled along the streets leading to the Vulcan Bar chatting about old times.

"I fucking hated it," Wullie said.

"Me too," Brian said.

"You're not the only ones," Al said. "But you and Beth definitely got the worst of Mammy."

"Evil bitch," Wullie said as he clenched and unclenched his fists. "She fucking had it in for me and Beth."

"I know, there's no excuse for it," Al said.

"One of these days I'll fucking kill her," Wullie said calmly.

"You don't want to do that," Brian said.

"Oh, I do," Wullie said with a manic snicker. "I'll shove both barrels in her mouth and blow her fucking head clean off."

Al had become increasingly concerned about his brother, Wullie's, behaviour. He would talk enthusiastically about how he killed the wildlife designated as pests. Al had come to an early conclusion that Wullie enjoyed taking the lives of the animals.

"Anyway, it's Saturday night and we're out on the town so let's park all this up," Al said as they approached the Vulcan Bar.

"But it wasn't right though, Al, and you know it," Wullie said.

"I know, Wullie, but just leave it for now and spend some of that money in your pocket," Al said.

Wullie grunted, groaned and muttered something to himself that Al couldn't make out.

"I'm going to get totally rat-arsed tonight and with any luck I'll not be going home alone," Brian said as he took a deep breath and puffed his chest out.

Al opened the door and was greeted by the sounds of *'You to Me Are Everything'* by The Real Thing.

"Now that's more like it!" Al thought, as he stepped into the pub.

On seeing Al, Brian and Wullie arrive, Davey, who was sitting in the far corner with Sandra, Beth, Little Irene, Big Irene, and Rommel, got up and pulled another table and four chairs over.

The pub was ram packed with twenty something's all out having a good time.

"Hello Jack," Graeme said quietly. "Will you and your boys be needing a bit of the good stuff tonight?"

Graeme was a drug dealer. On hearing how the lads were spending, he had made a point of introducing himself to Al and the lads a few weeks earlier. Al had created a line in the men's room and inhaled the cocaine. He had never been attracted to drugs, preferring to spend his money on whiskey. However, the cocaine experience had made him feel euphoric, mentally alert and hypersensitive to sight, sound and touch. The effects disappeared, for him, within the hour, so he would just buy a few grams for the girls that expressed a desire to have the high. Davey had recommended that he buy and use amphetamines as it helped them all to work through the long nights.

"Yeah, sure," Al said as he handed Graeme a bundle of notes. "Go and give it to the brunette, Babs, over by the jukebox."

"Sure thing," Graeme said, pocketing the money.

"Young Hearts Run Free" by Candi Staton began to play. Al looked over to see Graeme handing Babs the small sachet of white powder. She looked up in a bid to find Al in the busy pub. When her eyes finally found him, she smiled and gave him a suggestive wink.

"I'm on here," Al thought.

At the table Big Irene was arm wrestling Rommel for a five-pound note. She resisted his attempts to force her arm over, and then tightened the grip on his fingers. Al could see the look of extreme pain in Rommel's eyes. Seconds later Big Irene slammed his hand down onto the table.

"Whoo-hoo!" the girls yelled as Irene picked up the five-pound note, stood up and took a bow.

Al was about to sink his third whiskey when Davey pulled up a chair next to him.

"For fuck's sake Davey, you've got that look of doom and gloom about you again," Al said as he put his glass back on the table.

Davey shook his head.

"It's all been going off," Davey said.

"What has?" said Al.

"Well, you know that the Pegs have been robbing the leading firms," Davey said softly.

"Yeah, and they came unstuck against us, right?" Al said decisively and then clenched and unclenched his fists.

"Yeah, I know, but the Pegs had a run in with Joey Flemming and the Balgrayhill Boys. Anyway, the Pegs have spent all morning robbing poor bastards and then Joey Flemming has turned up mob handed. Well, Joey's reputation for violence is well known everywhere. He's a fucking head case and has stabbed at least ten people that I've heard of," Davey said, taking a sip of his drink. "They're all fucking mental and constantly high on 'mulkies'.

Mulkies was a highly dangerous mixture of milk and gas. Local lads would take a half bottle of milk and place it under the gas lamps in the closes in Petershill Road, turn the gas on, fill the milk bottle up, shake it and then drink from the bottle. This combination was renowned for making the drinkers short tempered, angry and prone to extreme violence.

Al turned to see if he could see any of the Springburn Pegs in the pub. When he'd scanned the room completely and failed to spot a single lad he turned back to Davey.

"So, what happened?"

"The Springburn Pegs just folded, and I mean they didn't put up any kind of fight. They saw that it was Joey Flemming and they just handed over everything they had. Joey made them empty all their pockets too. He turned them over good and proper, mugged them right off," Davey said with a sly grin.

"Well, what goes around comes around," Al said, reaching for his drink.

"It doesn't stop there," Davey said.

"So what then?" Al said.

"The Pegs have named you, me, Brian and Rommel as the most active leading firm," Davey said.

"And?"

"They will want in. I know what Joey Flemming is like and you have to believe me when I say that this fucker will not take no for an answer. He's dangerous and I don't scare easily but this lunatic will cut you up in a heartbeat just to make some kind of point," Davey said.

"We'll deal with it if or when it happens, "Al said resolutely. "Now, if you don't mind, Davey, I'm out tonight to have a good time and enjoy myself."

"Yeah, sure. I'm just keeping you in the picture," Davey said.

"Consider me informed," Al said, as he motioned to the landlord to pour him another drink.

"Is it alright if I sit down?"

Al turned to see Babs grinning and looking down at him. In the background he could hear *Let the Music Play'* by Barry White.

"Sure," Al said with a broad smile.

"I don't think I've seen your place yet," Babs said, fluttering her eyelids with a sexy, suggestive, smile.

***

A couple of nights later Al was returning from the pub. It had been a good night and he was feeling on top of the world. He shouted out down the road. It was something that Al, Brian and Wullie had agreed to do since the Springburn Pegs had declared war. The brothers would know that it was Al on his way home. Al put his hands around his mouth again, staggered and recovered, and shouted out for a second time. He nearly fell clean over as he looked up at the sound of a window slamming open and a huge, white, Pyrenees Mountain dog plummeted towards him. Al looked down at the large working dog with its drooping ears and rolling gait lying by his feet. It was Glenn, Mammy's dog. The dog's body was mangled, contorted and its neck had been broken. The dying dog whimpered and tried to raise its limp neck.

"Glenn, what the hell have you done you stupid dog," Al thought. *"I can't bear to see you in so much pain, boy."*

Al thought, for a brief moment, that he should end the dog's life and put it out of its misery. But as he crouched down and put his hands around Glenn's neck, the dog died. Al closed his eyes and shook his head. When he looked up, he saw a bus had come to a halt.

"What the fuck is going on?" one passenger yelled as he stepped off the bus.

"What the hell is going on here?" another passenger shrieked.

"This bastard is killing a dog in the middle of the bloody road, and he doesn't give a fuck who sees him!" an elderly woman said as she stumbled off the bus onto the road.

"No, it's not like that," Al said as he heard the tottering of high heel shoes.

A woman in her mid-thirties reached down and pulled off her high heel shoe and attempted to batter Al with it. She narrowly missed his head.

"Calm down, it's not what it looks like," Al said calmly.

"This cunt is killing the dog!" another distraught passenger shouted.

"You nasty bastard!" a passenger shouted out as he launched a kick.

AL grabbed the man's leg and tossed it to one side.

"I fucking told you lot, you've got it wrong!" Al said as he stood up straight to face to the growing, angry, mob of passengers and passers-by.

A Ford Zodiac MK2 came to a screeching halt alongside the bus. The driver's door slammed open and a guy with a Teddy Boy quiff hairstyle, white T-shirt and tight blue jeans got out of the car carrying a large butcher's knife. He looked at the dog lying dead on the road and then clenched his teeth, gripped the butcher's knife and strode towards Al, slashing wildly at the air.

"Fuck, I'm done for here," thought Al.

"Waaaaa!"

Al and the crowd turned to see Brian and Wullie yelling at the top of their voices while racing down the road wielding axes, swords and a dagger.

The Teddy Boy stopped in mid stride, turned and ran back to his car. The bus driver tried to usher everyone back on the bus. The older woman refused to budge.

"What's going on here?" Brian said as he stood beside his brother with an axe in one hand and a dagger in another.

Wullie held his sword up high with his right hand. He was ready to slash at any sudden movement. In his left hand an axe dangled down by his leg.

"Right, let's just calm the hell down," Al said as he raised and lowered his arms.

He explained what happened and that the dog was a family pet. The passengers returned to the waiting bus and the woman in the heels apologised before giving Brian a suggestive smile.

With the crowd dispersed, Al reached down and picked up the dog. He carried the dead animal in his arms through the front door, up the stairs into the flat. Al looked over at the open window.

"Glenn must have heard my voice, got excited, and jumped out of the window," Al thought.

Wullie put the kettle on.

"We'll have to bury Glenn," Brian said.

"Yeah, I know," Al said, looking down at the dog lying on the white sheet Brian had laid out for him. "We'll do it in the morning."

The three brothers drank their tea and then returned to their home carrying the dog. En-route they discussed burying Glenn and decided that they should do it that evening so that no one could see them and avoid another misunderstanding with angry animal lovers.

It was 2.00am the following night when the brothers decided to bury Glenn.

"Look at the state of him," Brian said, pointing to the dog. Rigor mortis had set in. Glenn's legs had set sticking up in the air, his jaw was open with his teeth were showing.

"He looks like he's making some kind of a hideous grin," Al thought.

"He's as solid as a concrete bollard," Brian said, gently pushing the dog's leg.

"He's got to be buried," Wullie said.

"Yeah, I know that Wullie," Al said curtly. "Grab the other end and give me a hand then."

The brothers lifted the dead dog in the white sheet and climbed down the stairs. Brian held the doors open. Once they were in the back garden, they put Glenn down on the ground.

"Where are we going to bury him?" Wullie asked.

"Over there should be alright," Al said, pointing to a spot by the fence.

The brothers didn't have any traditional garden tools and were forced to try and dig the grave with a claw hammer, butcher's knife and an axe. The heatwave had made the ground bone dry. They bashed, stabbed and attacked the ground for over two hours and only managed a shallow opening.

"I've never worked so fucking hard in my life," Al thought as he pounded the ground with the axe.

"This will take forever," Wullie said.

"Let's just go with what we've got," Brian said.

Al looked at the shallow grave and then at Glenn with his rock-solid legs still sticking up in the air.

"Yeah, okay but it might be a tight fit," Al said.

Al grabbed one end of the sheet and Brian the other. They carried the dog over, lay him in the grave and began to cover him up with the soil.

"The dog's too bloody big," Wullie said.

"The hole is too small," Al said, looking at Glenn's head and tail still sticking out.

"So what do we do now?" Brian said.

"Cut Glenn's head and tail off," Wullie said calmly. "We can bury them separately."

"What?" Brian said.

"It's not like Glenn will feel anything, he's dead!" Wullie said. "It's either that or we leave him out like this for the kids to see when they're out playing in the morning."

"Look, its late and we're all tired," Al said. "Let's just go back inside and discuss who will cut Glenn up."

Once inside the flat Wullie put the kettle on. No sooner had he poured the boiling water into the mugs when three police cars screeched to a stop outside. They battered down the door and steamed into the room mob-handed, carrying spades and shovels.

"What the hell's going on here?" Brian said calmly.

"Right, you lot," the burley police sergeant said. "Who have you done in and buried out the back? We've had a phone call. You were overheard talking about burying Glenn."

Al began to chuckle.

"Lad's you've got this all wrong," Al said with a wry grin.

"Don't give us any of that. You were heard!" the Sergeant said.

Al explained to the police officers that Glenn was the family pet. The officers, armed with shovels and spades, proceeded to dig Glenn back up again.

The police sergeant shook his head when he looked down at Glenn's hideous grin.

"Chuck that dog in the bin," the sergeant said, waving his men to pack up and leave.

Once the police left and the neighbour's curtains stopped twitching, Al and Brian lifted Glenn back out of the shallow grave and put him in the bin. Al looked back as the brothers walked back towards the tenement.

"It's like Glenn's grinning at me," Al thought.

The morning came quickly, and Al was sitting by the window drinking a cup of tea when he heard the dust cart arrive. The air brakes gave a loud hiss as it stopped outside the block. Al opened the window and listened.

"Oh my good lord, look at this," one dustman called out.

"What kind of person does a dog in and leaves him in the bin?" another said.

"Bastards," the third dustman said. "That's the kind of person that does something like this, bloody bastards!"

Al took a quick peek out of the window and caught the final sight of Glenn's grin before he was thrown into the back of the dust cart.

***

Two days later, Al, Brian, Wullie, and Davey were out, as normal, stealing the lead from the homes due for demolition. Al was holding a piece of lead in his hand.

"I just love the touch, smell and the fun of stealing this lead," Al thought. *"There's nothing quite like it."*

The day before, Brian had been out with a girl he'd met at the Vulcan when several Springburn Pegs pounced out on him. He was alone, unarmed and outnumbered. The girl, Betty, had been scared for both herself and Brian. There was an unwritten rule amongst all the gangs of Glasgow that said that no gang should ever, ever attack a rival if he's with his wife or girlfriend. The Pegs had been tooled up with blades and were looking to prove to others that they didn't just cave in to their demands. They also wanted to try and retrieve whatever credulity they could muster after being publicly robbed by Joey Flemming and the Balgrayhill Boys. Fortunately, the Pegs abided by the unwritten rules and let Brian leave with Betty, with a stern warning that next time he would be hurt.

Al's leading crew would carry candles at night to work from. The rationale was that torches could be seen for miles, raise potential suspicion from the police, or attract those intent on robbing the thieves.

"Look," Davey said as he pointed over to a torch light across the road.

The four lads crouched down by the window and peeked over as the torch light and an outline of several lads approached the house. There was a crashing noise from downstairs as the front door was kicked open. The lads could hear a voice barking out orders to check the rooms downstairs.

"Through the hole," Al whispered.

The three lads nodded and carefully crept across the floor towards the hole in the wall they had created earlier, which led into the adjacent property. Al stepped over the rubble and disappeared through the hole, promptly followed by the others. The lads stood either side of the hole and listened as doors were being flung open downstairs. Then the sound of the stairs thudded as the lads made their way upstairs. Al looked over at Brian. He was holding a machete above his head and over the hole's entrance. Finally, voices could be heard in the next room.

Al spoke.

"Who is out there?"

"We're the Balgrayhill Boys and I'm Joey Flemming. Come back in here so we talk," Joey Flemming said.

Al could hear a few of the Balgrayhill boys chuckling.

"Listen, there's plenty of money in this for everyone so there's no need to fight," Al said in his best reasoning voice.

"Just come through so we can talk," Joey Flemming said.

"Fuck off!" Brian shouted as he gripped his machete tighter.

"Don't you know who I am?" Joey called back.

"Yeah, I know who you are," Al said firmly. "You're the bloke who got your reputation beating up drunks."

"Why, you cheeky bastard!" Joey Flemming yelled as he clambered towards the hole in the wall.

Brian brought the machete down. The huge blade twinkled as the Balgrayhill lad's torch caught the steel.

"You come in and I'll cut you to fucking ribbons," Brian said as he brought the blade down again over the hole.

"You're fucking dead, the lot of you!" Joey Flemming threatened as he stepped back from the hole in the wall. "Believe me I will hunt each and every one of you bastards down and make you pay."

Al and the lads listened as the Balgrayhill Boys finally stomped off down the stairs and left the property. Al peered back over the window to make sure they had left.

"Fuck me that was close," Brian said with a chuckle.

"I should have brought my shotgun," Wullie said with a slightly insane smile.

"No, no, this isn't good," Davey said, shaking his head wildly. "This is not good at all. That mad fucker Flemming will stop at nothing. I know him and I know his reputation and we've pissed him off big time. He will come at us, and we've got to find some way to smooth all this over."

"I tried to reason with him," Al said with an open handed gesture. "I told him there's plenty enough for us all."

"I'm going to have to find a way through this," Al thought. *"I'm on the run and I don't want to draw any attention from the police."*

"We have got to make some kind of deal with them," Davey said. "I don't want them turning up at my house with my wife and bairn."

"Alright, Davey," Al said. "Stop fretting. I'll reach out and try to find some way of resolving this."

"Good, good. We need to do this sooner rather than later," Davey said.

"For fuck's sake, Davey, the man has just told you that he's going to get it sorted so give it a fucking rest will yer!" Brian said, as he slid the machete down his trouser leg.

Once the sun was up, the leading firm carried their haul back to Davey's and waited for the scrap-man to arrive. He paid out over five hundred and thirty pounds.

"This is good money," Brian said as he counted his share of the haul. "It's well worth fighting for."

Davey started to shake his head nervously.

"He's winding you up, Davey," Al said, patting Davey on the back. "If it can be sorted then I'll sort it."

Al and Brian were still buzzing from the amphetamine and the excitement of making a few quid leading. They washed up and went to the café for food while Wullie stayed at the squat and slept.

"Do you fancy a swift drink?" Brian said.

"Yeah, why not," Al said.

The two lads strolled down to the Vulcan Bar on the corner of Vulcan Street. They knew they couldn't get properly on it as they would be out again in the evening and then off to work as soon as the pub closed.

"The landlord poured two pints and handed them over the bar.

"Cheers," Al said as he reached for the glass.

"Are you with me tonight or are you seeing what's her name, Betty?" Al said as he handed Brian the pint glass.

"You mean the beast?" Brian said, taking a sip of the ale.

"Beast?" Al said with a quizzical expression.

"Yeah, the beast. You've seen her, fucking hideous," Brian said, wiping the ale froth from his lips.

"That's a bit strong, Brian. She might not be the best looking of girls but she's alright, you know," said Al.

"It's a pig, Al, a fucking beast. You have to tell it as it is," Brian said.

"If she's so bad why are seeing her?"

"Port in a storm comes to mind, not on the game and... she reckons she was a virgin... so, untouched," Brian said, taking a large gulp from his glass.

"That is harsh, Brian." Al said.

"She reckons she might be pregnant," Brian said casually.

Al nearly choked on his beer.

"What?"

"Yeah, might be in the family way. Unbelievable really," Brian said. "I only did the deed a couple of times."

"Why the fuck didn't you use something?" Al asked

"What can I say? It just seemed like a good idea at the time to go bareback," Brian said.

"Are you sure she's pregnant?" Al asked.

Brian nodded.

"I'm as sure as you can be," Brian said.

"I don't want this to sound funny, Brian. But are you sure that it's yours?" Al said.

"Al, you've seen the beast. Blokes are not exactly queuing up around the block to give it a tug," Brian said.

Al shook his head, then wandered over to the Jukebox. He took a coin from his pocket, slid it into the machine and made his selection. Just as *'Howzat'* by Sherbet began to play he returned to his brother at the bar.

After the second pint, the lads decided to go back to the squat and grab a couple of hours sleep. They stepped out of the pub and into the sunshine. They turned and began to walk slowly when they suddenly found themselves surrounded by five Balgrayhill Boys. One of the lads stepped forward and pulled out a knife.

"We're going to cut you boys up," the lad said as he swung the blade from left to right.

"Fuck I've been caught out," Al thought as he patted down his pockets. *"I've got nothing but my fists!"*

Al and Brian stood together. The brothers clenched their fists and gritted their teeth, ready to fight for their lives when a red two door 1500GT Cortina MK1 with oversized steel wheels came to a screeching halt beside them. The window was wound down and a guy in a white polo shirt threw his cigarette to the ground.

"Are you boys Springburn?"

"Yes mate," Al replied.

The car door was flung open, and the guy stepped out onto the road. In his right hand he held a military bayonet. He strutted towards the Balgrayhill lad brandishing the blade and before he could make any kind of move, he was stabbed in the stomach. The Balgrayhill lad yelped out in pain as the blade entered his body. He dropped his own knife and buckled over in excruciating agony.

"Right, who wants it next?"

The Balgrayhill lads held up their hands.

"We don't want any trouble, mate," one of the lads said as he helped his injured friend back onto his feet.

"Good, because this is Springburn territory, so fuck off!"

The Balgrayhill lads scampered across the road and down an alleyway.

Al looked down at the blood on the pavement and then at their rescuer.

"Alright, lads? I'm Archie Jones," Archie said as he pulled a white handkerchief out of his pocket and wiped the blood from his bayonet. "Cheeky fuckers coming down here like that."

"Cheers mate," Al said as he shook Archie's hand. "I'm Jack Wilson and this is my brother Brian."

"We appreciate you stepping in like that," Al said.

"We Springburn lads have to stick together," Archie said. "Anyway, I've got to be somewhere so maybe I'll see you about."

"Yeah, sure," Al said. "We drink at the 'Fling' or the 'Vulcan Bar'. We'd like to buy you a drink."

"Sounds good to me," Archie said as he climbed back into his Cortina and slammed the door shut. He turned the ignition key and the sporty 1500cc GT engine fired up. Archie revved the engine a couple of times, slammed the shifter into first gear and then dropped the clutch. The racy, four cylinder motor roared as the car slid away sideways with thick grey smoke belching out from the rear wheel arches.

"Tasty motor," Brian said.

"Brian, we can't ever get caught out like that again," Al said. "That could have got real nasty and all because we weren't carrying something."

"I'm not having that happen again," Al thought. *"Next time I will be ready."*

***

The week went well with the leading firm pulling in another record week. Al had taken some time to see what else could be salvaged from the homes destined for demolition, when he came across the copper piping that fed the water tanks. The sun had just risen, and Al was sitting on the roof looking at the way the clouds were forming. He was thinking about his best friend from childhood, Larry White. He had heard that Larry, aged only 20, had died of cancer.

"You were a great friend Larry, and I'm sorry to hear you're no longer with us," Al thought as he looked up towards the clouds.

His brother, Wullie sat down beside him.

"Have you ever heard voices talking to you, Al?" Wullie said as he lay back on the tiles.

"No," Al said.

"What kind of question is that?" Al thought.

"Why, do you?" Al said, turning to his brother.

Wullie nodded.

"What kind of things?" said Al.

"They tell me to hurt people, you know, really hurt them," Wullie said.

"Do you?"

"Sometimes I hurt people and it feels good, you know," Wullie said.

"I only see violence as a last resort," Al said.

"You've been missing out then," Wullie said.

There was a moment's awkward silence.

"Do you remember that incident over the plate of cheese?" Wullie asked.

The image of Mammy opening the food cupboard door came flooding back. She had expected to find the plate with the cheese waiting for her. She immediately turned to Wullie and accused him of stealing it. Wullie had vehemently denied taking it, but Mammy was having none of it. She grabbed the dog chain and began to belt Wullie repeatedly until he fell to the floor with both hands protecting his face. Mammy stood over him with a contorted expression of pure hatred on her face, while he screamed out in agony and begged for mercy. She hit him again and again. Finally Wullie whimpered that he had taken it and Mammy stopped beating him. She then returned to the cupboard and opened the door opposite only to find the missing plate of cheese. Mammy turned back to Wullie who was still on the floor whimpering from the beating. She yelled out that he was a no good liar and grabbed the chain again. Wullie was beaten so badly that he couldn't stand for almost an hour.

"I remember that, Wullie, and plenty more," Al said. "It was wrong."

"I will kill mammy one of these days," Wullie said with a sneer.

There was a second awkward silence before Wullie clambered onto his feet and looked up at the sky.

"There's Jesus, Al. He's up in sky and looking down at me," Wullie said as he reached up to the sky.

"Alright Wullie, let's just get the fucking lead," Al said bluntly.

"I'm getting worried about you Wullie. You're sounding like a bloody psychopath and off your rocker," Al thought.

Al needed to get the lead sold, get himself washed up and then take care of some business. The unresolved matter with Joey Flemming and the Balgrayhill Boys had been escalating.

Two days prior Al had left the pub after closing and had been caught out on his own. He was tooled up with a large blade but there had been six of them. Seeing that he was outnumbered, Al shot off down the street with the Balgrayhill Boys giving chase. Al was in good physical shape and ran up and down the streets looking back occasionally to see If they were still chasing him. He sprinted past a house party where *'Wooly Bully'* by Sam the Sham & The Pharaohs was playing. To his left was a steep hill. Al looked back, then darted left and dug deep as he charged up the hill. At the top of the hill, he looked back again to see that all but one of the lads were doubled over trying to catch their breath. Outside one of the tenements was a rubbish skip. In the skip was a broken wooden table. Al quickly climbed up into the skip and pulled desperately at the heavy wooden table leg. With a final tug it snapped, and Al was armed. The lone Balgrayhill lad reached the top of the hill. With his hands on his hips, he bent forward panting and gasping for breath to fill his exhausted lungs. When he eventually looked up, he found Al standing by the rubbish skip holding the heavy table leg. The lad immediately turned and bolted away back down the hill. Al dashed after him. Al passed by the house party again and heard that *'Wooly Bully'* by Sam the Sham and The Pharaohs was being played again. The Balgrayhill Boy sprinted down the road with Al, brandishing the wooden table leg, in hot pursuit. The lad turned the corner. Instinctively Al slowed down as he approached the corner. He bent down behind the wall and crept along until he could safely see around the bend. The Balgrayhill Boys were standing in the middle of the road, waiting with pickaxe handles, and machetes and one lad had an axe. One of the boys shouted that he'd seen Al and once again the chase was on. Al hurried back down the street with the screaming gang of lads behind him. He passed by the house party and *'Wooly Bully'* by Sam the

Sham and The Pharaohs was playing a third time. As Al turned the corner he dug deep into his physical reserves and hurtled up the hill, not stopping until he reached the top. He stood at the brow of the hill looking down upon the worn out, exhausted Balgrayhill Boys who were less than halfway up the hill.

"They must love that song," Al thought as he recalled hearing it three times.

Al had washed and got changed. He took a small pocketknife and slid it into his jeans pocket. He made his way across town and waited patiently outside a factory that produced train equipment. A whistle sounded and a flood of working men in overalls left the factory. Al saw the lad he was looking for and came out from behind a car.

"Kurt," Al said.

Kurt turned quickly on his heels and clenched his fists.

"It's alright," Al said. I'm not here to cause any trouble. I just want to talk. Can we do that?"

Kurt nodded his head.

"Look all this bad blood between us just isn't good for business and making money is what's it's all about, isn't it?" Al said calmly.

Kurt cautiously nodded his head.

"We can both make good money from this leading game. There's no need for anyone to get hurt. Now I'm happy to let bygones be bygones, just forget what has happened in the past and then move on in a way that can benefit us both," Al said.

"Okay, what do you propose?" Kurt asked.

"Look, this is just an idea, but why don't you do leading on Mondays, we'll do Tuesdays and so on. That way we don't need to bump into each other. What do you think?"

Kurt rubbed his chin and thought for a moment.

"You seem like an alright kind of guy for a Springburn, and I do agree that making money should be what it's all about, but Joey wants you boys, and he wants you bad," Kurt said.

"You and I both know there's no money in violence. You do one of us and we'll do one of you. Where's the pay day in that? I'm reaching out here, Kurt. I didn't turn up with a blade to cut you up as my enemy but instead came with sound reasoning and good sense in the hope that you can relay this back to Joey, as his number two, so we can park up all this territorial bullshit up and just fill our working-class pockets with money. What do you think?"

Kurt paused for a moment.

"Between you and me, none of us want all this aggro. You and your boys are all game lads, and we respect that and personally I see the benefit of us finding a way to co-exist and make money while we can, but Joey is a whole different animal. He would sooner see you lot in the morgue and take it all for himself. But that said, I will speak with Joey and I will do my best to find a compromise because, like you, most of us see the benefit in us all making money," Kurt said.

"I can't ask for any more than that," Al said holding out his hand.

Kurt shook his hand.

"I can't make any promises," Kurt said.

***

Al returned to the squat where he found the gas cooker rings on full to keep the room warm and Wullie sitting on the settee cuddling his shotgun.

"This is my baby," Wullie said.

"You are worrying me," Al thought. *"Brother or not, you're definitely losing the plot Wullie."*

Brian took a deep draw on cigarette, looked at Al, and slowly shook his head.

Al bolted upstairs to his bedroom, pulled back the carpet and lifted the lose floorboard. He reached in and took out a bundle of notes. He sat down with his back resting against the bed and counted out one thousand pounds. Al stuffed the money into his pocket, put the floorboard back down and then went into the bathroom and took a new, unopened toothbrush from the cabinet.

"I'm going back out," Al said as he opened the front door. "I'll see you later."

Al made his way across the city to Glasgow Central train station where he rented a deposit box. He put the thousand pounds in it, along with the toothbrush.

"If it all comes on top then this is my getaway money," Al thought.

Chapter 20

"What the hell is this?" Davey said as he swung the living room door open.

Al, Brian, Wullie and Davey had just broken into an abandoned house. The plan was to dig through the wall upstairs so they could return the following day to start stealing the lead, brass pipes and door handles. However, the front room was stacked from floor to ceiling with brand new washing machines, television sets, fridges and freezers.

"This looks like a hiding place for someone's stash," Brian said as he wandered into the room and ran his hand over the white goods.

"We've fallen on our feet here," Al said with a broad smile. "We need a van, and we need it quick, Davey."

"Yeah, right, my sister's boyfriend has a van. They only live a couple of roads up," Davey said as he followed Brian through the maze of brand-new television sets.

"Good, give him a few quid and get that van back here as quick as you can. There's some good money here and I know just where to get rid of it," Al said as he began to mentally tally up how many pieces they had in the room.

"Right, I'm on it," Davey said as he bolted out the door.

"What do you reckon, Al?" Wullie said.

"There's got be a good thousand quid in here for us," Al said as he cast his eyes over the haul for the second time. "Yeah, at least a thousand quid I'd say."

"Nice one," Brian said as he patted the top of a fridge.

"We'll have a couple of these for the squat," Al said as he tore the side of the cardboard covering the television set. "Yeah, we'll have a television, washing machine and a fridge. We don't need a freezer."

"Sounds good to me," Brian said.

"So what happened to you last night?" Wullie asked.

"You mean up on the roof?" Al asked.

"Yeah, with a yelp like that I thought a cat had been run over outside in the street," Brian said with a chuckle.

"Hey, it wasn't any laughing matter. I climbed up on the roof through the skylight, secured the rope around the chimney and began to slide down the roof to start cutting the lead away when there was this almighty crash as the skylight from the next house burst open and this bloke has started climbing up with a bloody great butcher's knife in his hand shouting 'don't you go nicking my lead!' I lost my grip and began sliding down the bloody roof. I thought it was all over. If it hadn't been for the rope, yours truly would have been splattered all over the concrete."

"Did the bloke with the butcher's knife try to help you back up?" Brian said.

"Did he fuck," Al said. "I managed to get a firm hold back on the roof and set about convincing him that we wouldn't be nicking his lead."

"Here," Brian said, as he pulled himself up onto a small fridge, "it's a good job we didn't go through the wall first. Imagine him standing there in the dark waiting for us."

"Yeah, well that's a thought I could do without," Al said with a relieved smile.

Davey was back within the hour with a twin wheel transit van. The lads filled the van to the back door with goods.

"We'll need to make several trips with this lot," Davey said.

Al nodded as he looked at the stolen goods.

"Davey, you're with me. Brian, Wullie, you stay here and keep an eye on our stuff. I'll be back as quick as I can," Al said as he opened the passenger side door of the transit van and got in.

Al gave directions to his contact. They made four trips in total to Al's buyer and a fifth to take some of the haul back to their squat. Al's contact tried to get away with an offer of eight hundred quid, but after a bit of haggling Al squeezed the thousand pounds in cash out of him.

"Here, Al," Brian said, "Happy birthday."

"Yeah, right. I almost forgot about that," Al said as he divided the money into four equal lots and handed it out.

"Money can make you forget a lot of things," Davey said as he fingered through his wad of notes.

"So what time are we meeting at the Vulcan tonight for your twenty first birthday party?" Brian asked as he looked down at his watch.

"About half seven," Al said as he pocketed his share of the money.

"I'll see you later then," Davey said as he climbed into the driver's seat of the van, closed the door and wound down the window.

"See you later," Al said as he watched Davey start the engine and drive the van away.

Al, Brian and Wullie had bathed and dressed in their best clothes in readiness for the evening's twenty first birthday celebrations.

"Have you arranged to see Betty tonight?" Al asked Brian as he checked his hair in the hallway mirror for the third time.

"If she's there, she's there," Brian said casually.

"Has she said any more about, well you know, being pregnant?" Al said as he stepped away from the mirror so that Brian could check himself out.

"I haven't seen her," Brian said.

"Will Mammy be there?" Wullie asked as he leant back against the wall and put his hands into his trouser pockets.

"Yeah," Al said.

"I will kill her one of these days," Wullie hissed. "I'll let her have both barrels straight in the face."

"Sure you will, Wullie," Al said. "Just not tonight though, okay? It's my birthday and for once it would be nice just to go out and have a good time without any of the usual bullshit."

"Alright, Al," Wullie said.

"You are very definitely getting worse, Wullie," Al thought.

The three brothers strode down to Cowlairs Road and onto the corner of Vulcan Street.

"It's ram packed in there already," Brian said as he looked up at the shadows through the obscured glass windows.

Al smiled as he opened the door. As he entered the pub he was met by the sound of *'December 63 (Oh What a Night)'* by Frankie Valli and the Four Seasons and several cheers from around the bar.

"This place is packed," Al thought as he scanned the room. *"And it's full of girls!"*

News of 'Jack's' twenty first birthday party had spread far and wide. Al and his mates were known as great fun, generous and big spenders.

Several girls dancing together by the jukebox raised their hands and waved as Al made his way through the pats on his back and birthday wishes. Al reached into his pocket and put a hundred pounds on the bar. The landlord, on seeing Al enter, had begun to pour him a double whiskey.

"Happy birthday," the landlord said as he put the drink in front of Al. "It's on the house."

"Cheers," Al said as he picked up the glass and took a small sip. "Can you stick this behind the bar?"

The landlord nodded, picked up the money and placed it in a black jar by the bottles of spirits. Al took another small sip of his drink and then turned around. To his left, at the far end of the bar, he saw Mammy chatting with his aunties Doreen and Mary.

"Can you send down whatever they're all drinking," Al said to the landlord, pointing to the three women.

'Let Your Love Flow' by the Bellamy Brothers blared out from the jukebox. Al looked over to see the new girls chatting.

"Happy birthday mate."

Al turned to see Billy Jones, the lad who had bottled it when he heard that the Springburn Pegs had an interest in their business.

"How are you, Billy?" Al said as he motioned the landlord to get Billy a drink.

"Yeah, alright I suppose. I've been running this bloke about, doing a bit of chauffeuring," Billy said.

"Nice work and it'll keep you out of trouble," Al said.

"The bloke I drive about is a nightmare when he has a drink. I mean we all like a good drink, but this fella doesn't know when to stop. The other day he had me running him about from bar to bar in Edinburgh, and slowly but surely this fella is getting pissed. He's slurring his words and patting me on the back while I'm driving and telling what a good lad I am," Billy said. "I'm on the payroll so I do what I'm told.

Anyway, he's come out after eating some foreign shit and got in the car. I could see in the rear-view mirror that he wasn't right. He was out of it and the drunkest I've ever seen him. It was the last drop of the day and he's told me to get him back to Glasgow. We've pulled away and I'm constantly checking the rear-view mirror to see if he's okay. Then once we're out on the open road I could see that he had his eyes closed but was starting to stir and groan. I could hear his guts going ten to the dozen from the driver's seat. I asked him if he was alright and he's just writhing about on the back seat holding his stomach. Then he's looked up and believe me when I say I'll never forget the look of sheer horror on his face.

He screams 'stop the car, quick!' I've checked my mirror to see what's behind me, indicated, and then tried to pull over to the side of the road. Before I could stop, he yelled out and unleashed the bowels from hell. I could hear the dirty bastard filling his pants on the back seat. He's pulling at the car door frantically but it's too late. That noise as his pants filled has given me fucking nightmares, I tell you.

Then the rancid smell of hot shit assaulted my nose. I mean it literally burnt my nostrils and the back of my throat. I heaved, and then heaved again, still pulling frantically at the car door. Finally it opened, and I've fell out onto my hands and knees by the side of the road. I'm gagging and retching my stomach up but there's nothing to be sick and still that horrendous smell of shit is trapped inside my nose. I've wiped the tears away and managed to sit myself up and take deep breaths of clean air. I've finally pulled myself together and got back on my feet. I couldn't hear anything from the back of the car, so I've stuck my head in and asked if he was alright and that smell has hit me again like a bloody great steel wrecking ball in the face.

My legs buckled and I've grabbed my throat and all I see was my boss laying out on the backseat unconscious in a pool of his own shit. It was the worst day of my life and I still had to drive him the hundred miles back to Glasgow. I had all the windows down and pulled my jersey up over my nose and still that noxious smell of shit persisted. I don't know what he'd been eating there but it wasn't fish and chips that's for sure."

Brian, Wullie and Davey had joined the conversation and all four of the lads were in fits of laughter.

"I think you need danger money," Brian said, still laughing.

"No, I've given up chauffeuring," Billy said, putting his empty glass on the bar. "Can I have a job back with you guys?"

"You mean you've given up running a drug dealer about and want to get your hands dirty with us again," Al said.

Billy nodded.

"Nah, that isn't going to happen, Billy. We only have game lads on our firm, the kind of lads that face trouble head on, and we all know that's not for you. So, mate, I'll get you a few drinks as it's my birthday but that's about it," Al said.

"Don't Go Breaking My Heart' by Elton John and Kiki Dee had just started to play when the pub door opened and one by one, eight hard-core Balgrayhill Boys followed Joey Flemming into the pub. Al spotted them immediately and nudged Brian. Al caught a glimpse of Kurt, Joey Flemming's second in command, as he passed by a group of dancing girls. He looked directly at Al and shook his head. Al took that as his sincere offer to find some kind of compromise with Joey Flemming had failed. He turned back to the bar and picked up his drink.

"That bastard Joey Flemming is a legend in his own mind," Al thought.

The birthday celebration continued without interruption. The drinks flowed and Al managed to spend some time chatting with his favourite aunts. He spotted Graeme, the drug dealer, nodded, and held up a batch of notes. Graeme smiled and handed a couple of small bags of cocaine to Babs to share with her friends.

As the evening wore on, Al found himself surrounded by just his close friends, Davey, Little Irene, Big Irene and his family, Brian, Wullie, Sandra, Beth and Mammy at the bar. The drinks flowed and the music played in the background. Everyone was laughing and enjoying the evening. Al looked up to see Joey Flemming walking towards him. He put his drink back on the bar.

"Is anybody invited to this party?" Joey Flemming said, now standing just a few feet away from Al.

"Yeah," Al said as he looked directly at the gold cross hanging from his ear. "Anybody but you!"

"Who the fuck do you think you are walking up to me like that?" Al thought. *"Oh, fuck it. I should try and make some kind of peace here."*

"Forget that Joey, come here, I'll buy you a drink," Al said as he motioned Joey to follow him down the bar.

Al bought Joey a beer and put it on the bar in front of him. Joey sneered, lifted the glass and swallowed the contents down in three large gulps. He wiped his mouth on his sleeve and then put the glass upside down on the bar.

"You have no idea who I am, do you?" Joey said.

Al knew that putting an upside glass in front of somebody was an invitation to fight them.

Al didn't hesitate. He threw a left hook, followed by a powerful right cross and then a hefty uppercut that sent Joey Flemming sprawling back onto a table of drinks. The pub erupted into an all-out brawl of bloody violence as the Balgrayhill Boys steamed across the pub, punching and kicking at everyone in their way. Brian grabbed a beer glass and smashed it clean around the head of one of the lads. He yelped out in pain and fell to the floor holding his bleeding face. Brian kicked him in the stomach twice before finding an open spot and kicking the lad right in the face. The sound of the lad's nose breaking was sickening.

Wullie had thrown a table to one side and steamed forward into a lad who was slashing the air with a small knife. He side stepped the clumsy lunge, grabbed the lad around the neck and held him in a choking position. The lad lashed out with the knife, but Wullie had him firmly around the throat. As the lad gasped for breath, he dropped the blade. Wullie pulled the lad down onto the floor, climbed onto his body until he sat on the lad's chest. He reached down and grabbed the lad's ears.

Holding them firmly he raised the lad's head and then smashed it back down on the floor several times.

Mammy quickly reached into her bag and pulled out a dog chain. A large lad with a thick black beard stumbled over the fighting. Mammy bolted over toward him. She grabbed him by the beard and yanked his face with such force that she had a handful of facial hair in her hand. Mammy swung the chain, whipping the lad around the face, and then she whipped the lad again and again. In a bid to escape her attack, the lad tried to turn, but a final swing of the chain connected with the back of his head. The lad's legs gave way and he stumbled. Mammy smashed the chain across his head again, until he finally lay on the ground unconscious, a thick pool of blood pouring from his head wounds.

Joey Flemming had managed to stagger back onto his feet where he was met with a swift kick between his legs. He buckled and grabbed his groin. Al grabbed him by the hair, pulled his head back and delivered a succession of targeted, high powered, thunderous blows to his face. Joey's nose and mouth bled more and more as each blow found its target. With one final dynamic head shot that must have rattled his brain, Al let Joey fall back to the floor. He looked down at the man that had been the cause of so much aggravation. Joey spluttered and tried to get back on his feet.

"I'll fucking do you good and proper," Al thought as he stomped his foot down on Joey's back.

He tried again to get up, but Al raised his right leg, took careful aim and then jumped and brought his foot down with such a vigorous force on Joey's arm that it broke the bone. Al could hear the sickening crack as Joey's arm lay lifeless on the ground.

He looked up to see Big Irene throwing punch after punch at their attackers, while little Irene kicked a lad on the floor who had been trying to scramble away from the carnage.

The fighting stopped. The Balgrayhill Boys and their infamous leader, Joey Flemming, were beaten. Al, his friends and family watched as the wounded and beaten lads helped each other up and out of the pub. As the last of them left and the door closed firmly, Al, his friends, family and most of the pub let out a huge victory cheer.

"Right," said Al as he stood up straight and stuck out his chest. "Its drinks all round!"

"Whoo-hoo!" the pub yelled out as one.

Play That Funky Music' by Wild Cherry hammered out of the speakers while the landlord and bar staff ran up and down the bar serving drinks. Al pulled a wad of notes from his pocket and handed them to the landlord.

***

Al and Brian were the last to leave the pub. The landlord tried to hand back twenty-four pounds from the jar, but Al insisted that he share it with the bar staff for the fine job they had done.

"I thought you might have taken Babs back," Brian said.

"Nah, not tonight," Al said as he staggered out into the cold night air.

"It feels too early to go home," Brian said.

"Really? I feel pissed as a fart," Al said, as he stumbled out onto the road.

"We did well tonight, Al, and showed them Balgrayhill Boys who the guvnors are," Brian said.

"Yeah, but that won't be the last of it," Al said.

"You think?"

"People like Joey Flemming have a huge ego to feed. He won't give up," Al said.

"Well fuck him," Brian said.

"Yeah, fuck him," Al said with a short laugh.

"Here, I've got an idea," Brian said, as he came to an abrupt stop.

"What?" Al said with a slur.

"Do you remember when we first broke into the Trebor factory and nicked that box of Mars bars?" Brian said.

"How could I forget? The taste of those chocolate bars will stay with me forever," Al said.

"Probably the biggest meal we had eaten up until then," Brian said.

"Yeah, probably," Al said.

"Why don't we go to the Trebor Factory and do it again just for old time's sake," Brian said with a drunken smile. "It'll be fun!"

"Nah, we can't go robbing a place for a few chocolate bars," Al said.

"Yeah, we can," Brian said. "It's your twenty first birthday, come on."

"Oh, alright then," Al said with a drunken slur.

Al and Brian traipsed across town until they found what was known as the Trebor Factory locally, even though it was a confectionary distribution centre. The two drunken brothers clambered over the wall and into the yard where they forced open the back of a delivery truck and took one single box. In fits of laughter, they climbed back over the wall, out into the street, and down the alley opposite just as they had so many years before. At the end of the alleyway was the same play park where they had first eaten their haul of Mars bars. The two men sat on the ground by the swings. Brian tore open the cardboard box, revealing the popular Marathon chocolate bars that were covered with peanuts and caramel. Al looked at the wrapper, smiled and then tore the end off with his teeth. The two brothers ate several bars each before staggering off back to the squat.

Chapter 21

Al was still a little hung over from his birthday celebration when he decided to go out and check some of the homes due for demolition. He had been inspired by finding the large haul of television sets and white goods that netted him and his team a cool one thousand pounds. Al used his shoulder to force open the front door. Once inside he ran from room to room to see what could be taken later that evening. As he left, he spotted two police officers.

"Come here you," one of the officers said.

"Who me?" Al asked innocently.

"Alright son, what were you doing in the house?"

"Oh fuck, I don't want to get nicked," Al thought.

"This is a bit embarrassing, lads, but I got caught short and needed to take a crap," Al said. "It must have been a dodgy beer or something."

"Don't give us all that old tosh, son. What's your name?"

Al hesitated for a moment and then smiled.

"Jack, Jack Wilson."

"What, are you on the run or something?"

"No, nothing like that" Al said, shaking his head vehemently.

"We've heard your name, Jack Wilson, and you don't come up on our records, son."

"I've not been in any trouble with the law, sir."

"Don't give us that, you lying little cunt. You and your mates are at it. We know it, everyone fucking knows it. Your name just keeps coming up again and again."

Al remained quiet.

"So, let's just cut straight to the chase, shall we?"

Al nodded.

"You lads are out there stealing lead and you're pulling in a lot of money. Now don't go trying to deny it or you'll only piss us off. We've spoken to the scrap-man, and he put your name in the frame as the biggest earners. So, we will be wanting our cut."

"I don't know what you mean," Al said.

"Don't try to fuck with us, Jack-fucking-Wilson. We don't give a flying fuck what you and your mates do, but for us to turn a blind eye, it will cost you one hundred pounds a day to operate."

"A hundred quid a day, that's a lot of money," Al said.

"You'll get value for money. You can operate freely and if a rival crew gives you problems, then we'll get round their place and nick them."

"Okay," Al said.

"What's more, we'll give you information."

"Information? What information?" Al said.

"Right now, Dibble has got a right fucking hard on for you, Jack Wilson."

"Dibble? Who is Dibble?" Al asked.

"Dibble isn't his real name. We all call him that because he looks like the cop in 'Top Cat', the cartoon series on television. You must know him?"

"Yeah, yeah, I know who you mean," Al said.

"We've heard Dibble talking about you and your little firm and he wants you badly. So, Jack Wilson, if you want to stay out of prison and keep making money, it's going to cost you one hundred pounds a day. Do we have a deal?"

"I'll need to speak to my boys," Al said.

"Good, you speak to your boys, because the clock starts ticking tomorrow. Inside that house you've just come out of is a fireplace. Every day you put one hundred pounds up inside on the inside shelf."

"Isn't that a bit dangerous? What if someone breaks in and nicks it?"

"Then you will owe us another hundred pounds. Either way we will get paid."

"I'll speak to the boys and let you know here tomorrow morning at the same time," Al said.

"Good, and make sure you bring our first payment. Now, on your way," the police officer said, motioning Al to move along.

Al met up with Brian, Wullie and Davey at the café. He told them, over breakfast, about his run in with the police and what they wanted. Brian was in favour of just boycotting them while Davey was keen to pay and to keep on operating. Wullie didn't care either way as he would be going back to his job as a gamekeeper in Aberdeenshire soon.

"What do you think?" Brian said before putting a piece of sausage and fried egg into his mouth.

"I think that one hundred pounds a day is just twenty-five quid each and that's a small price to pay to keep operating safely and to stay out of prison," Al said as he raised his hot mug of coffee.

"Well that's it then," Brian said. "We pay."

***

The following morning Al got himself down to the same house and put one hundred pounds on the inner shelf up inside the fireplace and then waited outside for the two police officers. They arrived right on time.

"I've spoken with my lads," Al said, "and they've agreed to pay. The money is inside the fireplace just as you wanted."

"You've made a wise decision. Now, next Tuesday Dibble is planning to turn over David Campbell's home, so make sure there's no lead there."

"Right, thank you," Al said with a shocked expression.

"You see, as we said, this arrangement can work well for us all."

***

Al told the lads about the impending police raid on Davey's home. They all agreed that paying was a wise investment. Davey had expressed concerns over the Balgrayhill Boys and Joey Flemming in particular and hinted that it was a problem that could be solved through their new alliance with the police. Al, having heard a number of rumours about how Joey Flemming was planning to carve him up, dismissed it, stating that he had his own plans.

***

Al had asked around and found out where Joey was living. He had forced open the derelict house opposite Joey's home and watched him through the window while making mental notes of the times he came and left the house.

Al had armed himself with a twelve-inch piece of lead piping which he filled with dirt and compacted down before taking a hammer and bending the ends over to make a heavy, solid, weapon. He hid behind a Morris Minor. The buzz in the pit of his stomach began to rise as he heard the front door of Joey's home open and close. As Joey strode out onto the pavement and passed by the end of the car, Al shot up and smashed the lead bar across the back of Joey's head.

THUD!

Al could feel the rush of adrenaline race through his body as he pounded him a second and then a third time.

SMACK!

SMACK!

Joey had dropped to his knees. Al stepped around to his right so that he faced his nemesis. As Joey looked up, Al took another mighty swing with the lead pipe.

CRACK!

Joey's jaw broke, and several of his broken teeth shot out onto the concrete

CRACK!

Al had taken an almighty swing and smashed the lead pipe into Joey's upper arm. Then he stepped back and got a tighter grip on it. Joey was slumped over and whimpering as he coughed and spat blood onto the concrete pathway. Al booted him in the side of the head so he lay on the ground. With the lead weight firmly gripped in his right hand, he lowered himself down onto one knee, gritted his teeth and stared at Joey.

"If I ever have to come for you again, Joey Flemming, I'll fucking kill you," Al said as he rested the heavy lead pipe on Joey's head.

***

The police raid on Davey's home, led by Officer Dibble, produced nothing. He was angry, upset and pissed at not finding stolen lead and making the arrests he so desperately wanted. Three days later, still angry and driven to make an arrest, Dibble and two other officers caught Al moving lead inside one of the abandoned houses. He was arrested, handcuffed, and forcibly taken to the police station. Dibble had arrested him for stealing lead and assaulting three police officers. Al was angered by the false charges and offered to fight each of them one on one in the cell. While still handcuffed, the three officers, led by Dibble, proceeded to beat, kick and punch Al until he lay bloody on the cell floor.

The news of Al's arrest quickly spread back to his family. Mammy, on hearing what had happened to her son, waited outside the pub where she had been told Dibble, still wearing his police uniform, drank at. She waited patiently until the last bell rang and Dibble staggered out of the pub. With the metal horseshoe in her hand, she confronted Dibble. Before he could say anything, she smashed him around the face, again and again, until he fell to floor. Mammy continued to smash him around the head while hissing 'this is for what you did to my son, Al'. Mammy left him unconscious in the road in a pool of blood.

Al was told what Mammy had done while he was still locked away in his cell, and how Dibble had been taken to hospital with a fractured skull. In his report he stated that he had been attacked by six armed men

Al had been fingerprinted and was sweating on the results coming back showing that he was Al McIntosh, wanted for being on the run from London and not Jack Wilson as he had claimed. The weekend passed quickly and with forty pounds bail he was released on the Monday morning before the fingerprint results came back. Al left the police station quickly and went back to the squat where he packed a few things. As he came down the stairs, he noticed the letter plate opening and two barrels appear. Al quickly dived down beside a fully dressed mannequin dummy that Brian had brought back a few nights earlier after a drunken night out.

BANG!

BANG!

Two shots were fired. Then as the barrels disappeared back through the letter plate, Al rolled over behind the wall. The dummy was facing away from the front door. Al could hear the letter plate open again.

BANG!

BANG!

Each shot hit the motionless mannequin dummy.

As the letter plate closed for the second time, Al raised his head and peeked out of the window with his heart thumping violently against his chest. It was Joey Flemming, carrying a shotgun under his arm. His battered and bruised face contorted with anger.

"That's it," Al thought. *"It's all come on top here, what with the police and now this. I've got to get away."*

Al picked up a few items, including the key to the safety deposit box at Glasgow City's Central Train station, and then bolted out through the front door and down into the city.

"Brian knows the rules, thought Al. *"I told him that I might have to just get up and go without notice and this is it. He'll tell the boys that I was on the run from London, and they'll understand."*

Al opened the deposit box, took out the one thousand pounds and the new, unopened, toothbrush and bought a train ticket to London.

Books by Al McIntosh

With Dean Rinaldi

Villain – No Remorse

Villain – No Remorse II

Villain – No Remorse III

Follow or Contact Al McIntosh:

Facebook: Al McIntosh Author

Facebook: Krays, Gangsters & Crime in British Time

Printed in Great Britain
by Amazon

78126111R00183